To, Uncle Victor
with love & best wishes
from
Lucie
x x x
Christmas 1987.

£3.50

THE WORLD OF
FLAT RACING

THE WORLD OF FLAT RACING

TEXT BY BROUGH SCOTT
PHOTOGRAPHY BY GERRY CRANHAM

PEERAGE BOOKS

CONTENTS

THIS IS an odyssey, not an encyclopaedia. It's the end result of photographer Cranham and scribbling ex-jockey Scott sailing their racing interest to assorted corners of the globe. It's not a gospel, not a tract. It's an impression in words and pictures of what we saw, heard and, since the subject is horse racing, sometimes smelt. Our hope is that it amounts to a rare travelogue of one of the world's most extraordinary activities – at the same time glorious, absurd, athletic, seedy, consuming and, above all, visually superb.

That this last emphasis has been reflected so well should not surprise anyone who knows Gerry Cranham and his work. Suffice here to say that the racked-up energy that once brought this heavily-built six-footer the Southern Counties junior half-mile running title two years in a row also revolutionised sports photography and reduced this writer to pulp long before the final turn.

Cranham is one of the great originators and his skill has brought him acclaim and awards. The Victoria and Albert Museum once featured Cranham's work in the first exhibition of its kind ever held by that institution. And the qualities he possesses were once admirably set out in connection with another highly esteemed exhibition entitled Man and Sport, arranged under the auspices of the Baltimore Museum of Art in the late 1960s. Cranham was one of 10 top photographers from all over the world most prominently featured and the catalogue said of their craft: "Sports photography... demands an in-ordinate amount of energy and imagination. You cannot possibly photograph a sport unless you understand it completely and understand the men who play it. The indefinable aspect is devotion and caring. The same intensity they have to play the game you have to have to record it. Not stop it but suspend it forever in time. This is the whole art."

INTRODUCTION

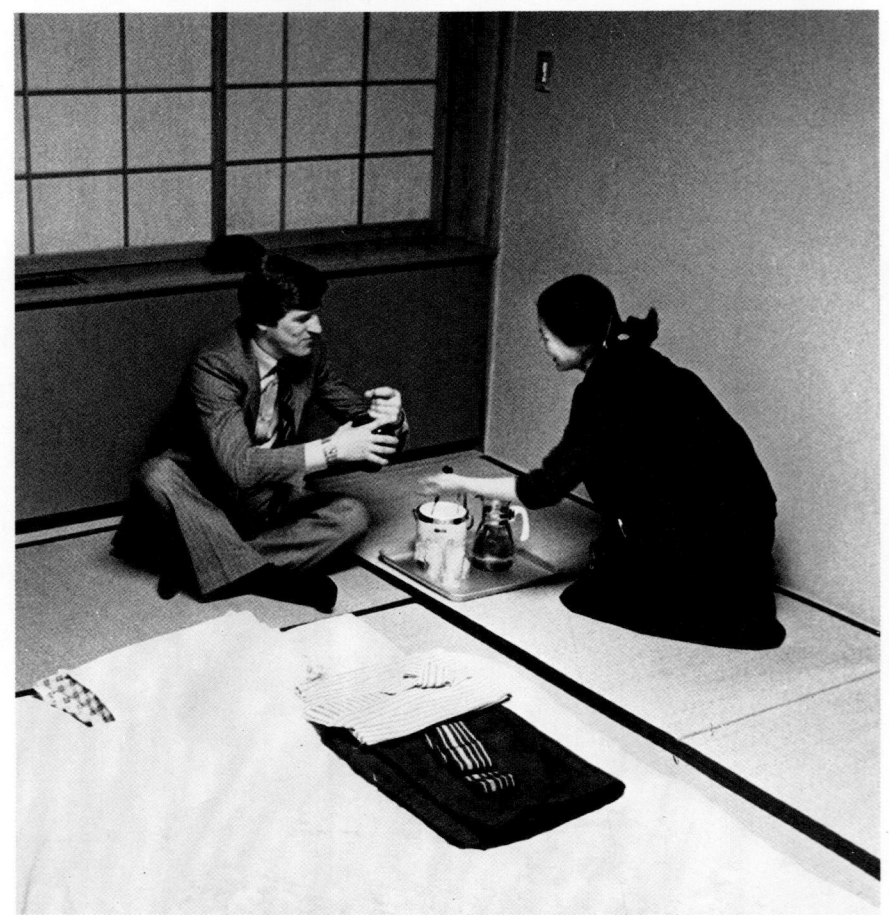

Brough Scott in Japan: an odyssey made possible by the racing world's unfailing hospitality

After he came out of the Army in 1953, Cranham threw in a career as a draughtsman to pursue that art, cycling first to athletics meetings with a camera slung on his back. *His* pictures had to put you right in the action. It no longer became good enough just to record the event and in the pursuit of his grail Cranham would run to every corner of a stadium to catch the vital, fleeting image.

Inevitably Cranham, his fast eye and his empathy for sport began to blend with the colour and excitement of horse racing. In 1978 he brought out (with Richard Pitman) The Guinness Book of Steeplechasing, a volume likely to remain as a unique evocation of that most dramatic of sports. But following a visit to Newmarket to shoot a photographic essay Cranham became obsessed with the idea of bringing out a book on the extraordinary assortment of images flat racing presents around the world.

Indulgently World's Work and its enterprising managing-director Chris Forster took him on. Then I cockily agreed to do the writing with no idea of the enormity of the task. It was not just the size of the racing world, which would need not four years but forty without covering the half of it, but the all consuming problem of controlling the runaway lensman.

If Cranham sees an image, little local difficulties, like regulations, tend to crumble. During his steeplechasing phase fences sprouted strange, half-hidden lenses so often that the rules governing photographers were re-drafted by the Jockey Club. Moreover, though we have not dared enquire what the latest laws are in Hong Kong, some of us will never forget the night at Happy Valley racecourse when the runners for the seventh race had the unrepeatable experience of having Cranham photograph them, gorilla-like, from right on top of the starting stalls.

Worst of all were the dawns. From Chantilly to Chicago, from St. Cloud to

San Isidro, there were terrible alarm calls and then Cranham, festooned with Nikons and notebooks, waiting in the hotel entrance, saying: "The light will be fantastic in half an hour. Horses in silhouette. Magic." Most people were very helpful but there was no reason why everyone should understand. One desperate morning at Japan's Miho training centre, they did not. "I must go to the other side of the track to shoot the horses against the early light," said Cranham. "But I am very sorry Mistah Cranham, it cannot be permitted," came the reply.

A picture might be lost and there was only going to be one winner. The lensman stormed off through the sand with the benighted official spluttering helplessly in our wake.

It was some wake. Over the four years of this erratic, bow-legged journey round the globe Cranham, equipped with a range of cameras and lenses from a fish-eye to an 800mm, shot a total of 1,164 rolls of colour film and 390 of black-and-white, giving a grand total of 55,944 camera shots. Kodak must have thought Christmas had come to stay.

The result cannot pretend to be more than a personal window on the world of racing because no two people should expect to lay much more than Puck's "girdle round the earth." The book can I believe justifiably lay claim, however, to being a unique journalistic account of flat racing in the late Seventies and early Eighties, a record of an era which may, in time, prove to have been crucial in the development of the sport internationally. As we go to press, after having logged between us some 750,000

miles, visited a score of countries and 100 racetracks, including almost all the racecourses in Britain and Ireland, it is inevitable that some of the book will become dated immediately. Maybe, but it remains a journey which we hope all sorts of readers can enjoy.

To have done all this could not have been achieved without the extraordinary generosity of a whole range of

First published in Great Britain in 1983 by
World's Work Ltd., The Windmill Press

This edition published in 1987 by
Peerage Books
59 Grosvenor Street
London W1

Edited by John Lovesey
Art Direction, Design and Typography by Peter Nash
Illustrations by Michael Davidson
Index compiled by Indexing Specialists of Hove

Photographs copyright © 1983 by Gerry Cranham
Text copyright © 1983 by Brough Scott

ISBN 1 85052 080 1

Printed in Hong Kong

people. First of all my own employers at ITV and The Sunday Times, who reacted with magnificent British phlegm when ideas were suddenly sprung on them to report events from Sydney, Saratoga or New Zealand. There were my friends on the International Racing Bureau, who were an unfailing source of hope and who through the good offices of the remarkable Jean Romanet at the

Société d'Encouragement in Paris have produced the statistics at the back of the book.

There was the lady in the Bury St. Edmunds museum who allowed Cranham to pull out of its case her oldest and most treasured coin in order to photograph it. There was the book's editor, John Lovesey, as special a mentor as any writer ever had, and the book's art director and designer, the remarkable Peter Nash.

There were PanAm, who pitched in with some flights, a lady called Kay Rees, who smoothed our paths across the Atlantic and elsewhere.

There were George Ennor and Patsy Collman who were separate towers of strength and of course all those wonderful, hospitable members of the racing family on whose doors we would hammer at all times of day and night.

Understandably, there were occasional moments of tension but, overall, our travels only served to confirm that the tremendous freemasonry of the turf is as extensive and strong as any on this planet. It is one of which Charles II would surely have approved when he began to get things moving at Newmarket 300 years ago. The "Merry Monarch" may have had faults and there have been all sorts of high- and low-born rogues since then on two legs and on four, but one thing almost excuses them – they loved this crazy old game. And so do we.

BROUGH SCOTT
MAY 1983

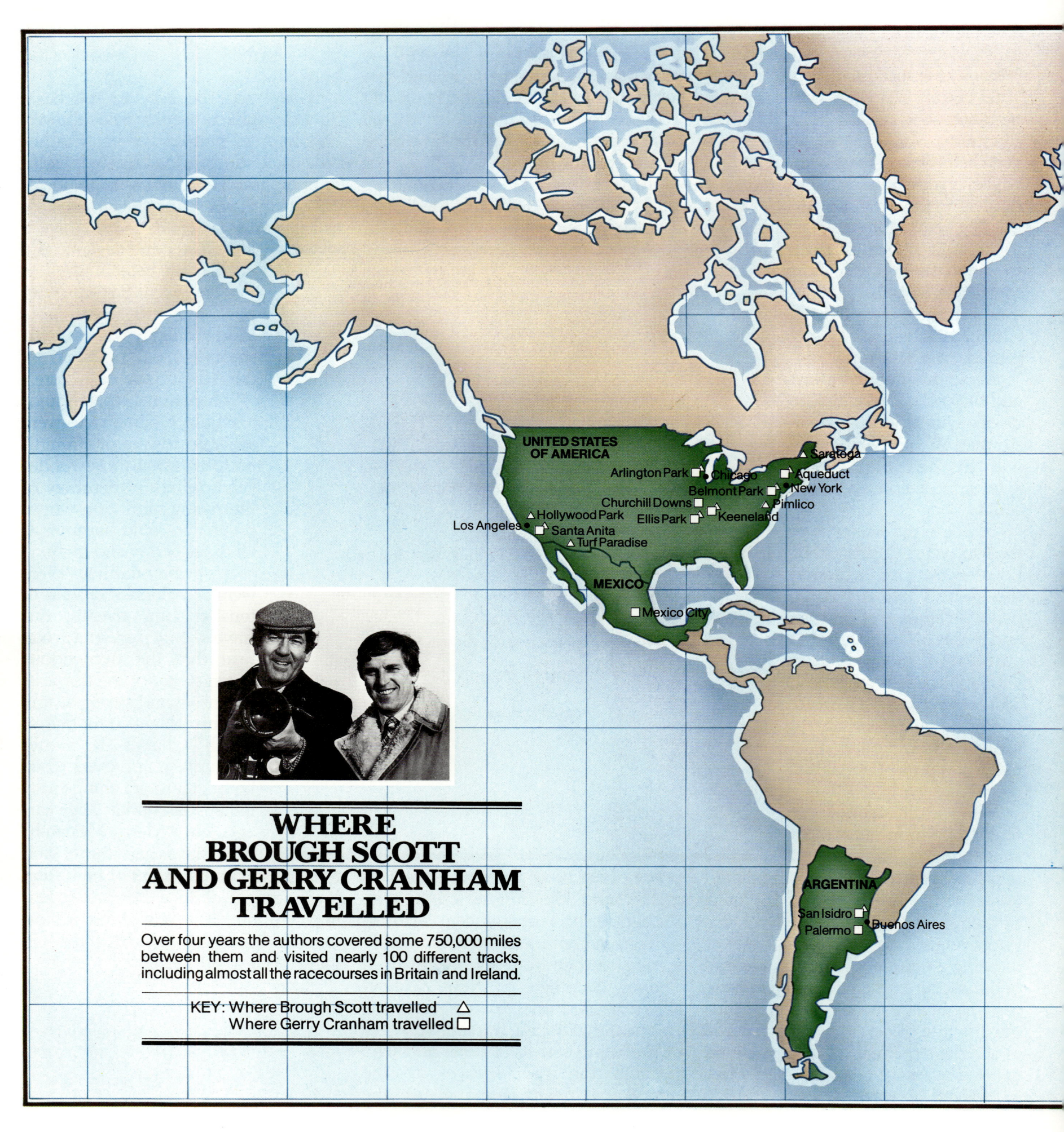

UNITED STATES
OF AMERICA

△ Saratoga

Arlington Park □ □ Chicago □ Aqueduct
Belmont Park △ New York
Churchill Downs □ □ △ Pimlico
△ Hollywood Park Ellis Park □ □ Keeneland
Los Angeles ● □ Santa Anita
△ Turf Paradise

MEXICO

□ Mexico City

ARGENTINA

San Isidro □
Palermo □ ● Buenos Aires

WHERE
BROUGH SCOTT
AND GERRY CRANHAM
TRAVELLED

Over four years the authors covered some 750,000 miles
between them and visited nearly 100 different tracks,
including almost all the racecourses in Britain and Ireland.

KEY: Where Brough Scott travelled △
Where Gerry Cranham travelled □

Once race meetings abounded on the beaches of the Emerald Isle. Now, the only official survivor is a summer meeting, held at low tide, at Laytown, 40 miles up the coast from Dublin, and where there are few points on the track that are not underwater when the sea is in.

Racing is not all about horses but people and ambient atmosphere. Never is this more in evidence than at the Royal meeting each June at Ascot, on the only course owned by the Crown. Burned into the memory by the black-and-white scene in *My Fair Lady,* the style is unfailingly topper-and-tails and summer frippery. In such fashion a lady, with a pretty parasol, may certainly become a focus of as much attention as a horse.

As piquant as the local food, racing in Mexico City does not seem any slower or less exuberant than competition at sea level. In the thin air at 7,350 feet, the oxygen-depleted atmosphere in which Mexico's capital noisily thrives, horses and men are as hell-bent as ever for the winning post.

Etched into a pink dawn a South African trainer, observing from a typical viewpoint, reviews his horses as a general might the cavalry. Training started at 4 a.m. to beat the fierce heat of the now rising sun, for the aspirations here are the same as where it all started. Indeed, this wide open land near Johannesburg is also called Newmarket.

At St Moritz in Switzerland when the winter ice on the lake is thick enough they schedule a race meeting. It is no tinpot operation either. There are changing tents, bars, a wooden grandstand and huge braziers cooking sausages and other goodies. When the runners, fitted with studded shoes, gallop round the tight, six-furlong circuit they are brilliantly set against the snow and the town stretching away up the mountain, one of the most splendid backdrops in the world.

Immortalised by George Stubbs and Sir Alfred Munnings and countless other artists, the horse bewitches man. Race the noble animal on a course, generously splatter colours from the whole spectrum and the spell is complete, even at Kempton Park, close to London. There, not even the spread of suburbia has managed to destroy the pretty, leafy charm of the place. In high summer it can seem like a multi-imaged dream.

The hoi polloi and the monied, more than 100,000 people, pack in for the USA's amazing and marvellous Kentucky Derby Day on Churchill Downs. Three miles from the centre of Louisville, pulses quicken there each May as the big moment of this festival draws close.

Bust a gut, perhaps, but get up the hill at Sandown Park in England whatever it costs. The spectators who now merely form a frieze of blurred images against which the horses and jockeys work their skill, will want to know the reason why if you don't. Vociferously.

Even the frosty air on the morning of Melbourne Cup Day in Australia cannot cool the passion and the heat expended on this most famous of Australian races, as one of the country's greatest jockeys and one of its finest horses have a final, limited workout, a last sharpening before the cut-and-thrust of the afternoon's major event.

1
BEGINNINGS

'Business in Exning in early medieval times wasn't too good, so a few of the sharper wits set up their stalls four miles away on the Icknield Way to sell their wares to passing pilgrims, and this New Market developed its own identity. It even acquired an Inn called the Griffin, and it was at this hostelry that King James I of England rested his funny stumpy little body after a long day's hunting for hare and partridge across the sweeping East Anglian countryside in 1605.'

A Plan
of
NEWMARKET HEATH,
and the
COUNTRY ADJACENT;
describing,
all the RACE COURSES now used.
Surveyed
by I. Chapman.

LONDON,
Printed for W. FADEN, Geographer to the King,
Charing Cross,
March 31.st 1787.

NOTE.

Round Course .... 4 Miles.
Dukes Course .... 4 Miles.
Beacon Course .... 4 Miles.
Rowleys Mile .... in the Flat.
Bunburys Mile *is the last Mile in the R.C.*
Two middle Miles .... in the B.C.
Two Year Old Course *from R.M.P. to the
Post in the Furs half a Mile.*
The new Flat *from the D.D. to the end of R.M.P.*

REFERENCES to the COLOURING.

Blue, Dukes Course.
Red, Beacon Course.
Yellow, Round Course.

MR 284

HORSE racing as we know it started in England. Well, you can start from a 500 BC Greek urn, from a later Roman mosaic or even from the Irish Book of Kells in the 8th century AD if you like. But since Newmarket became the first big centre of thoroughbred racing rather than of chariot or charger racing, let us begin just outside that Suffolk town, and standing knee deep in the supposedly magical water of St Wendred's Well.

The Well is said to be made up of seven springs, and at the bottom of a big beech-treed bank about three miles from Newmarket, the water still bubbles up as clean and clear as it did 13-odd centuries ago when the blessed St Wendred was held in such esteem. Not only did they name the spring after her, but when she died her body was carried around in a golden coffin to bring good luck in battle. St Wendred's magic may have given us inspiration, but it certainly didn't warm up Gerry Cranham and myself on a raw February afternoon that sent every shivering ghost on Newmarket Heath through our bones and left us wondering how on earth the Iceni tribesmen from these parts, and their Queen Boadicea, managed without thermal underwear.

So to spell out the connection with the sport of kings, the Melbourne Cup and the million-peso punters in Venezuela, in simple terms, it's almost a historic version of 'There was an old lady who swallowed a fly...'. Because of St Wendred's Well, a holy settlement grew up at Exning, half a mile away. Business in Exning in early medieval times wasn't too good, so a few of the sharper wits set up their stalls four miles away on the Icknield Way to sell their wares to passing pilgrims, and this New Market developed its own identity. It even acquired an Inn called the Griffin, and it was at this hostelry that King James I of England rested his funny stumpy little body after a long day's hunting for hare and partridge across the sweeping East Anglian countryside in 1605.

That royal involvement with Newmarket, through James I, his son Charles I and grandson Charles II, gave us the first direct link to the racing we have today. For when Charles II settled into his deceptively hedonistic stride, he became, through his many visits to Newmarket, the major catalyst in a crucial stage of horse racing's evolution.

Organised and impromptu races had, in the natural scheme of things, been taking place since man first shackled up the horse as a beast of burden. In England specifically there are records of a Roman garrison holding races at Wetherby in Yorkshire in 210 AD. The Venerable Bede, circa 720, also records some; there were races at Smithfield Fair at the gates of London in 1174, a match (at Newmarket) between the Earl of Arundel and the Prince of Wales (later Richard II) in 1377 and, in 1512 the City Fair at Chester in North-West England, had a wooden ball as the first recorded race trophy. But it was only from the 16th century, with Britain at last free of the wearisome internal strife of the Wars of the Roses, thet race meetings, really began to develop.

To this end, Henry VIII started royal stud farms near London at Eltham and Greenwich, and his daughter, Elizabeth I, began another further afield at Tutbury in Staffordshire. In these establishments and many others like them, it soon became clear that if you wanted to breed horses to run quicker you needed horses of Eastern

The antecedents of Newmarket and horse racing as we know them today are many and varied. At Exning in Suffolk the church of St Martin (Right), with its Early English chancel and some lancet windows that date back to the late 13th century, and a west tower recognised as being of approximately the same period, is one such small spot in the corridors of time. For Exning not only predates the home of racing but it was some of its inhabitants who established the New Market, four miles away, in early medieval times. Exning itself was born because of St Wendred's Well, the source of which are springs found at the bottom of a big beech-treed bank where Mr Robert Fellowes, agent for the Jockey Club (Far Right), can even today stand knee-deep. And perhaps appropriately enough it was in this flat countryside, where the ghosts of men and horses can be imagined in the mists, that Queen Boadicea in her horse-drawn chariot and the Iceni tribesmen gave so much trouble to the Romans. The coin (Above), was discovered in the area and was part of the currency of those brave Britons.

blood. And it's fascinating to look back across four centuries and see the matter-of-fact way Arabians, Barbs (from the North African Barbary Coast) and Turks were ordered up on what must have been an immensely long journey from Southern Europe, just as if they were Continental automobiles being imported today.

The process, therefore, of breeding to lighter, faster stock, and the fashion for going to the races (Elizabeth I had a special stand built for her at Croydon), was already well advanced before Charles II not only made Newmarket races the most important and best organised sporting event of the time, but actually rode in them.

He was also no mean performer between the sheets, and a cold morning looking at horses from Palace House Stables can be brightened by the thought of how Nell Gwynn, the most active of all Charles's amours, used to creep through a secret passage to the royal bed-chamber within a few yards of where the horses now stand. The Merry Monarch remains the only ruling English king to have actually ridden a winner, and although the pace of such races as the Newmarket Town Plate, which he won in 1671, were, with first a heat and then a run-off of over four miles, some way from the speed of, say, the last quarter in the Kentucky Derby, Charles's involvement meant that the sport developed immensely.

There was money in it too. Not just in the matches which were the most common form of race, with two horses pitted against each other and sidestakes often into four figures. There were also plates, where the prize was the total entry money, and betting could reach dizzy heights. Roger Longrigg's encyclopaedic and incomparable History of Racing quotes from Evelyn's Diary of February 28, 1699, that 'the Duke of Devonshire lost £1,900 at a horse race at Newmarket'. Allowing for inflation, that figure makes even the biggest-hatted Texan punter seem quite modest.

All this enthusiasm spurred the search for the best available blood, and at the start of the 17th century the first permanently influential stallions, and subsequently the first great racehorses, appeared. Although such names as Turks and Barbs are also used, the really influential Eastern horses were what we would now call Arabs, some were the spoils of war. The most famous of these was the Byerley Turk, which in 1688 was lifted by the enterprising Captain Byerley at the siege of Buda from some Hungarian with whom we might commiserate if it weren't for the strong suspicion that he had himself taken the animal from a Turkish gentleman.

The well-run legend has it that hostilities didn't end at Buda for the wretched quadruped. He had to carry the newly-promoted Colonel Byerley at the Battle of the Boyne, from the after effects of which Ireland is still suffering, before retiring to the sultan's life at stud where he became, through his great great grandson, Herod, one of the three stallions whose blood, remarkably, is traceable in all the 200,000-odd thoroughbreds now thundering around the globe.

The other two original patriarchs have equally colourful life stories. The Godolphin Arabian, foaled in the Yemen in 1724, was imported via Syria and Tunis to France as a present to Louis XV,

and then was supposedly stolen and used as a carthorse before ending up at Earl Godolphin's stud near Newmarket and becoming the grandsire of the immensely influential Matchem. The Darley Arabian was also well-travelled, having been born in Aleppo in 1700 and bought by a Mr Darley and dispatched on the long haul to his brother's stud in Yorkshire, where the horse sired Flying Childers, the first truly great racehorse.

Flying Childers, foaled in 1715, was never beaten, and a contemporary writer described him as 'the fleetest horse that ever ran at Newmarket, or, as is generally believed, ever ran in the world'. Be that as it may, the really interesting thing as we search for historical perspectives is that he was an absolutely pure-bred Arab. From that time on, the mixture of selective breeding, of better care and feeding, and perhaps of the cross with local stock, produced a hybrid, the English Thoroughbred, which became a distinctive type in itself, infinitely superior in speed to the original Arab. The English Thoroughbred remains the fastest weight-carrying creature the world has ever seen.

If the horses were beginning to take shape, so too were the tracks. Epsom, the future home of the Derby, was already holding meetings in the mid-17th century, as indeed was another Newmarket in Long Island, New York, and by George II's reign (1727-1760) there were 16 tracks officially allowed to run King's Plates. There were also so many little village meetings that in 1740 was passed an 'Act to restrain and prevent the excessive increase of horse races', with a main provision that no race should be worth less than £50.

Ascot had been started by Queen Anne in 1711, and Doncaster had also been going for over half a century when in 1776 a sweepstake was run there named after Lieutenant-General Anthony St Leger. It is a measure of the change during this period that this 'St Leger', the first of our 'classic' races, was over only two miles and was for three-year-olds, whereas at Epsom only seven years earlier the debut of Eclipse, one of the greatest horses to look through a bridle, had been as a five-year-old and in a race of four-mile heats.

Three-year-old racing, which had begun only in the 18th century, received its most famous boost in 1780 when a race named after Lord Derby was run on Epsom Downs, and by the end of that decade two-year-old racing had also become established. Some sort of order had begun to be made of these developments by the establishment, in 1752, of the Jockey Club as the controlling body of the sport, by the introduction (1773) of a Calendar as official record of races, and by the publication (1791) of their Stud Book in which, very soon, all thoroughbreds had to be registered.

But let's not have the orderliness of print delude us that the evolving sport was clear of corruption. Wherever you go in the world there are people eager to bend, bribe or bluster their way through the racing rule-book, and in the 18th century they got up to some fearful tricks. Horses were poisoned, races were fixed and even the Prince of Wales (later George IV) was made unwelcome after his horse, Escape, hacked up in

(Above) Nell Gwynn and Charles II

(Top Right) Racing on Newmarket Heath in the mid-18th century, captured in a painting by John Wootton looking towards 'The Gap' in the Devil's Dyke. George III is shown, among courtiers, looking on from a carriage.

(Bottom Far Right) Byerley Turk: His blood is traceable in many of the 200,000 thoroughbreds racing today.

(Bottom Right) Flying Childers: 'The fleetest horse that ever ran at Newmarket'.

a race at Newmarket in 1791, after being easily beaten the previous day.

The prime instigator of the prince's self-exile was Sir Charles Bunbury, one of the great reformers of the Turf. Besides campaigning against the usual wickedness of the game, he pioneered rather less severe training methods. The 18th century had such an obsession with sweating and purging horses–and people–that those old sporting prints of strange, scrawny, little racehorses may not have been much wide of the mark.

Bunbury has another claim to immortality. It was he who lost that famous spin of the coin in 1779 with Lord Derby, so that the world's most famous race is called the Derby and not the Bunbury. His horse, Diomed, took the first running of the Derby. Diomed was such a failure at stud in England that his fees were reduced to two guineas a mare, and at the ripe old age of 21 he was shipped off to Chesterfield, Virginia. But whether it was the sea voyage, American air or good old Virginian potatoes, the nicest of miracles happened to Diomed. He had eight more magnificently virile years, and became the most significant horse ever taken into America.

Bunbury's mantle as battler against corruption was donned in 1840 by Lord George Bentinck, an able if at times hypocritical aristocrat who, if he had done nothing else, would be remembered as the man who invented the horse box. In this light, horse-drawn van, he shipped Elis up to the 1836 St Leger to the horrified surprise of the bookies, who had happily laid the horse at long odds after seeing that it was still down in Sussex earlier in the week.

Bookies at that stage were a pretty unsavoury lot, the most notorious being William Crockford, who would try to bribe everyone from the jockey to the starter. But at least Bentinck put some teeth into racing administration, introducing the flag start and a system of keeping a check on betting defaulters. Perhaps his greatest triumph was the unmasking of the scandal of the 1844 Derby, in which the winner Running Rein was discovered to be a four-year-old.

Bentinck was followed by another autocrat, Admiral Henry Rous, whose meticulous naval training put some much-needed logic into the Rules of Racing, and in particular some science into the haphazard methods of handicapping horses by assessing the weight they should carry to give each one an equal chance. It seems so bland to write that now, but it's worth remembering that things had been so chaotic that many of the first handicaps had been worked out on the basis of size, a system that existed in the Philippines and which, quite apart from its irrelevance to actual running ability, leads to all sorts of lovely ruses to make a horse measure smaller than it actually is. Indeed, Rous himself once declared that a public handicapper would find the task of truly assessing a horse's ability impossible.

The old admiral made his breakthrough by insisting on the right of the authorities to discipline or suspend those who raced dishonestly, and his researches also came up with a scale of the weight that should be allowed for age between the different generations of horses that has remained one of the constant reference points. Rous died in 1877 and, looking back across the intervening century, we can begin to see other constants of the sport as we know it now.

For a start, the horse had settled into a definite standard and height, measuring normally between

15-2 and 16-2 hands, as it does today. Rous estimated that since 1700 the racehorse had grown by an inch every 25 years–that is, a whole hand in the century–and in 1850 he maintained that 'the best racehorse of 1750 is inferior to the common plater of today'. To judge merely by the times available (for instance the 1½-mile Epsom Derby course took the 1880 winner, Bend Or, 2 min 46 sec, and the 1970 winner, Nijinsky, almost 12 seconds less) similar improvement has been made since Rous's day. But more forceful riding tactics, and improved training facilities, have been more important factors over this period, and it is unlikely that such great 19th-century heroes as Ormonde and St Simon were in purely athletic terms much behind the top horses of today.

Plenty of other things had achieved something approaching their present pattern 100 years ago. Matches were by then a rarity. Races were for the distances and age groups that we are used to today, and the gruelling practice of running them in heats and a run-off had been discontinued. Grandstands had been built, courses were railed off and no longer did the owner and his cronies gallop along behind the race to see how their money went.

Jockeys also had to wear owners' identifying silks, and the exact entries, and weights to be carried, were published not only in the official Racing Calendar, but in newspapers whose interest and coverage of horse racing made it England's first truly national sport. Derby Day became a national holiday, when Parliament would rise and what seemed like most of London would make the long, dusty trek to be part of the great multitude on Epsom Downs.

In fact, it is in the area of public involvement that we see one of the two major changes from the 19th-century sport to the many-faced but understandable world-wide entity which this book looks at in various parts of the globe. But let's start with the most visible change, the actual running and riding of the races themselves, and although it may shake the British ego, one has to admit that almost all the force for change has come from abroad.

For if you stand out at Newmarket races today and imagine the races a century back–and it's not difficult with all the sporting prints available–you will notice that the whole rhythm has tightened up. No longer the battle of wits with the starter and his flag, but the mechanical stalls start, pioneered in America, Australia and even France before it was finally adopted here in 1963.

At the other end of the race, there is now a photo-finish system. The jockeys are better protected because of chin-strapped crash helmets, more identifiable because of distinguishing numbers beneath the saddle cloth. And they ride with much much shorter stirrup leathers, with their point of balance over the horse's shoulder, not back through its middle.

All these improvements originated outside Britain, and are now in common use worldwide, all were treated with profound scepticism when first introduced into Britain. None more so than the change to a 'shorter' riding style at the turn of the century, when the arrival from America of the first great exponent, Tod Sloan, was greeted with jeers of: 'Monkey up a stick!' Even that style was still many holes longer than the even more perched-up method adopted since the use of starting stalls over the last 20 years. Sloan had many faults, greed, arrogance and total dishonesty among them, but he and other Americans who followed him had the ultimate answer to their critics – they won. In fact, within a few years British jockeys had adopted not only the new style, but the new tactics of forcing the gallop all the way, rather than the old pattern of everyone waking up for the last desperate rush with whip and spur.

So the alteration of the rhythm of the performance has been one great change. The other has been the relationship with the spectator. For while, 100 years ago, racing was already drawing big crowds in England, France, Germany, America and Australia it was always a very patrician affair. The owners received nearly all the consideration. Since the public had begun to pay to go in, they were entitled to consider the races were run to some set of rules, but that was about where their involvement ended.

The blue blood may now be thinner, but the sheer cost of training fees means that most owners of racehorses tend to be plutocratic, and because they are the *owners,* they are still closest to the action. But all over the world the public have become very much party to the deal, a huge supportive mass who must be informed, and stimulated into putting their money not only through the turnstiles, but, most importantly, through the betting windows on and off the course. For the most important truth the 20th-century racing world has to accept is that it is locked into a dependent relationship with the public.

It's interesting to look back at how this relationship developed. Racing found the public a tolerable necessity, provided enough of them paid at the gate to keep the racecourses afloat, and governments were sometimes prepared to allow their gatherings provided they didn't breed too much villainy. But as 20th-century 'progress' caused the running costs of both racing and government to rocket after the Second World War, so at last the basic slice for the average man was increased. It was as if light bulbs went off in the authorities' brains, and prompted the idea that if the average man was that keen on betting, racing and government could siphon off a nice share of his indulgence for themselves.

The different agreements between governments and racing have provided the author with some of the most remarkable contrasts in this flip around the world. But what is certain is that the whole communication side of the business – public-address, camera-patrol films, betting-indicator systems and massive radio, press and television coverage – has given the game an

openness that the Victorians would have found quite unacceptable, and would have made old Queen Elizabeth tilt back her red head with laughter in her box at Croydon.

Yet the new openness has not removed the mystery, the tantalising end-of-the-rainbow magic of trying to find the winner. So long as that mystery holds, racing will too, but the progress that has been made means that when you look at the racing game around the world, you look first at the people. For me at least, that has been an education.

(Centre Left) Tod Sloan: 'Monkey up a stick!' they called him but he had the perfect answer for his critics – he won.

(Right) Sir Charles Bunbury (shown with Cox his trainer and stablelad): He gave Prince of Wales his come-uppance.

By Courtesy of Fores Gallery England.

2
BRITAIN

'When you see the light in the eyes of Oswald and the stud groom, Eric Scallon, as they watch their newest product wobble round his box, for all the world like a camera tripod on an ice rink, you realise that this is something much more than a business. And that's confirmed when Michael Oswald dashes across, through the dark of the stable courtyard and telephones almost direct to the owner. From the sound of it, the call is received with all the joy and interest of news of a first-born. It is a business that is a hobby that is a passion. Or vice versa. Perhaps it ought to be added that the owner – caring, enthusiastic and immensely well-informed despite her most rigorous of business schedules – is Her Majesty the Queen'.

MICRO CHIPS are wonderful things, but no one has yet grafted them on to the human skull. Until that happens, information will continue to outrun knowledge, and those who talk of a shrinking world will tend to a swelling around the head.

That's a rather pompous way of saying that it is as much a problem of brain-power as of bank balance that limits the scope of this book. Having spent 20 working years in the game, and travelled to racing countries all over the world, the overwhelming impression is of how vast and varied a globe you are dealing with, even in what many may see as the simple confines of the horse-racing business. So there comes a time when you need to return home to take stock, to sift through your information, and maybe even to give the lie to G.K. Chesterton's pessimistic note: 'It is a pity that people travel to foreign countries, it narrows their minds so much'.

Therefore, beyond the harsh statistics, our canvas does not in this volume even attempt the successes and problems of the Canadian racing scene, where the legendary E. P. Taylor bred Nijinsky and launched the greatest breeding operation of the age, but where also the future is threatened by government-sponsored lottery schemes. We have also not yet been to the vast Indian sub-continent, where racing now flourishes in four major centres despite excesses of climate and extremes of poverty. Panama, Venezuela, Brazil and Chile similarly set the luxury of horse racing in what sometimes appears to be a political powder keg, but sadly they too remain mere spots on some future itinerary, even if the likes of Pincay, Velasquez and Cordero have put Panama permanently on the riding map.

Some of those countries would merit a book to themselves, as certainly would the great continent of Africa, with all its huge assets in men and resources so perilously linked with the danger of self-destruction. As with everything else in that area, it's South Africa, with its money and its climate, which is infinitely the strongest racing country and which has, in Hawaii, bred a horse of world-wide influence. But having watched sad-eyed white settlers look askance at black jockeys in puttees and bare, bleeding feet in newly independent Kenya some 20 years ago, it is even more interesting to see how racing has prospered in that territory and in others less blessed by political stability. Proof, if you needed it, that the original thrills which inspired the Merry Monarch and his court in England three centuries ago, can still work in almost any age and environment.

Indeed, when we come now to look at the British scene, it is this same astonishing vitality, under financial and social pressures, which shines out as the most significant feature of recent years. Looking back, it has its funny side, because at the start of the Seventies, all of us pundits were predicting doom and despondency, the mass

exodus of all top horses and owners to France and America, with Britain sure to be reduced to the status of some equestrian banana republic. Yet turning into the Eighties, and despite a terrifying economic recession and a disadvantageous tax and betting system compared with all other major countries Britain, for all its woes, still had, at 7,000, a thousand more Flat horses in training than in 1976, and at over £12½ million, almost double the total prize-money on offer.

The British have moaned that French racing receives six per cent of total turnover, American between five and seven per cent and Japanese an amazing 15 per cent, while poor old 'Blighty' has 0.7 per cent. But both the two most recent independent enquiries (the Economist Research Unit, commissioned by the Jockey Club in 1976, and the Rothschild Report, sponsored by the government in 1978) concluded that our pitiful little slice was enough.

The truth is that we are landed with our system, and must make the best of it, which means, more than anything else, using this direct connection between the exclusive (sometimes, as we have seen in France, *dangerously* exclusive) world of the Turf and the man in the street. After all, there is nowhere else in the world where, on any weekday of the year, you can walk into a shop in any corner of the land and have a bet right up to the 'off'; and then listen to the commentary. Anyone who devises some

brilliant new computerised totalisator scheme has first of all to jump the hurdle of whether he is actually giving the punter a better deal, and it has been racing's greatest failure that there is so little representation of those whose betting provides up to 50 per cent of the whole prize-money, and without whose interest the whole circus would collapse in a twelvemonth.

What's more, despite a drop in racecourse attendances from almost 27 million in 1976 to 25½ million in 1981, and a failure of the betting turnover at over £2½ thousand million to keep pace with inflation, Britain still took more interest nationally in horse racing than any other country in the world. Each of the national newspapers (some 20 million total readership) carried every weekday racing programme, and the two rival TV channels screened up to 11 races live every Saturday. This is an extent of coverage which may not endear itself to the puritans, but which for the ordinary punter, 95 per cent whose gambling is done in one of some 10,500 betting shops, gives an opportunity to share in the so-called Sport of Kings unequalled anywhere else in the world.

Such a glowing tribute to betting shops and media coverage isn't just me puffing up my fellow hacks and paying my gambling debts. It is a strong belief that establishment thinking here, and more particularly abroad, does not realise how lucky Britain is. Of course, infinitely more money would

come back into the sport if we had something akin to the brilliantly run Australian off-course tote

(Preceding Spread) Training the racehorse. The beauty of the morning or the start of the headaches? You have to be stony of heart not to be stirred by the sight of one of Newmarket's 100-horse strings filing out across the Heath.

Newmarket had its first recorded horse race in 1622 and there are still two separate racecourses on the land owned by the ruling Jockey Club. These pictures of the original Rowley Mile, named after Charles II's favourite horse, show the international aspect of present day racing:

(Above) The 1967 2,000 Guineas, and the Australian star George Moore is seen winning on the Newmarket-trained Royal Palace from the French-trained Taj Dewan, ridden by the French crack, Freddie Head. Third is the Irish-trained and ridden Missile, owned by the American Raymond Guest.

(Top Right) Guest's young compatriot, Steve Cauthen is seen winning at Newmarket in 1981, beating the eleven times local champion Lester Piggott.

(Centre Right) Both Piggott and Cauthen were unplaced in the 2,000 Guineas in 1981. This classic has always been the first leg of the English Triple Crown, run in one mile, straight across the Heath.

(Bottom Right) The runners were certainly close enough at the finish in 1981 of this 2,000 Guineas, in which the Irish-bred, Greek-owned To-Agori-Mou wore down the English-bred, Indian-owned, Newmarket-trained Mataboy with the American-bred, Saudi-owned, Wiltshire-trained Bel Bolide. Not for nothing is Newmarket called the HQ of racing.

system. But the time to do that was back in 1962, when betting shops were legalised. Having failed to organise a deal then, having also failed with all shades of government since to obtain a larger share of the total betting turnover for racing's support, we are stuck with what we have got.

We hear a lot from the Jockey Club, quite rightly, about its concern for trainers, owners, breeders and horses, but how much better if every pronouncement was prefaced on behalf of the great unchampioned mass outside. In default of such an attitude, and because the big bookmaking chains recruited Lord Wigg, who as chairman of the Levy Board had been the finest tribune ordinary racing people ever had, we now have the absurd situation where it is the big bookmakers who speak most loudly on behalf of the punter. Well, it's nice that someone represents the sheep. But the wolf? That must be ridiculous.

Equally odd is the way losing betting-shop punters impugn everything from a trainer's honesty to a jockey's parentage. You would imagine that such a jaundiced view of proceedings would soon kill their enthusiasm, but it is one of racing's extremes of good fortune that people return again and again to the fray in the belief that one day they will unlock the key to this mysterious

world, and the whole cornucopia of riches therein, even if their task in Britain probably demands more knowledge less easily gained than anywhere else in the world. After all, the 34 flat-race tracks around the country hardly ever operate for more than two days consecutively, and the 6,000 horses who perform on them disappear between engagements to training stables so disparate that information gained is at best haphazard, and at worst deliberately misleading.

But it is a parallel and necessary good fortune that such healthy punter cynicism is probably less justified in Britain than elsewhere, and that the sport has in consequence kept a good enough face to attract, when it needed aid in the early Seventies, the support of business interests and oveseas investors. That new bunch of owners, and Robert Sangster's demonstration that the top British prizes were the best show-place for major stallion syndications, will one day be seen as the watershed of the Seventies.

But if the investors have changed, the outward look of the business has hardly changed at all. A good thing, too, because there is no sport in the world that passes down such a richly varied and beautiful tradition. The downland glories of Good-wood and Salisbury, the regal splendour of Ascot,

the historic city-walled circuit at Chester, York's great sweeping Knavesmire, Ayr's balmy gulf-

Newmarket's training grounds have 28 miles of grass, sand and peat-moss gallops and extend over 2,000 acres of Jockey Club-owned heath. Besides size the place has age. The Devil's Dyke in the background (Top Right) is an 18-foot high, 15-mile long earthwork which once formed the boundary between East Anglia and Mercia in Saxon times. The horses about to canter up Warren Hill (Below) on the other side of town comes from Bruce Hobb's Palace House Stables where in the 17th century Charles II (the only king to ride a winner) once consorted with well-known orange-seller, Nell Gwynn. Bruce Hobbs first made headlines by winning the 1938 Grand National on Battleship, but his successful career is now confined to the flat. So is that of Berkshire trainer Peter Walwyn (Centre) whose Lambourn yard has sent out classic winners like Grundy, Humble Duty and Polygamy. Here, over breakfast in 1978, he talks things over with his then assistant Jamie Douglas-Home, with Pat Eddery, who was associated with many of Walwyn's major triumphs before taking a retainer from Vincent O'Brien in 1980, and his wife Virginia Walwyn (universally known as 'Bonk'). Another vital member of the team is head lad Ron Thomas (Bottom Right) pictured with equipment for cleaning out his horse's box, and saddle pad and crash helmet for riding out. (Note: the two rings of the martingale, a common aid in morning exercise but not on the racecourse.) Ron is one of Walwyn's 50 strong staff, who look after 120 horses, all of whom need mucking out (Bottom Centre).

stream climate, Newmarket's enormous rolling heath, Epsom's crazy climbs and turns. All of those 100, some as much as 300, years old. All different, some right-handed, some left, and some almost dead straight, and with variety you bring hope.

Mind you, all racing peddles hope as if it were Turkish-market hash, but British flat racing, with it's five-month break between November and March, and its horses all warming up at their separate stables, is about as brazen with the powders as you can get. By the end of February, every hard-luck story has been smoothed into total credibility, every potential star has the world at his feet, and of course 'this is the nicest bunch of two-year-olds we have ever had'. To go round evening stables, the yard all swept, the horses held soldier-like to attention in their boxes, the smell of hoof-oil and sweet fresh hay, is an almost dangerous pleasure. Look at gleaming thoroughbred after gleaming thoroughbred in an atmosphere that is heady with belief (not to mention the trainer's whisky), and you will need a heart of stone not to leave convinced you have seen the winners of all five Classics and every big handicap from the Stewards' Cup to the Pitmen's Derby. One false move and you will have ended up buying a share in one. Beware, it's not only marriage that often fits the definition: 'A moment of pleasure for a lifetime of regret.'

Yet this is marvellously intoxicating stuff. Go to Newmarket one March morning, 1,700 horses, 40 stables and 30 miles of gallops on what, with its three main training areas and 2,500 acres, still claims to be the largest slice of tended grassland in the world. This is a universe of long files of horses scudding past cool, watchful men, the trainers who are the hub on which the whole horse town and its

Epsom, when staging the Derby and The Oaks is much more of a funfair occasion than Royal Ascot. The gipsies and fairground amusement promoters set up shop to tempt visitors on to such delights as the big wheel. The cockney pearly kings, traditionally from the East End of London, raise money for charity. Many of the visitors on the Downs travel from London on old, open-topped buses, which are often the scene of some pretty raucous entertainment. There is a good view of things from the top storey on a nice day, but it must be a squash down below if it rains. Epsom does not really have the cachet for dressing up, which is such a feature of Ascot and nowadays morning dress is worn only on Derby day itself. There is also some racing and top-class runners taking part. Sea Bird was poised on the heels of the leaders coming round Tattenham Corner in the 1965 Derby, (Centre Far Right) which he went on to win with immense ease, persuading many that he was one of the truly great horses of all time. Not so good, maybe, was the 1980 Derby winner Henbit (red spots on blue) but he did not lack courage as he struggled home with a broken bone in his leg to beat Master Willie, Rankin, Pelerin (rails) and Garrido. Willie Carson, who rode Henbit for Dick Hern, also won on Troy (24) seen going to post for 1979 Derby, and the Queen's filly Dunfermline, who won The Oaks, most appropriately, in her owner's Silver Jubilee year of 1977; no wonder he grinned. There is nothing new for some jockeys to be in the number board for the Derby but many of the names in 1977 (Top Left) are history already.

3RD RACE		DR			
	V. SAINT MARTIN	4	12 F. DURR	23	24 A. MURRAY	18
1	J. CRUGUET	22	13 E. HIDE	1	25 T. MURPHY	11
2	L. PIGGOTT	10	14 G. LEWIS	15		
3	J. MERCER	14	15 B. TAYLOR	24	25 RUNNERS	
4	P. WALDRON	5	16 G. MOORE	12	BLINKERS 7.8.21.	
5	J. GORTON	7	17 E. ELDIN	25	WHITE.	
6	R. PARNELL	2	18 G. BAXTER	21	L. RED H'S on BODY	
7	P. EDDERY	19	19 E. JOHNSON	8	2. BLACK CAP.	
8	P. COOK	20	20 W. WILLIAMSON	17	10 YELLOW - GRN SL'S	
9	A. BARCLAY	9	21 G. STARKEY	13	YELL' ARMLETS-GRN CAP	
10	W. CARSON	6	22 M. THOMAS	16	OFFICIAL GOING	
11			23 F. HEAD.		FIRM	

ING PRICES

APPROX. ODDS							
HORSE No.	12	11	15	3	1	14	BAR
PRICE	11/2	5/1	10/1	12/1	8/1	10/1	20/1

STAND
KMO 293
121 CGF

Coca-Cola

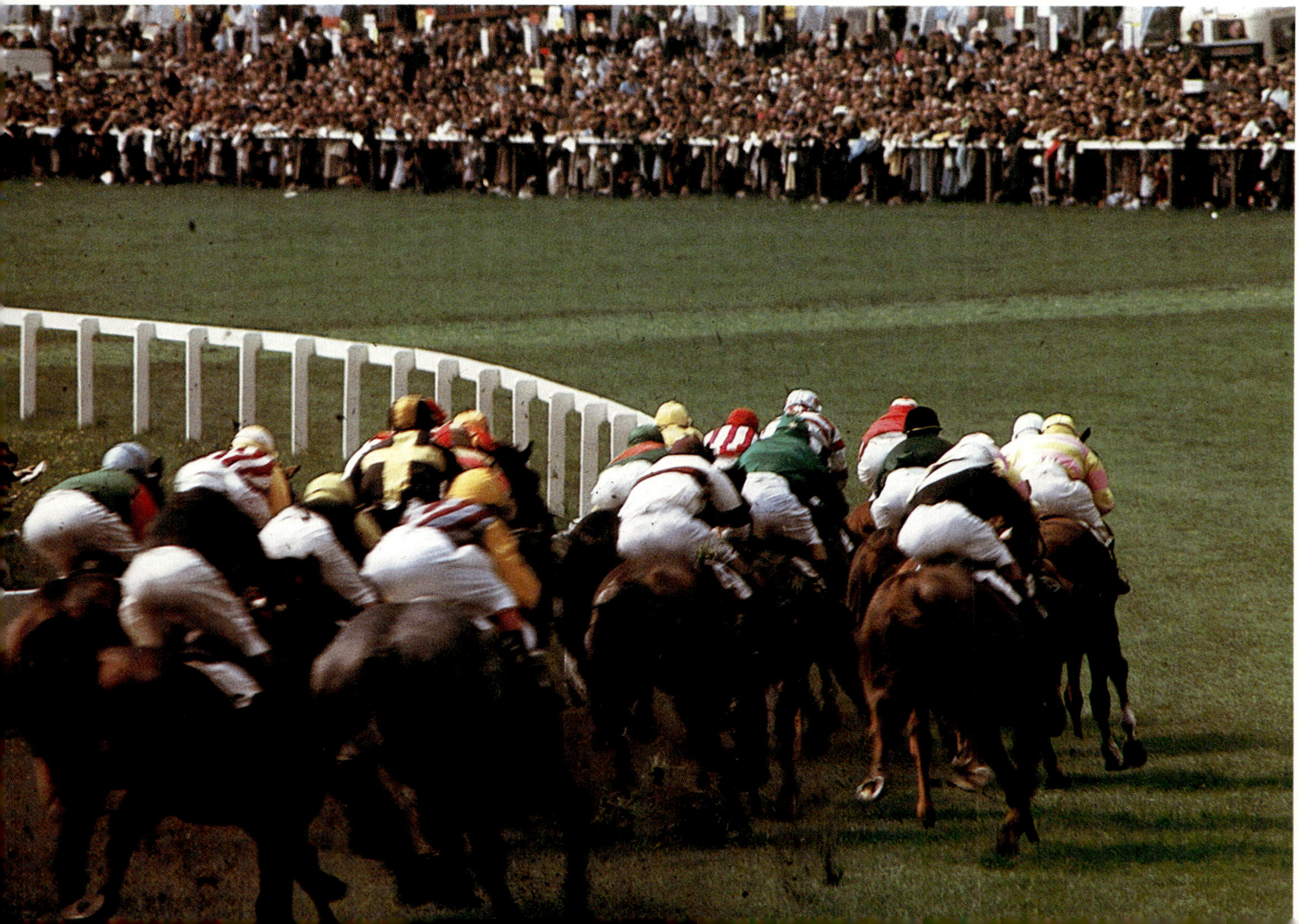

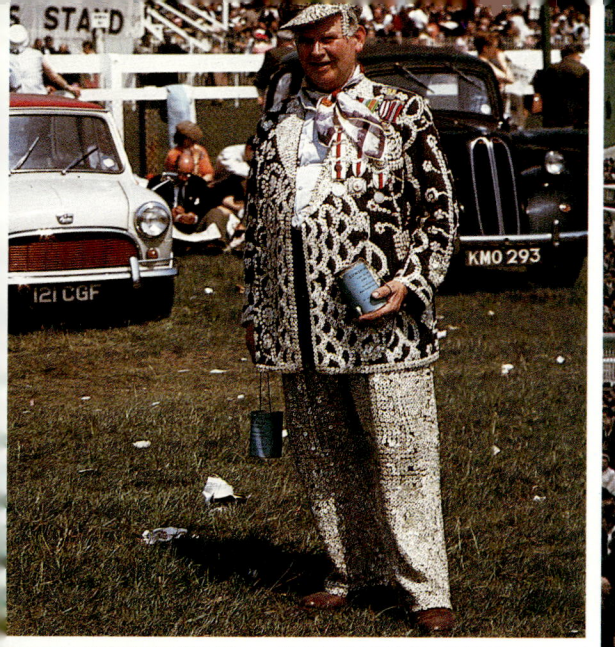

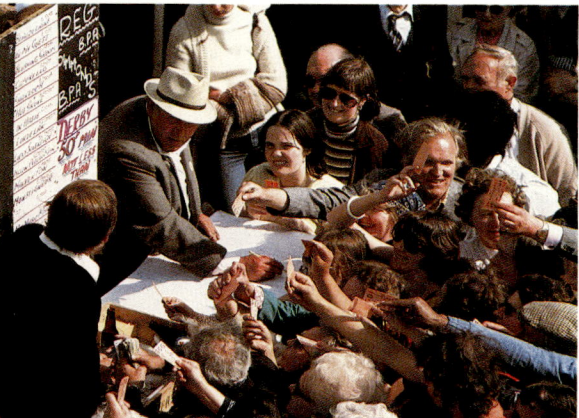

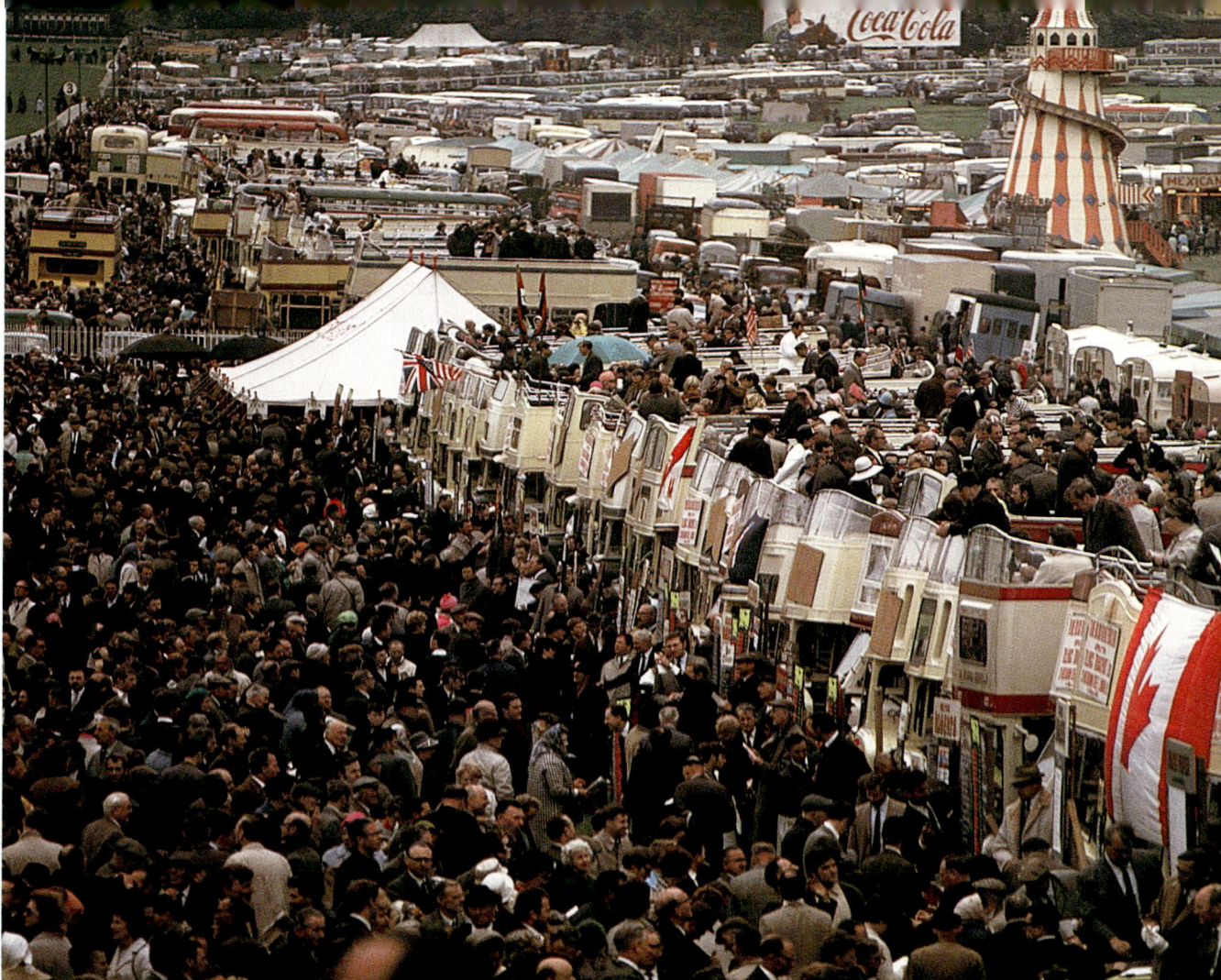

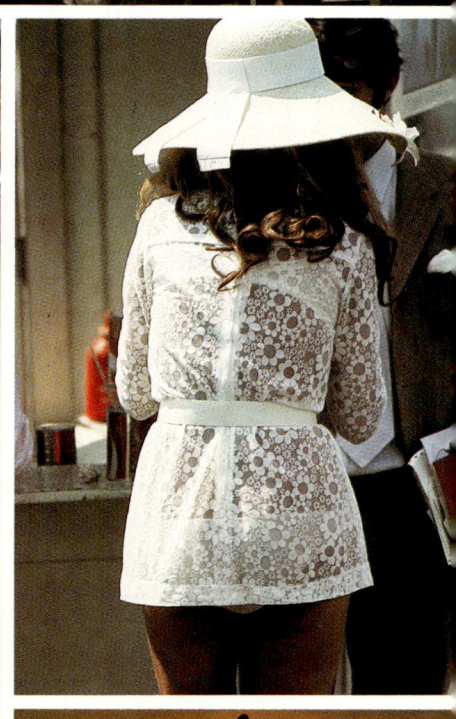

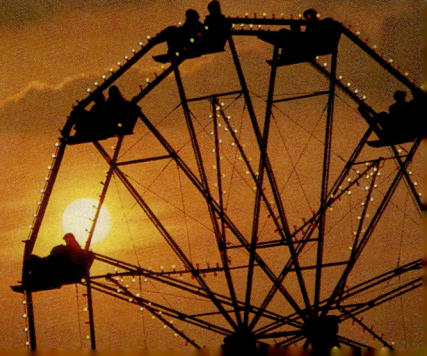

2,000 ancillary jobs depend. Men like Henry Cecil, already twice top trainer in his early thirties, lean, dark, pensive and casually elegant. Bruce Hobbs, still as tall and magnificent in the saddle as when he rode Battleship to win the Grand National way back in 1931. Michael Stoute, the new lion who conditioned Shergar to roar home by a record 12 lengths in the 1981 Derby at Epsom. And Frankie Durr, the little simian figure just turned from a long career as a jockey and now putting his love of gadgetry into every training aid.

Don't stop at Newmarket, with its 300 years of Turf history. Travel on up to Richmond, in Yorkshire, where the castle has stood proud above the River Swale for fully 900 years and where, up on the high moor, Bill Watts now carries the torch which has been taken to Classic success by three generations of his family.

Come to the Berkshire Downs, those ancient, contrarily named uplands where St George once slew the dragon and where the first primitive men made their encampments above the swamps. Lambourn has almost 1,000 horses, led by the great 100-strong battalions of Peter Walwyn and Barry Hills, both of whom trained major Classic winners in the Seventies. Move 10 miles east along the ridge, and you find the Royal trainer, Dick Hern; every inch the old-fashioned cavalry officer as he rides out with his string, but every ounce the professional as he prepares for another record-breaking season.

It was from West Ilsley that Dick Hern turned out Brigadier Gerard to win 21 out of 22 races in 1970-72, and it was one of those story-book coincidences with which racing abounds that in the same generation there was, in Mill Reef, another equally brilliant colt trained 15 miles across the Downs by another Royal trainer, Ian Balding, at Kingsclere. After one decision in the Brigadier's favour, the revenge match never happened, but the rivalry between the camps was so strong that you could almost imagine the two heroes neighing out their challenges across the Berkshire air.

Kingsclere was the setting for the animal classic, Watership Down, but even the most fanciful fictional caperings could not match the

Pause for thought. Trainer John Dunlop sits and watches some of his mammoth string walk through the oak trees at Arundel, six miles from the Sussex coast. This tranquility is in direct contrast to the jet-setting hassle which makes Britain's top trainers the busiest in the world. During one week in July, 1982, Dunlop saddled the winner of the Scottish Derby, spent three days at the Keeneland Sales in Kentucky, touched down briefly in England before going on to Belgium to supervise another winner before returning to Ascot for yet another victory. In 1982 Dunlop had a published list of 146 horses in training, the largest string in the country, and won over £500,000, £200,000 of this sum overseas. In the best British tradition, this success has been achieved with a blend of new and old. Dunlop's yard, which he took over in 1966, is based on the old stables of Arundel Castle, seat of the Dukes of Norfolk, owners of the oldest title in the land and the Earl Marshals of England.

of the arm to where his horses are cantering, and add: 'And look at those, the best bunch of…king horses in the country'.

Even we hardened racing hacks find it difficult not to be bowled over by the sheer timeless beauty of these early mornings. Ten miles along from Ryan Price there is the picture-book little town of Arundel. It has old, gabled streets, and a massive grey Norman castle up behind which, for over 500 years, has been the home of the Dukes of Norfolk, the Earl Marshal (senior nobleman) of England, and in whose stables and grounds John Dunlop's modern-day racing army goes about its manoeuvres. Dunlop has the tall, clean-cut look of the British military officer down the ages, but he didn't assemble the biggest string in the country (140 horses in training) by being an army block-head. Nor has his long list of successes in England and all over Europe been achieved without a comprehensive knowledge of the latest methods in his profession. After all, even if the beauty of the place in the morning might gain you a few owners, it is what you do with the horses that keeps them. For all its great cloak of privilege and tradition, British racing is still answerable to that severest of disciplines – the need to produce winners.

The extent to which British trainers have adapted the old methods to the new technology available is best seen a dozen miles up the road from Arundel at Pulborough, where Guy Harwood has developed by far the most impressive self-made training centre of recent years. Because he had an engineering, rather than a military, back-ground (his father ran a garage), and because his whole yard and gallops have been newly built rather than long-established, it is easier with Harwood to see the modern-day precision beneath the well-worn routine.

Other trainers (Dick Hern for one) have for some time laid store on a horse's weight, but it has taken Harwood to say it loud and clear. Other trainers and vets have been trying to get our reading of a horse's blood tests as exact as the Australians and Americans do, but Harwood and Brian Eagles (who stayed some months with the great blood guru, Percy Sykes, in Sydney), wave the banner of their profession's competence more vigorously than equally able but more reticent

real-life character of Captain Ryan Price and his band on another set of Downs 100 miles south-east at Findon, in Sussex. For to say that Ryan is larger than life is a bit like calling the Mad Hatter predictable. A former commando who won the war single-handed, Ryan became one of the greatest jumping trainers of his time before, like Vincent O'Brien, switching to the Flat with equal success. But where O'Brien conducts his operation with a reserved, almost inscrutable, watchfulness, Ryan wears his great heart not just on his sleeve, but somewhere way out beyond his cuffs, and for years

the ancient Stone Age camp of Chanctonbury Ring has reverberated with the roar of 'the gallant captain' instructing his string of a morning.

These downland settings are unique to British racing, and to stand on the Findon Downs and look out and see the farmland stretch down to the little town of Ferring and the English Channel beyond, you find it hard to disagree when the captain takes your arm and, with a characteristic superlative, says: 'Look at it, most beautiful place in the world'. And then, if he is in one of his wonderfully bom-bastic moods, he will give another theatrical sweep

The human element. Charm or anachronism? It may be the computer age but these shots from Lingfield racecourse, 30 miles south of London, reflect the number of jobs still needing manpower. Handpower in the case of the late Billy Macdonald, using Tic-Tac, the bookies' sign language to telegraph the latest news from one betting ring to another. The white glove is used for visibility and when the attention is attracted, the Tic-Tac gives the number of a horse and then its betting price. The raised right arm, for example, is the sign for 5–1. Whatever its efficiency, there is an old-fashioned feel about the Tic-Tac, just as there is about the number board and the stewards' race scrutiny (Top Left). At most English racecourses the individual numbers, the jockeys' names and other necessary information are still pulled up by hand.

15.RUNNERS
BLINKERS
7.9.12.17.18.22

Official GOING

STRAIGHT COURSE
GOOD TO SOFT
ROUND COURSE
SOFT

teams. And other training establishments have new American-style barns and all-weather woodshaving training tracks, along with all their 20th-century office equipment, but none of them has yet packaged it into such a fine, unblushing brochure as Harwood has done. It may not be everybody's style, but it reminds potential critics (as well as investors) that just because British racing has the longest history, it doesn't have to be out of date.

In 1981 came the ultimate justification of the Harwood method, and a terrible blow to all of us who have long used such good-sounding phrases as 'furnished', 'let down' and 'looks twice the horse he was last year' about some three-year-old Classic hope. 'That's nonsense!' said Guy in the last week of February, 1981. 'It's a myth that a three-year-old is going to be a whole lot bigger and heavier horse than he was as a two-year-old. If he runs enough for you to find his best racing weight, you will discover it is almost exactly the same. If he is much heavier, he is unfit. If he is lighter, he is sick.'

Since Harwoood had To-Agori-Mou heading for the English Guineas, and Recitation for the French equivalent (La Poule d'Essai des Poulains),

we could sit back and judge by results. Recitation duly won his trial race at Salisbury, but when To-Agori-Mou, the previous year's top-rated two-year-old, got well beaten in his comeback at Newmarket, there was no lack of grandstand critics pouting their lower lips in disapproval. All the more so when a quite-unabashed Harwood insisted that To-Agori-Mou's weight, 1,160lbs in February, 1,105lbs at Newmarket and 1,090lbs the previous year, proved that he was not yet fit. 'And', he added, 'the horse only lost ten pounds in the race and the journey. Most of them lose thirty pounds on this first trip of the season. It just shows how much work To-Agori-Mou needs to get to his peak.' Again the colours were nailed to the mast, and one can only report that To-Agori-Mou, like Recitation, did not let his master down. Both of them won their respective 'Guineas' at the weights predicted, and To-Agori-Mou continued at that same poundage to prove himself one of the gamest and most consistent milers for many years.

This emphasis on weight suddenly provides a new, measurable guide to a horse's well-being where before everyone had to rely on goodwill and guesswork and rumour as much as research. It also

makes one wonder when each racecourse will be equipped with a weighbridge, and the horse's

The little armies prepare for war. A military parallel can often be applied to the British way of training, especially in yards set in their own land, like these two: Ian Balding's at Kingsclere in Berkshire (Bottom Left) and John Dunlop's (Above) at Arundel in Sussex. If horses are to handle adequately a wide variety of differently shaped tracks, the equivalent of a little drill is needed. Ian Balding, in front on the right (Right), leads some of his 60-strong team back from exercise on the famous Kingsclere Downs. There he has already trained Mill Reef to win the Epsom Derby and Prix de L'Arc de Triomphe in 1971, on land where six other Derby winners have been conditioned over the past 100 years. But it's not all downland work and three horses breeze along the specially-laid Dormit woodchip gallop. This gives consistent going if the turf becomes too firm or too boggy. In the centre picture John Dunlop's calming of a young two-year-old is much in the manner of his father, a distinguished surgeon. This is January and for the two-year-olds the early drills consist of trotting and hacking around the indoor riding school, 49 bundles of hope scampering round together. It is a sight that might have given old-fashioned, keep-your-distance trainers something like apoplexy, but the obvious success of the session merely confirms the old truth that a horse is a herd animal. He is at his best when he can be allowed to remain so.

As well as the obvious testimonial to the trainer's skills, and perhaps to the demanding nature of the downland gallops at West Ilsley, the fact that Brigadier Gerard's achievement (and that of Royal Palace in 1967) was possible at all, surely emphasises the need for keenness of mind, as well as fitness of body, on the broad, green tracks of Britain and France. For while it must be true that the European Classic contender is not as physically fit as his Australian or American counterpart (he will have done half as much flat-out galloping), you can also bet your last ticket that if overseas-style work-outs were the answer, the likes of Hern, Cecil and Walwyn would be on to it. When you have got five-figure prize-money, and seven million in stallion values at the end of the line, you will try anything.

Newmarket is a good place to study the problem. The huge, open grasslands may have been a perfect place for Boadicea to whirl about in her chariot, but put a racehorse at one end and when you set off, the sight of such infinite space tends to go to his head like whisky on an empty stomach. With pretty few exceptions (High Top in the 1972 Two Thousand Guineas), it's usually best to settle a horse ('rate' him, in US jargon) in a race, and use his punch at the finish. When you puzzle over the completely different rhythms of the Kentucky Derby (10 furlongs) and the English Two Thousand Guineas (eight furlongs), you only have to compare the two tracks they are run on – Churchill Downs dead flat and a mile round; Newmarket's Rowley Mile a mile straight, with a marked descent at The Bushes two furlongs out, and a definite climb out of the dip in the last furlong. Newmarket gives no place to hide, no bend to help, and if you go down to the track to

racing weight made known to the public. It is a crucial piece of information which would do more for our knowledge of a horse's fitness than all the quotes and excuses from trainers, jockeys and their staff. For much of the fascination and frustration of this early part of the season, and the lead up to the first two Classics at the very beginning of May, lies in how completely in the dark we all are. Before the Kentucky Derby, run on the same day as our Two Thousand Guineas, and also the first leg of the triple crown, a horse may have up to six races earlier in the season, whereas a top English Guineas contender will hardly ever have more than one, and sometimes, as in Brigadier Gerard's case, none.

That we feel our way around at all says much for the closeness of the racing family. Because without knowing the horse's weight, without any official record of such common aids overseas as exact work-out times, and without even a glimpse of the wretched beast for the previous six months, it is possible for an outsider to get some idea of its condition. There is usually a press man close to the stable from whose pieces you can glean some clues; there is the cynical eye of the betting market, which will soon send a horse's price sailing out if it gets a

whiff that he is not ready; and most of all in this seemingly inexact end of the business, there is still the evidence of statistics telling you who does, and who does not, win races first time out.

A computer freak called Peter Jones has developed a highly original business with his Trainers' Record, logging the exact results of every stable, the number of horses, the number of starts, the winners, the tracks, the jockeys and, of course, the winners first time out. For instance, Jones's 1980 opus records that no fewer than 17 of Dick Hern's horses won on their first appearance of the season, a pattern which he has long maintained. Brigadier Gerard's owner-breeder, John Hislop, recounts how he never queried the policy when told that Hern planned to run his horse first time out in the 1971 Guineas. Hislop had been crack amateur rider, enviably literate author and *eminence grise* of the racing press, but the plan is still inconceivable in Australian or American terms, for don't forget this was Brigadier Gerard's one chance to win a Classic, and the showdown not just with Mill Reef but with the previous season's champion two-year-old, My Swallow. And the horse was to face it without having had a race for six months.

My Fair Lady to life. Everyone dresses up for Royal Ascot whether they are in the Royal Enclosure, like owner's wife Mrs. Harry Demetriou (Top Right) or in one of the less exotic enclosures. The four days of the meeting in the middle of June have for long been as much fashion show as sporting event and while hats have always been a feature of the finery, the famous Mrs. Shilling (Centre) has taken the whole thing to ludicrous lengths not unconnected with her son's millinery business. Still many ladies get it precisely right and those men who like to have chauvinistic jokes about seeing how their fancies move enjoyed the 1977 reappearance of the mini skirt. The very first day of racing at Ascot took place in 1711 on August 11 and in the presence of Queen Anne and her Court. The royal connection has stayed and the meeting is always started each day by the carriage procession of the Queen and her guests down the course (Bottom Far Right). The royal party will have been driven from Windsor Castle, 6 miles away, where Her Majesty always has a house party for the races which still have direct connections with the sovereign and where the members' enclosure is re-christened the Royal Enclosure for this meeting. Entry to this area can be obtained only by completion of a voucher form, with a guarantor, six weeks in advance from St. James's Palace. The screening process is nowadays defended on the simple basis of a need to limit numbers. Barring of divorcees from the Royal Enclosure is now mercifully a thing of the past and even children are allowed entry on the Friday of the meeting.

ROYAL
ASCOT
FULL
FORM
RATINGS AND FORECASTS

watch the race, you can appreciate why it claims to be the fairest test of the thoroughbred in the world.

That's no bad boast, but it's a pity that it has to be tempered by the thought that this is just about the unfairest test for a spectator anywhere on the planet. The Two Thousand Guineas is bad enough, yet that is only one mile straight. Imagine a race like the Cesarewitch two-and-a-quarter miles, with just one slight dog-leg in the middle. They literally start in Cambridgeshire and end in Suffolk, there is time to order another glass and damn near drink its contents between the 'off' and the field coming into the view of anything less than a radio telescope. At least there is a competent running commentary these days (many disapproved when it was started as recently as 1954), and there are several TV monitors in the bars, but this still means that the average racegoer in the grandstand has paid all his travel and entry money to see far less than he would at home on his television set. It's a ludicrous situation, and the moves at the beginning of 1982 towards renting a massive Diamond Vision portable TV board to place opposite the grandstand need to bear rapid fruit, or the customers will start to vote with their feet.

So the Two Thousand Guineas (for colts) and One Thousand Guineas (for fillies) are won and lost (both of them, by the way, now worth something like 20 times their original value). Punters pick over their pockets, we all start sucking up like mad to the winning connections, but sadly the horse who has actually done the running tends to disappear off to the dope-box, and out of our lives, as quickly as he or she entered it. If you *do* follow them, you will be rewarded by sharing some of the best moments with some of the happiest people in sport. Which is how, in 1976, I came to

They also race horses at Royal Ascot and there is no one more knowledgeable or more pleased to have a winner than the Queen herself. Her highly successful stud and stable has produced Ascot winners like Buttress whom she and the Queen Mother are pictured greeting (Bottom Far Right) after Willie Carson had ridden him to victory in the 1979 Queen's Vase. The Queen and her mother are flanked by the royal racing manager, Lord Porchester (left) and the senior royal trainer, Dick Hern (right), who are both hatless, traditionally so in the sovereign's presence or even when cheering on a great horse like the stayer Le Moss, seen winning Ascot Gold Cup (Bottom Near Right) for the second time in 1980. The Ascot circuit is just over a mile-and-a-half long from where the runners turn away from the stands and its undulations include a marked climb towards the finish. The winner's circle is the most coveted racing spot of the week, and no man has been there more often in recent years than Lester Piggott (Bottom Left), pictured talking to trainer Paul Cole (black topper) after his victory on Crimson Beau in the 1979 Prince of Wales Stakes. The famous Ascot Lawns makes a magnificent sight but it should be remembered that Ascot has 25 days racing outside the royal meeting. It is home, at the end of July, of Britain's richest race, the King George VI and Queen Elizabeth Stakes, whose 1975 finish between Grundy and Bustino (Centre Far Right) was an unforgettable epic at the end of the fastest (2 min 26.98 sec) mile-and-a-half ever recorded in Britain.

meet Jean-Pierre Fourchault, a 25-year-old Paris-born bachelor with a swarthy, smiling South Pacific face, and George Winsor, a 26-year-old Cornishman, whose daughter Kerry had her fifth birthday on Two Thousand Guineas day. That Thursday evening at Newmarket, they were tending equally different horses – Jean-Pierre's a tiny chestnut filly whose tail nearly touched the ground, George's a narrow but taller colt with spots on his bottom. They were half-a-mile apart, with the London Road and some of the racecourse between them, but their joint glow of pride could have lit beacons all over Cambridgeshire. The two horses were Flying Water and Wollow, the brilliant winners of that year's Guineas.

The glow was freshest up at The Links (the visitors' stables adjoining the golf course), for it was only two hours after Yves St Martin had brought Flying Water through with her devastating challenge, and since the filly had only arrived at Newmarket at 10 o'clock that morning after a three-hour stall-to-stall journey from Chantilly, she must also have become the fastest-travelled classic winner of all time. 'She's so good that there isn't really anything for me to do', said Jean-Pierre, as Angel Penna's travelling head lad, Jacques Caron, put the anti-phlogistine paste on Flying Water's precautionary tendon-support bandages. 'You just lead her anywhere you want, into the box, the plane, round the paddock, the parade. She seems to like it all. And look at her now, completely calm'.

Over at Henry Cecil's modern barn-type stables (this was before Cecil succeeded his father-in-law, Noel Murless, at Warren Place), Wollow was under equally fervent admiration. 'Wollow got the mood all right', said George Winsor, looking at the empty champagne bottles from the previous night's celebrations. 'Normally he gets a bit funny with more than two people in his box, but yesterday they were all over the place, and he was as good as gold. It was the same at the races. Leading him across from here, he was playing the fool, rearing up and squealing. Once he got to the course he was quiet as a sheep – right until the parade, when he began to want to get on with it'.

Neither of our lads rode a winner as a jockey. Fourchault did have 15 mounts as a Maisons-Laffitte apprentice, but Winsor had none at all, as he was already 8st 4lb when he joined Cecil's stepfather, Sir Cecil Boyd-Rochfort, in 1966. Yet both lads rode well enough to have experienced the two Guineas winners' most clearly viewable asset – a light and perfectly-synchronized action which made that week's rivals look leaden-footed even on the way to the start.

'As soon as she came to us last year, you could feel that she could go fast', said Jean-Pierre of Flying Water, as he took off the dark blue stable coat that is the Wildenstein livery. 'She's only small [the assessment of 1.55 metres, 15 hands 2in, looked on the generous side] but she can always out-run them'. George Winsor sensed Wollow's high class before he fully felt it, for he had led up the colt's sire, Wolver Hollow, to win the Eclipse Stakes in 1969. 'This feller was perhaps a couple of inches shorter [just 16 hands] but otherwise he was the spittin' image of his father, right down to the way the top of his mane won't lay over the right side of his neck'. He added, with real affection: 'Wolver Hollow was a great ride, but this fellow is even better. You can sit behind anything in a gallop, and when you want him to he will go past like a Rolls-Royce. It's a tremendous feeling'.

So how confident were our two heroes before the most important lead-ups of their careers? Jean-Pierre really doesn't seem to have worried: 'I knew she would be behind early on, and once Yves moved her out and I could see how fast she was closing on them, I was quite happy'. Conversely, George wasn't quite as easy. 'It was all right in the parade because Dettori was so relaxed. Some jockeys get terribly nervous. But when I had loosed them off, I suddenly realised that this was it and I could feel my heart going thump, thump, thump. It was the same when they first called him in the race, and afterwards I could feel the old ticker going hard against my shirt'.

Naturally there was a financial reward in all this. George Winsor had received nearly £1,000 from his 2½ per cent share of Wollow's winnings the previous season, with a similar amount going to the head lad, Paddy Rudkin, and the rest of Cecil's enthusiastic team. They were to receive another £1,200 from that Classic victory, and although their French counterparts get merely 1½ per cent of all winnings to the general pool, their dapper turn-out was a reminder that in the past year Penna's horses had collected more than 3½ million francs.

This was just a year after the bitter scenes of the stable lads' strike had caused a near riot at the Newmarket Guineas meeting, and at one stage had threatened the Two Thousand Guineas itself. It was clearly the job at its best. 'It's the Derby next', said George, with wonder in his eyes, 'I've never had a runner there before, but I expect we will be all right. It's just that I never thought that this could happen to me so soon. It's something that comes once in a lifetime'.

The Derby dream didn't come off for Wollow, who finished fifth after an unlucky-looking run. But George has continued to make his way, and is now travelling head lad to Cecil's mighty team, a living tribute that with luck and application the racing ladder can be climbed. He is, of course, at the glamorous pinnacle of his trade, and no one should forget that for the average lad there are no fat percentages, no glittering perks, just a pitifully low basic wage. Yet its 1981 level of £65 for a 40-hour week was twice its level of four years earlier, and the fact that some of our worst fears have not been realised suggests that the shared involvement with the racehorse, whether it's a Classic winner or selling plater, binds stables together even in circumstances when other businesses would surely fall apart.

No doubt the Derby dreams are the strongest tonic of all, and for four giddy weeks after the Guineas any three-year-old with four legs, a tail and the Derby engagement has a chance of making the headlines. For unlike the Preakness Stakes, the second leg of the American Triple Crown, which at 9½ furlongs actually goes down in distance, the Epsom Derby is a whole half-mile farther than the Two Thousand Guineas, bringing with it not just the possibility of a different result but a whole new batch of stamina-bred runners. As in 1980 and 1981, the Two Thousand Guineas winner may not even be a Derby runner, and therefore May is an exciting, if somewhat hysterical, month for anyone following the British flat-racing scene.

But it is also a beautiful time, and anyone locked on to the Derby Trial circuit will certainly get a guide to historic England, even if he never sees anything that turns out to be any use at Epsom. For instance, the Chester meeting in the week after Newmarket is the oldest in the country on its original site, there being records back to 1540, which was 45 years before old cloak-throwing Sir Walter Raleigh founded Virginia in the name of Elizabeth I.

James Gill's unique book on British racecourses claims Chester may well have raced some time before then, and with all due respect to the grandstand, you can well believe it, for the track is bounded on one side by the ancient Roman Wall, and on the other by the River Dee, after which the Romans called their city Deva. Just a mile round with only a furlong straight, Chester is a little 'bull-ring' by our standards, but the premium it puts on handiness has made it a popular Derby trial for trainers, and Henbit and Shergar both had their final pre-Epsom race in the mile-and-a-half Chester Vase.

The richest Derby trial in recent years has been the Mecca Dante Stakes, run at York the week after Chester and won in 1978 by the subsequent Derby hero, Shirley Heights. York, too, is riddled with history, having been the Roman city of Eboracum, the gateway to the far north, and the racecourse goes back over 250 years, even if doubling up as a public execution ground for part of that time. Losing punters struggling off for the London train may think little has changed....

What York's fine, flat, fair galloping course cannot claim to be, is much of an imitation of Epsom's cambers and turns. Neither can Goodwood, whose Predominate Stakes is on the trial circuit, for although it has got plenty of undulations, it bends round right-handed rather than left. If you are into topographic similarity, you have to go to Lingfield, in its leafy corner of Surrey, or Brighton, whose track is stuck eccentrically up on the Downs above the old Regency seafront. It would be nice to say that these places give us firm guide-lines to Epsom. In fact, often they give us

evidence of a conflicting nature, which means that the sports headline writers have to dust down such hardy old cliches as Classic Trial Shock and Big-Race Hope Flops.

So much public attention is focused on the Derby at this stage that it is easy to forget the very private moments when the candidates first appear. And so, in one of those weeks of failed Classic hopes, we trekked off up to Norfolk, and at last found a Derby hopeful with everything going for him. He was bright, determined and beautifully bred, but as he was just 10 minutes old when we saw him that Monday night in 1980, those Classic bets had to wait until 1983. By then, we reasoned, the first staggering Bambi steps should have developed into the effortless, ground-devouring stride of Grundy, his Derby-winning father. The original instinct that had the foal up and searching for his mother Escorial's milk should have been re-channelled into the burning will to run. And the little pink-rimmed eyes that blinked out unseeingly in the first minutes of life should have

that 'Look of Eagles' that only a confident and highly-tuned racehorse carries.

Four thousand six hundred and seventy-seven thoroughbred foals were recorded in England during 1980, and this was the 37th of the 40 expected on the stud. As all horses date their birthday from January 1, this one was getting on into the season, but late foals can often make up the lost ground very quickly.

Naturally, the 1,000-odd studs around the country vary from small 'couple of mares in the back paddock' outfits to huge commercial combines where the value of the bloodstock is counted in millions of pounds. This particular one is right at the top of the tree, with a history stretching back through the centuries. It and its sister studs under the same ownership have produced 22 English Classic winners, and a polished brass plaque on the box opposite our foal commemorates it as the birthplace of the 1900 Derby winner, Diamond Jubilee.

The present values of bloodstock have reached

dizzy proportions, even if the costs in England have soared to the point where the expense of getting a yearling to the sales was estimated at £7,200 in 1981 – some £1,000 higher than the average price at auction. Britain suffers from discriminatory taxation compared with its main rivals, and few incentives within the industry, but is still playing with big numbers at the top level. For instance, Shirley Heights, winner of the Epsom and Irish Derbies in 1978, was already on to the 43rd of the 47 mares at a fee which was officially £8,000. But demand was seeing nominations change hands for

Captain Nicholas Beaumont, clerk of the course and as such in charge of racing at Ascot, sits in his office with the Gold Cup roll of honour behind him. The Ascot Gold Cup is run over 2½ miles on the Thursday of the Royal Ascot meeting. Although races over such extreme distances have gone out of fashion this great test of stamina is still regarded as the climax of the whole of this famous meeting. Captain Beaumont's duties, however, extend way beyond the glitter of the royal occasion. He took over his post in 1964 and now has 13 days flat racing to manage as well as nine days of jump racing.

immensely well-informed despite her most rigorous of business schedules – is Her Majesty the Queen. The Royal studs have been something of a success story during this reign, but it is typical of the cussedness of fortune that whereas the Queen has now won every other Classic, she has never come closer to the Derby than when Aureole was second to Pinza in the Coronation year of 1953.

Nonetheless, the Derby is very much a Royal occasion, even if, with up to half a million people stretched across the Downs, it is also the largest annual public event that Her Majesty regularly attends. In many ways, the Derby is the perfect example of the most attractive side of British racing. It involves investing something as trivial as a horse race with quite ludicrous importance, but then getting away with it by transforming it into a sort of folk festival that works at all levels.

The actual race, which had its 200th anniversary when Troy slipped his field in 1979, is still the most coveted prize for three-year-olds in Europe. The prize money, even at £100,000 to the winner, may not be the highest, but this is the race where you are into £5-million stallion valuation the moment your colt passes the line.

The spectacle is still remarkable by any standards. Thirty thoroughbreds streaming up, round and down the old horse-shoe-shaped course. Just two-and-a-half minutes of action, of which most people at Epsom will only catch the merest

It's off to work for horses at Newmarket (Bottom Left) as they make their way from stable to gallops. Newmarket is the largest training centre in England, with 2,000 horses housed in its 50 yards. They vary in every respect, of which numbers is not the least factor. Trainers like Henry Cecil and Michael Stoute have well over 100 horses every season, but at the other end of the scale numbers can be as low as ten.

(Top Left) In sharp contrast to Newmarket, Pulborough, a sleepy little town in Sussex was barely on the racing map until Guy Harwood decided to start his training career there in the mid sixties. Since then he has blossomed into one of the leaders of his profession. Dealing with virtually virgin territory and with nobody to answer to but himself, he was able to do precisely what he liked – a considerable advantage in his case. His stable today has many of the most modern facilities in the country and his winners, like the 1981 2,000 Guineas hero To-Agori-Mou (cantering) have established his ability beyond doubt.

(Top Right) Lambourn in the Downs above Newbury in Berkshire, is second only to Newmarket in size but, unlike Newmarket, has about an equal proportion of flat and jumping yards. Its hilly terrain, in contrast to Newmarket's much flatter country, is a big help in training jumpers who so often need much more strenuous work to get them fit as they get older.

(Centre Left) This is not the most usual view of the grandstand at Epsom, even if it is winter, but it's one which Philip Mitchell and his staff get every day of their lives. Mitchell's yard is alongside the Derby start and any runners he has at his local meeting need to do little more than step out of their boxes to go to work.

(Bottom Right) There's nothing very glamorous about sweeping the yard as the lads are doing at Ian Balding's stables in Kingsclere, but it's all part of the job.

twice that value. And if that sounds like expensive procreation, remember that Grundy's fee was £15,000, so our little foal's value would be well into five figures even at birth. That means there's lots of pressure – it's all on checks and thoroughness, charts and tables.

Sixteen men and two secretaries are employed on this and its sister stud four miles away, which is the court of Bustino, Grundy's great rival on that astonishing Ascot Day in 1975 when Grundy won the King George VI and Queen Elizabeth Stakes by a neck in 2m 26.98 sec, the fastest mile-and-half time ever recorded in Britain. When you consider all those staff wages, the rocketing costs of animal foodstuffs and the values mentioned above, you can see why some think of horse-breeding as the ultimate in rich men's hobbies.

Yet when you understand from stud manager Michael Oswald that these studs have made

enough in the past few years to pay the running costs of up to 20 of its graduates in training, you appreciate that these two at least are a sound commercial venture.

Finally, when you see the light in the eyes of Oswald and the stud groom, Eric Scallon, as they watch their newest product wobble round his box, for all the world like a camera tripod on an ice rink, you realise that this is something much more than a business. And that's confirmed when Michael Oswald dashes across, through the dark of the stable courtyard and telephones almost direct to the owner. From the sound of it, the call is received with all the joy and interest of news of a first-born. It is a business that is a hobby that is a passion. Or vice versa.

Perhaps it ought to be added that the studs referred to are the Royal ones at Sandringham and Wolferton, and the owner – caring, enthusiastic and

glimpse – but they will have been there on Derby Day. Without giving you the whole of Henry V's speech at Agincourt, and not suggesting that many of us are usually odds-on 'to outlive this day and come safe home', the real joy is that the Derby doesn't just belong to the owner, trainer or jockey who scoops the prize. It is a day out of time which belongs to everyone there.

You feel it most if you start earliest. Mind you, if you are travelling the 15 miles from central London you need to leave by 10am or you will be in a traffic jam that will last a week. Even the out-of-town routes get totally clogged by midday, and in 1971 Ian Balding set a personal best in the 10,000 metres by abandoning his car and footing it to Epsom in time to saddle Mill Reef for victory.

The perfect Derby Day begins at dawn, with the Downs beginning to stir, already decorated (or disfigured, if you are a local trainer trying to carry

on business as usual), by up to a thousand gypsy caravans set in the middle of the course. In almost caricature British style, there is also an army post set up under canvas which will punctiliously sound reveille while gypsies yawn and lurchers stretch. Up at the top of the hill, the fun fair's garish signs and structures await the afternoon's excitements, but already the 300 or so horses that are normally trained at Epsom are out on the hill amongst the assorted horrors which have invaded their privacy. Maybe 'privacy' isn't the right word, because the Walton Downs part of the grounds only survived at all after the great Stanley Wootton presented them to the nation in 1969 during Lord Wigg's period at the Levy Board.

Most of the exercise is fairly perfunctory on Derby morning, although you can have some fun if you are riding out, by galloping on the track and then pretending to gullible press men that you are

on a Derby runner. In fact, the great majority of horses running that afternoon only have a lead-out, or are just travelling up that morning from Lambourn or Newmarket, leaving the early birds to sniff the air of anticipation with which only Flemington on Melbourne Cup Day, or Churchill Downs before the Kentucky Derby, can compare.

The professionals arrive early, consciously ready for a special day even if, like jockey's valet Fred Dyer, they have been doing Derbies since Steve Donoghue's hey-day back in the 1920s. 'I think it were more fun in those days.' says Fred. 'But perhaps that's just age speaking. These boys seem more conscious of the money today.' Fred, and other valets like Stan Hales and Brian and Ivor Yorke, polish boots and lay out breeches and white scarves in an almost matador-like ritual, while the rest of the racecourse does its own preparations on the track, in the bars, and out in the fairground stalls

which have hardly changed in style, and less in intent, since Frith immortalised them in oil a century ago.

It's when the jockeys arrive, little snappy-suited manikins about to become the giants of the afternoon, that you really notice the countdown and begin to appreciate what a test you are putting men and horses through. Because for somebody not used to it–and, remember, even English jockeys only have nine days there a year–the Epsom track is little short of ludicrous. It rises 250 feet in the first half-mile, changing angles from right to left, and then sweeps across the Downs before plunging downhill round Tattenham Corner and up the finishing straight, which has a sharp camber running in towards the inside rail. After I had given one such guided tour to three French jockeys one of them pulled a long face and, plagiarising Marshal Bosquet's comment on the Charge of the Light Brigade, said: 'C'est magnifique. Mais ce n'est pas champs des courses'.

Such reservations are understandable, and every year many millions of words on hundreds of miles of newsprint discuss the pros and cons of individual horses 'getting the run of the race' and, most of all, whether they will 'act down the hill'. Such unanimity of wisdom is always suspicious, and while it is true that after the race you can find plenty of horses who got hampered, cut off, almost brought down, lost balance on the hill or steering on the bend, it is an interesting fact that the top rider of his day does not usually make excuses. There were not many whinges from Steve Donoghue in the olden days (he won six Derbies), and if Piggott has only won eight so far, he never seems to have traffic problems, and once said: 'It's all a lot of nonsense about the hill. The track's in good shape these days, and they all come round the turn the first time. It's the next year, if they run on to the course again, that they remember and check themselves'.

But not every Derby horse–and 32 are allowed–can have Piggott on board, and the demands on a horse need little magnifying. Epsom, with its gradients, its trouble in running, its five roads that cross the track, has often been criticised as too haphazard a course on which to hold the most important race of the year, and it has been suggested that the Arc de Triomphe is a truer

Epsom is the world's most famous racecourse and not just because it has been the home of the Derby since 1780. Its undulations, clearly seen at the finish (Top Left) have caused plenty of excitement. Jockey Geoff Lewis takes an acrobatic tumble (Top Right) in a race over the five-furlong track, which has a drop of 80 foot. But Lewis, in the white colours, is just a hard-working spectator (Bottom Right) as Willie Carson on Dibidale (left) races on though his saddle has completely slipped. This happened in the 1974 Oaks, when Dibidale actually finished third to Polygamy (out of the picture) and Furioso (right) but had to be disqualified since she shed her weight cloth as a result of the mishap and Carson was therefore unable to weigh in at the correct poundage afterwards.

championship test. Well, everyone to his own, but the Arc is very often as rough as any Derby, and the Longchamp going in October can be much inferior to the Epsom turf, which careful husbandry in the past few years has improved out of all recognition from the hard-baked strip on which Mahmoud set what must remain a pretty bogus hand-timed track record of 2mins 33⁴/₅sec in 1936.

Anyway, for a horse to be conditioned, run in and pull off the Epsom Derby in the June of his three-year season, must be as searching a single test as racing can devise, and at the highest level that is what racing was supposed to be about. All this, I might add, is written from the vast experience of having ridden the course at exercise, and having competed there just once, in the Moet and Chandon Silver Magnum in very early days as an amateur rider. The old horse was going quite well until a clod of earth hit him in the face at Tattenham Corner, and put us immediately into neutral. 'Hit him in the face?' said Frenchy Nicholson, my marvellous and much-loved mentor. 'Hit the jockey more like'.

In recent years, the performing has been in front of the television cameras, and the great honour of presenting the most famous race of all to a world-wide audience hasn't been without its moments. Of course, the triumph is with the heroes of the hour, but maybe just as memorable are the technical foul-ups. Like the exclusive interview with Piggott, beginning just as the band struck up across the track, immediately ending whatever hopes the viewers had of sharing the maestro's muttered comments, and the glorious moment when the communications all failed as we were trying to summon Willie Shoemaker from the weighing-room, and I was reduced to doing explanatory cobbler's mime on my upheld shoe.

Television and writing cannot match the thrill of riding, but they have given the opportunity of watching the English flat-racing year unfold, and there are times in high summer when you really have to pinch yourself to believe your luck. From Epsom, the trail winds on to Ascot, with all its My Fair Lady extravagance (except that the horses go the other way from the film), and with the best four days' racing of the year. After Ascot, the Irish Derby, then the first test of the three-year-olds against the older generations in the Eclipse Stakes up Sandown's long uphill straight. There are three

On a clear day you can see forever. Set high on the Sussex Downs, five miles from Chichester on Britain's south coast, Goodwood has a claim to be the world's most beautiful racecourse. The first meeting was held way back in 1802 and the frying pan shaped course has to fit itself so much around the contours of the rolling hillside that the runners have to swing sharply right immediately after the finishing post (left). There are 15 days racing a year (five meetings) and the picture shows horses parading before the 1979 Sussex Stakes. First run in 1841, this event is now one of the most important mile races in Europe and one of the highlights of Goodwood's principal meeting, at the end of July.

balmy days among the beech trees at Newmarket's July Course, whose stage directions ought to be 'another part of the same Heath', and then the supreme test of the generations at Ascot in the King George VI and Queen Elizabeth Stakes.

On then to Goodwood, set up with the larks on the Sussex Downs. You can't see much of the racing, but on a nice day the course is worth visiting for the surroundings alone. Into August, and we go to York, perhaps the best-run racecourse of all, even if it is so perilously close to a gooey-smelling chocolate factory that TV commentators are apt to suffer from excess palate moistening. York gets the largest crowds anywhere except Royal Ascot and Epsom on Derby Day, and certainly the people are the friendliest in the country. But for all that you cannot travel up to the Knavesmire, to Doncaster's St Leger meeting in September, or on to Ayr's famous Western meeting a week later, without noticing racing's version of Disraeli's 'two nations'.

The biggest stables, the most expensive yearlings, the best jockeys, the wealthiest patrons and the most impressive overseas connections are all based in the southern area of Britain. Not only does this mean that the southerners then scoop the biggest prizes, (there were just three northern Classic winners out of 50 during the 1970s), but with the mobility of the big motorway system they whizz up North to pluck the little fish out of hungry local mouths. You can see his point when a hard-working Yorkshire trainer like Tommy Fairhurst tells you: 'I had found a perfect little race for my filly at Catterick, and up comes something of Michael Stoute's that cost a fortune and has to break its maiden. What can you do?'

So far, the answer has been precisely nothing, but unless the Jockey Club is prepared to sacrifice whole blocks of northern stables on the altar of competition, a series of races confined to locally-trained horses may become a necessity. Protectionism may be a dangerous game, but when your actual product is threatened, as with the northern stables, and with the British-bred thoroughbred, it has seemed to many that action was needed.

There is a human side, too. For the North has been the part of the country most cruelly hit by unemployment, and where so many trainers were struggling that if the agreed minimum wage was actually paid throughout, another 40 per cent were in danger of going to the wall. True, the likes of Northern trainers Bill Watts, Peter Easterby and now the enterprising Steve Norton didn't seem to have any trouble running the ships, but many claim that the rest could at least be given some races to fight over.

It's in the unsung areas that British racing has the most serious financial problems, and where it tends to sing about them least. In British racing's pleas for a better deal from its Government (which have always failed despite the fact that it has the sort of case any American authority would drool over), there has been an obsession with comparisons of prize money, and not nearly enough with the need to give something of a deal to the racegoer and something like a respectable salary to officials who run the game. (Many earn only a third as much as their counterparts abroad.)

In travelling to other successful racing countries, it's the infinitely better conditions offered to the racegoer, and higher pay for the officials that strike you most. Since pleas to successive governments have been the deadest of ducks, British racecourses somehow have to generate their own money to try and offer better, and above all cheaper, facilities. They have made a start by being way ahead of racecourses in the rest of the world in attracting sponsorship, almost 20

The need for adaptability. After horses have reached the starting stalls they may be asked to gallop straight, right-handed, as at Kempton (Top Right), or left-handed, as at Chester (Below). Called the Roodee, Chester is just a mile round and, as such, the smallest as well as the oldest track in Britain. It has racing records stretching at least as far as 1540 and those walls are from Roman times. Yet the problem of marrying these old traditions with the demands of modern sport are also exemplified at Chester. Its May meeting may be one of the highlights of the whole racing year but there are only two other meetings during the whole season so this old course only sees seven days racing annually.

per cent of the prize money now coming from sponsors. It is a figure that astonishes the French and Americans, whose comparative riches have prevented them examining the subject seriously. To ensure British viability all other sources, and particularly the promised El Dorado of Cable TV, still have to be examined. There is a long-standing feeling that British racing has lacked business acumen because of the honorary nature of the main posts in the ruling Jockey Club. That would drop away if you suddenly had the racecourses actually making money.

What is worrying at the moment is how few of the British public actually go racing. Probably not many ever will. Travel costs and, despite unemployment, lack of leisure, often prevent the ordinary midweek racecourse looking much better than an empty shell, and you can't help feeling there is something phoney for a sport on such days appearing to be played for the favoured few on the track while the millions of absent friends bet at 'shops' or other outlets around the country. If the heart grows slow, the limbs deteriorate. The best hope Britain has is for a new aggressive management, operating American-style.

Maybe most of all British racing needs to muster a much better apology for existence. Internal squabbles between bookmakers, Jockey Club and Levy Board have left a nasty selfish image with their public. In fact, the circus actually generates £2,500 million for the general purse each year, employs more than 100,000, and attracts considerable overseas investment–all for not a shilling of government subsidy.

Moreover, the disputes within British racing have diverted public attention from another enormous service that horse racing can take credit for. Despite all its privileged upper echelons it remains, in this uneasy age, the most broadly based of all British sports. In a single week, I have been down a coalmine and into Buckingham Palace– and found immediate contact on the sport the people in both places knew and loved...their sport. That is no mean span across the country, and it is on that bridge that British racing must build its future.

The north of England also has its heroes, even if fashion and proximity to London dictate that most top trainers are located at Newmarket or Lambourn. Bill Watts, who started training in Newmarket, now continues a long family tradition on the moors above the ancient castle town of Richmond in Yorkshire. The horses train there on what was a racecourse in centuries past but now boasts a modern all-weather gallop (Top Right). As with all trainers, the early morning routine includes a check of riding plans for the morning work (Bottom Centre) with stable lads and apprentices who have earlier cleaned and reset their horses' beds. The straw carrier is the stable apprentice Nicky Connorton, who had ridden over 70 winners by the end of 1982 and looked like following his father in becoming a successful northern rider. But if behind every successful man there is a woman and behind every good trainer there is a head lad, Bill Watts is lucky to have the support both of his wife Pat with him in the picture on the left, and of the canny Gerald Curtis (Bottom Far Right).

3
IRELAND

'Now Gilbert and Sullivan's master-piece has had many homes since it opened in New York's Fifth Avenue Theatre on New Year's Eve 1879 but surely never before has the line, "I am the very model of a modern major-general," been put not just to an appreciative human audience, but to the ears of 80 mares and foals of a thoroughbred stud. For four successful nights, Sullivan's music bounced out in the Kildare dark, the borrowed pirate ship chugged up Tully's floodlit ornamental lake, top trainer Kevin Prendergast's daughter, Andree, played Ruth and every overseas breeding pundit had a fit'.

KING CANUTE may have failed to do it, but then he didn't have a decent reason to roll back the waves. James Black did. He wanted to build a racecourse, and of course he was in Ireland. When we reached James on that warm and hazy August morning, all that was visible of the famous Laytown track was the wooden winning post which James and his team had just finished hammering into the first stretch of sand about 10 yards from the water's edge. 'But we'll be putting the stakes in for the mile-and-a-half track out there', he said with a magnificent sweep of his hand towards a fine piece of 'begulled' ocean. 'The going should be fast, but the tide has brought in a lot of stones, so the straight mile won't be so straight this year.'

Laytown, started in the 1890s on this very strand, is the only official survivor of the once-frequent race meetings around Ireland's beaches. It is some 40 miles up the coast from Dublin, and if you continue on, as some riders unwillingly do, you hit the River Boyne, Drogheda or an asylum happily described as a 'giggle factory.' The only permanent building for the once-a-year festivities, is the gentleman's convenience, made of concrete. But before we were spirited off to lunch by one of

(Preceding Spread) Irish racing can be likened to this picture of Ballydoyle's ancient Norman castle serving as a backdrop to the perfectionist modern dream of Vincent O'Brien's training grounds near Cashel in County Tipperary. At the bottom level Ireland has proportionately more involvement in racing than anywhere in the world, with even the unlikeliest corner producing its own racehorse. Indeed, no fewer than 28 racecourses adorn the Emerald Isle, but this wide and happily haphazard base narrows to the spikiest of pyramid tops. At the pinnacle is O'Brien's Ballydoyle Stable and Coolmore Stud operation, Irish racing's biggest success story, but its very pre-eminence has suffocated competition and taken attention away from the very real problems at the grassroots.

Laytown is on Ireland's east coast, 40 miles up from Dublin, 20 miles south of the Ulster border and centuries away from the year-round activity of modern racing plants. Laytown races just once a year, either in July or August, depending on the tides, for the meeting is held on the sand. Started in the 1890s it is the only official survivor of the strand (beach) races that used to take place and often still occur, unofficially, all over Ireland. Laytown boasts that its only permanent erection is the gentlemen's lavatory. But come race day, a paddock is railed off, tents sprout to provide a weighing room and the usual racecourse facilities. The bookies use about 20,000 tea chests to stake out their positions in the day's engagement with the ever eager Irish punter. When the sea rolls back, a racecourse is marked out which includes a left-handed mile-and-a-half and a straight five furlongs. All Ireland's top jockeys have ridden at Laytown, as well as other notables; Prince Aly Khan was once among the winners. But there are problems and not only those associated with the fact that the sand gets in your eyes and there are deceptively deep puddles to catch the unwary who swing wide on the turn. Some years ago the famous Nicky Brennan rode a horse that ran away with him and set off out to sea, he having to clear the waves as if he had hold of a dolphin until some clever helmsmanship prevented him attempting the first four-legged channel crossing.

Ireland's most hospitable and race-keen judges, the field above the strand had already sprouted four tents, a paddock, a steward's box and about 2,000 tea-chests to do duty as defence works for the bookies line.

Over the meal we caught up on the legendary story of jockey Nicky Brennan, who some 10 years ago was 'carted' by his horse before the start and set off out to sea jumping the waves like a dolphin rider. The jockeys haven't forgotten Nicky, 'nor the sand that gets in your eyes', says Wally Swinburn, father of Walter Swinburn, as he pulls on his boots in the changing tent. 'Nor the puddles that you have got to jump', says hazel-eyed Joanna Morgan, just back from a swim by the two-mile start. She changes separately from her fellow jockeys, but is every bit as competent a professional as she is decorative a girl.

Outside, the tide has gone out, and the crowds have come in. Nearly 1,000 cars and some 8,000 people are crammed along the shorelines which earlier in the day had sported nothing more exciting than three sisters from the nearby nunnery dipping absurdly white ankles in the briney. 'It's a miracle nobody gets hurt', says Swinburn after winning the first race. 'You just gallop into a funnel of people, who part as you reach the winning post'.

In the next race, Gabriel Curran gets disqualified for missing a post, and Christy Roche for pushing him out. Swinburn wins for a second time to put him nearer another jockey's championship, and to close the happiest race day I have ever seen we had Joanna Morgan storming up the outside to win the last and finish soaking wet. 'It's those puddles', she says in soggy triumph. 'I trotted into what looked like a little one before the start, but it was deep, the horse stopped and I went straight on'.

Thus Laytown, a unique example of the Irish charm which still manages to be better at first hand than any tale could suggest. Yet it is still an extreme example, and it's significant that much more prestigious institutions also exhibit this same magically relaxed Irish genius which has made them, a tiny nation of three-and-half-a-million people, the most famous horse country in the world. Indeed, if you wanted to understand something of this secret, which in 1981 saw Irish-bred horses win nine of the 15 major European classics, you should have gone to the National Stud five nights after the Irish Derby in July, and you would have heard not a learned dissertation on worms or virus abortion but, of all things, a performance of 'The Pirates of Penzance'.

Now Gilbert and Sullivan's masterpiece has had many homes since it opened in New York's Fifth Avenue Theatre on New Year's Eve 1879 but surely never before has the line, 'I am the very model of a modern major-general', been put not just to an appreciative human audience, but to the ears of 80 mares and foals of a thoroughbred stud. For four successful nights, Sullivan's music bounced out into the Kildare dark, the borrowed pirate ship chugged up Tully's floodlit ornamental lake, top trainer Kevin Prendergast's daughter, Andree, played Ruth and every overseas breeding pundit had a fit.

For if you tried to stage as much as a poetry reading within hail of most British or French racing establishments, let alone their national studs, you would be locked up for deliberate sabotage. Yet in Ireland the man responsible is no escaped show-business maverick, but Michael Osborne,* the much-respected managing director of the National Stud itself and, far from fretting over the four-legged part of his audience, he produced the immortal answer: 'Didn't we do The Mikado last year?' before going on more seriously: 'I told a

*Osborne left the Irish National Stud in the summer of 1982.

couple of the lads to watch the stallions during rehearsal last night, and they said the horses stood there, just loving it'.

Now this isn't a suggestion that the D'Oyly Carte should have put Newmarket, Normandy and other breeding centres into their itinerary. Nor even that no foal will win a classic unless it has learnt 'Ruddigore' by heart before it makes the yearling sales. But Osborne is sure that the more relaxed approach to horses is part of the reason for Ireland's recent breeding success which in 1980 saw Irish-breds win twice as many Group One races as the home-breds in both Britain and France.

'Of course, Ireland has some tremendous advantages in climate, manpower and limestone soil', said Osborne, breaking off, in his red 'National Stud' sweater, from instructing some of the half-million schoolchildren who visit annually. 'And I am sure horses do best when we stick to basics, and don't worry about them'. And then, before you had a chance to think of this as mere crest-of-the-wave crowing, he proceeds to elaborate with all the precision of his veterinary background: 'Take water. Ordinary tap water has twenty five parts of calcium carbonate per million. The water here, drawn off a three-thousand-acre underground lake beneath The Curragh plain, has 360 parts per million. It may be useless for washing in, but it sure helps horses grow good bones'.

Osborne's reputation as a charismatic teacher, as well as an effective stud manager, is such that pupils flock from all over the world to attend the residential course he runs at Tully. Directness without bombast, detail without tedium, it's the classic teaching mix. 'Of course we are lucky that our grass grows right through the summer', he explained, 'but if the Irishman can look a bit haphazard, sometimes his natural suspicion of modern farming methods has helped the horse trade. You see, modern sprays tend to kill herbs like plantain,

chicory, burnet and yarrow, which horses love, and more intensive stud management keeps down the number of cattle, but most Irish farms have three times as many cattle as horses, and anyway horses here tend to be given much more space. Why someone like Piari Edwards [the happily bulky lady who bred To-Agori-Mou, Britain's top two-year-old in 1980 and outstanding miler in 1981] down in the Golden Valley [Co. Tipperary] would only have about six mares to two hundred acres'.

Michael Osborne need hardly add that the Irishman still has a natural affinity to the horse long gone in most of urbanised Britain and many other countries beyond. And with seven-and-a-half thousand brood mares to three-and-a-half million population compared with 8,000 to 60 million in Britain, horse-breeding is still a central part of Irish life. To that end, and to the considerable chagrin of hard-working British professionals, Irish breeders have gained considerable tax advantages. Bloodstock is zero rated on VAT (15 per cent in Britain), and since 1970 stallion earnings and the sale of nominations have not, as in Britain, been subject to income tax. 'Vive', as the French are wont to say after scuppering some Common Market plan in Brussels, 'le Marché Commun!'

If you want proof that this situation has brought better blood, just compare the figures. In 1970, when Charlie Haughey introduced the changed Agriculture Act, there were based in Ireland just 56 stallions based in Ireland who had won a race of International Group status. Ten years on, the figure was 106. And since Goff's moved Ireland's biggest yearling sales to their 21st-century premises at the unfortunately named site of Kill, Co. Kildare in 1973, the average price at their select sales has risen from £4,251 in 1973 to £17,289 in 1980, £ here signifying the Irish punt.

So Ireland's timeless gifts often adapt to the modern world, but while the success at Tully (the National Stud) is built on a site laid out at the turn of the century by a brilliant if eccentric English nobleman called Lord Wavertree (the boxes were positioned so that the horses could study the stars), the most remarkable of all Irish racing enterprises during the Sixties and Seventies was created out of the Tipperary turf by a quiet little man from County Cork. His name, now renowned the racing world over, is Vincent O'Brien.

So much has been written and filmed about the training grounds that Vincent O'Brien has developed at Ballydoyle near the ancient Irish city of Cashel, and the breeding empire that he and his son-in-law, John Magnier, have built up under the Coolmore banner, that there is no point in adding to it unless you try and put O'Brien into some sort of warts-and-all perspective both in his own land, and in the wider international scene. Despite a certain prickliness towards anything less than adulatory that is written about his organisation, Vincent would not have it otherwise.

The problem is to divorce the man from the machine, for if you don't you become snowed under by huge waves of American-style propaganda promoting the prospects of his horses as potential stallions, mares, foals or what have you. Successful though this may be, and in July 1981 his stable's Storm Bird was sold for £30 million without one race that year, it clouds over O'Brien's true fascination, his love and mastery of the thoroughbred horse.

You see these unique qualities best when he talks about the early days when he swiftly worked his way to an unprecedented dominance of the National Hunt game despite no original money, modern-day facilities or long-term experience. Seeing him now fully endowed with all these assets, and all the delights that they and a cultured Australian wife like Jacqueline can bring, is to peel away the outer veneer of success and see the shape

beneath. And the big surprise to one more used to a latter-day, almost woeful-looking, O'Brien is to learn how much he physically enjoyed his contact with the horse: 'I remember when I was first starting, we used to take the young horses out and just jump them round the farm, ditches, hedges, anything. That was wonderful fun'. He was sitting in one of those bright, flower-filled conservatories you find at some elegant villa at Antibes, but the talk takes you back to muddy triumphs at the Cheltenham Festival where he won 10 divisions of the Gloucester Hurdle, besides the Gold Cup and the Champion Hurdle, and to Aintree, where he pulled off the record feat of three consecutive Grand National winners between 1953 and 1955.

Yes, there's warm nostalgia about such great jumping names as Hatton's Grace, Early Mist and Knock Hard, but you can't miss the perfectionist edge which makes 'the infinite capacity for taking pains' very much part of the O'Brien genius. When he switched to the Flat, and within three years had won the Arc de Triomphe with Ballymoss, there were no half-measures: 'I had enough to concentrate on; I didn't want to confuse the system with having jumpers about'.

In pursuit of perfecting the system, he was also creating at Ballydoyle what has every right to be

The Curragh is Ireland's premier track and the home of all its classics, including the Irish Sweeps Derby; the 1980 race is seen (Above Right) being won by Tyrnavos (black with white spots). When the Irish Derby incorporated the Irish Sweeps in its name in 1962 it became the first European Classic to be sponsored. The Curragh plain has been going for an age or two longer, however, than this famous race, supposedly originating when the fabled St. Bridget was told that she could have as much land as she could lay her cloak over. When she spread it the folds stretched out to encompass the whole plain of Kildare. More than 30 days racing now take place on the huge 20-furlong U-shaped track, and the Curragh plain now houses over 40 stables and some 1,000 horses.

called the most complete single training complex in the world. There are gallops of every length, shape and constitution, as well as timing devices, viewing stands, weighing machines, computers, telexes and even his own flying horse-box. Despite it all being set in the greenest, most easy going, corner of Tipperary (in Cashel you could spend all day working your way down the line of pubs in the main street), Ballydoyle has such a crack-regiment air about it that when you are told, 'Mr O'Brien is a little late coming back from lunch', it seems the most natural thing that soon a chattering will grow in the sky finally to reveal a bright blue mechanized dragonfly hovering down on to the Tipperary turf. And then the great man steps out, and comes across to greet you, head tilted, polite, enquiring, more like, in writer Hugh McIlvanney's perfect phrase: 'One's idea of a kindly doctor than one of the most formidable racehorse trainers that the world has ever seen'.

O'Brien's unparalleled record, which by 1981 included five winners of the Epsom Derby and three of the Arc de Triomphe, cannot have been achieved without some razor-sharp steel within the scabbard. It's not a noisy explosion, like some trainers whose howls of rage can be heard half the length of the Berkshire Downs. But it sets grown men running like rats when Tabby's in the barn. One summer morning, some would-be wonder horse was having his final work-out before tackling a major English prize, and while we were treated with great coffee-pouring courtesy and shown the

stables, the gallops, even other horses working, we weren't just kept away from Vincent O'Brien, we were quite specifically kept out of his sight! But all was well. The horse, a massive great beast called Gregorian, worked well enough to travel for the Eclipse Stakes, in which he ran an honourable third, and we were invited in to breakfast on the beautiful walnut table beneath the oil paintings of Nijinsky, Larkspur and Sir Ivor.

O'Brien was then the 'kindly country doctor' again, as he invariably is if you ever get to him, but it has to be said that his most recent years as a trainer, (he was born in 1917, and his first training licence was issued in 1940) have seen a marked diminution in his once idyllic relations with the press, matters finally coming to a head in the summer of '81 when an official statement was issued from Ballydoyle temporarily severing relations with the Fourth Estate. Well, we scribblers take an awful lot for granted, and on the one hand it's hard to imagine anything more annoying than having to field endless, and often exactly similar, press queries while pondering the real work of training 50, or even 100, racehorses. But on the other hand, it's worth examining O'Brien's problems, for they illustrate a crucial shift of balance applicable not only to Ireland, but to the rest of Europe–an increased emphasis on the investment side of the game.

In what some may see as the good old days, a trainer's sole aim was to win races with his horse. The later stud value was almost coincidental.

In one of his lucid studies, Peter Willett showed that for many years the value of a horse at stud would be almost exactly level with its earnings on the track (Nearco won £50,000, sold for £55,000). And that in recent years the graph has taken off, until we arrive at the present remarkable position when the kudos and stud value of winning a prestige event are 10 or 20 times the actual prize itself. The winner of the Epsom Derby may collect £150,000 in prize money, but that is peanuts compared with a stud value of some £5 million. To take two specific examples from 1981, the top horse, Shergar, won almost £500,000, and was syndicated (at a premium, so the experts will tell you) for £10 million. And, most extraordinary and relevant of all, O'Brien's Storm Bird, the top two-year-old of 1980 but winner of a 'mere' £74,000 in prize money, was syndicated as a stallion for some $30 million.

From those figures, you don't have to be Pythagoras to deduce that reputation becomes every bit as crucial as performance, and therefore, if a trainer has a beautifully bred and already successful horse of which he now has a suspicion, to start sharing those fears, or even to risk their confirmation on the racecourse, is like making a bonfire with thousands of £50 notes. The dilemma is there for all leading trainers, but O'Brien is at the sharpest end of all. His 50 horses would be, pound for pound, the best bred and most expensive collection in the world. The syndicate of which he is part, and which Robert Sangster and John

Magnier initiated, has an annual bill at the yearling sales of over $4 million, and, thanks to Magnier's driving force, the Coolmore breeding empire, taking in during 1982 some four studs and 19 stallions, also has its fortunes inextricably linked with reputations on the track.

You see, then, how the quoted opinions of the most famous racehorse trainer of his time start to assume a quite unreal importance, and it's no coincidence that when he finally broke with Lester

Vincent O'Brien is lord of the promised land (Below) he has made for himself at Ballydoyle, Co. Tipperary, 120 miles south-west of Dublin. His talent was first displayed in the jumping game, where O'Brien won every top prize, including three consecutive Grand Nationals at Aintree. Having switched to the flat in later years, he now has to his credit three Arc de Triomphes and six victories in the English Derby and is hailed as the greatest trainer of modern times. His genius combines the timelessness of Tipperary, vital for the volatile thoroughbred, with the latest in modern technology (personal helicopter Top Far Right), crucial in the multi-million pound, jet-setting bloodstock industry today. It has brought O'Brien wealth, beautiful possessions and lovely horses, but also its share of heartache as prices have shot through the roof. Storm Bird, (Top Right) with O'Brien and stable rider Tommy Murphy, was the champion European two-year-old of 1980, failed in his only race as a three-year-old, yet still fetched a 30-million dollar valuation at stud. Storm Bird, by the top American sire Northern Dancer, had virus problems but he and others like him are in danger of becoming the ultimate absurdity – the racehorse too valuable to race. O'Brien takes breakfast (Bottom Right) with his wife Jacqueline and Brough Scott.

Piggott the crisis was reached not by any blunting of the extraordinary powers of jockeyship that had lifted home all those Derby winners, but by a failure of communication. Most specifically, after the 1980 Irish 2,000 Guineas when Piggott dismounted from the O'Brien classic failure, Monteverdi, and passed assorted uncomplimentary remarks about the horse which were immediately put into print. Candour, perhaps, but for O'Brien it was almost a case of arson.

If we try to put O'Brien into perspective, *don't* let's try to lessen his achievements. For if jealousy is racing's besetting sin, Ireland, for all its charm, is no more proof against it than any other place, and some people would have you believe that Vincent O'Brien has hardly served the nation at all, but is just an independent, internationally financed, little kingdom of his own, cut off from the rest of the country. The truth is that O'Brien's legacy to Ireland may be just beginning. For while in the past almost all his brilliant flat-race horses were American-breds, the settling of many of the most successful ones in the Coolmore empire should prove a historic addition to Irish bloodstock, and when you see that their 1982 mating list includes the Arc de Triomphe winner, Detroit, being bred to the brilliant miler, King's Lake, you can think that great home-bred successes may not be far away.

Nevertheless, for all the attention it necessarily warrants, it's important to realise that the O'Brien empire is only part, and an unrepresentative part at that, of the Irish racing world. Indeed, the whole breeding scene, with other Elysian places like Tim Roger's magnificent spread at Airlie, and the Aga Khan's two marvellous studs (five Derby winners

from Bahram to Shergar), wonderfully successful though it has become, is not typical of their racing, or indeed of Ireland itself. Besides their solvency, top breeders are into immaculate planning of both strategy and structure. On the racing front, the picture is very different. The game is almost broke, some of the racecourse stands and training establishments looks as if they were designed by Heath Robinson's Connemara cousin, and when you get into strategy that, for the vast majority of racing folk, means the relentless pursuit of that most delicious of triumphs, the winner only you and I knew about–'the touch'.

Don't let anyone think this is some pompous British condemnation. We have enough problems and dilapidations of our own, and although we have nearly 20 times as many people we put on only five times as many races and maintain only twice as many tracks as the Irish do. And anyway, no one on the British scene even begins to have the fun the Irish have in Ireland. Of course, trying to 'lay a horse out for a race' will always be a central part of racing's attraction wherever you go in the world. But whereas in some big betting territories– Australia, for instance, and more particularly Hong Kong–the pressure to get everything right can sometimes lead to tears, and while Ireland is in no way free of racing wickedness, nowhere in the world does the chat ('the crack', as they call it) match that of the Emerald Isle.

Naturally, in such a horse-orientated country, there are some great trainers around who can take horses to compete for the most international prizes of all. The ebullient Mr Punch-figure of Mick O'Toole is a frequent English raider, and his

Dickens Hill took the 1979 Eclipse Stakes. The gifted Michael Cunningham brought off his County Meath re-make of the Ugly Duckling story by developing little Cairn Rouge through to success in the 1980 Champion Stakes, and the highly qualified Dermot Weld devastated the British fillies when his Blue Wind ran away with the 1981 Oaks at Epsom.

But all these achievements don't get talked about in the bars, and on the long journeys to Limerick, Listowel, Wexford or wherever, a 10th as much as the horse which scored last week, and, hushed tones and a shake of the head, 'they had fortunes on him–fierce it was'.

Of course, such excitements mean that some horses' preparations are something of a tightrope between strategy and strangulation. It means that the stewards' inquiry reports published weekly in The Irish Field (now in a surprising but impressive way the best weekly briefing on the international racing scene) feature some elaborate protestations of innocence along the lines of: 'Jockey X stated that the filly performed best when left on the bit, and was inclined to sprawl if put under strong pressure', to explain what appeared to be a pretty uncompetitive performance. And, sadly, it also means that, along with the far greater reason of much higher prize-money in Britain and France, the international owner just wanting to promote his bloodstock tends to choose the more straightforward, as well as richer, scene over there than try to battle through the smokescreens in Ireland.

But the plus side of all this remains considerable. The Stewards somehow manage to run a pretty well-informed ship, which shouldn't

perhaps be surprising when you consider that men like Lord Killanin, Dennis McCarthy and Victor McCalmont are up on the bridge, and others like John Harvey and ex-jockey Paddy Powell are on the deck. And, most of all, the punters and the bookmakers continue to battle with a will that certainly gives the lie to anyone who thinks that the whole game is crooked from the start.

Accustomed to the far slower-moving, some would say apprehensive, betting rings of Britain, where the flourishing of a £10 note can sometimes get a bookie reaching for his cloth to cut the odds, the Irish ring is something of a mind-blower. After all, this is, statistically, a poorish country, but all over the nation's race-tracks you will see people marching in to bet with stacks of notes in their hands, and bookmakers like Ted Rogers and Sean Graham think nothing of taking a thousand-pound bet and not even altering the price. 'It's all about the strength of the market', says Sean through those plate-glass Belfast 'specs' of his. 'Over here, you have got several different big punters taking a view, and that means competition. And where there is competition and money, that's where a bookmaker can survive. In England, we don't think you have bookies at all'.

Some extremely slow-paying punters looked like clipping Sean's growing wings at one time, but his computer-print-out intelligence will probably always win through, just as one hopes it will for two of the legendary figures on the other side of the ring, the boyish-looking J.P. McManus, the man who once panicked an English betting shop by walking in with £10,000 in a sack and demanding to put it on the big-race favourite, and Barney

Curley, the bearded ex-monk who looks cool and sinister on the track, and yet can be warm and generous off it in the vast mansion his 'investments' have bought him up in County Monaghan.

The sheer physical scrum of an Irish betting ring is something British people don't see except at Ascot and Cheltenham, and 50 per cent of those punters at big English occasions are Irish anyway. The old 'battleground' cliché is perfectly accurate; bookies up on their stools against the rails with their boards out in front of them, while the punters come six to 10 deep to make bets. And at Galway, where the 1981 festival turned over more than £4 million in five days, the scrum is such that once you are into the ring you are like a French infantryman at Waterloo, and cannot get out again.

Unfortunately, little comes back into racing prize-money from all this activity despite healthy sponsorship from the big bookmakers. And the government takes out six per cent on-course, but a ruinous 18 per cent off-course, second only to the slice devoured in gambling-mad Japan. If in some ways this coup-planning turns racing in on itself, it also means that trainers get very highly skilled at their job, and the best criterion for the emergence of a truly skilled practitioner is the degree to which he and his supporters become feared in the ring. None more so than the late, great Paddy Prendergast, who in later affluent years, with practically every big race bar the English Derby to his name, would take you through to his lordly sitting-room where he would never miss a chance of pointing with real love to a horse on the wall. 'There he is', he would say. 'My first winner. I backed him with all I had, and doubled up next time. He

won five in all. He was the foundation stone'.

It remains only to add that there is another, infinitely sadder, infinitely more complex, Irish story with which nobody who visits Ireland can feel untouched, the troubles in the north. Sufficient to say that although other corners of some Irishmen's lives may be ensnared by the horrors of that sectarian and political impasse, the racing man's passport will still take him from the rolling hills of Unionist Antrim to the greenest fields of all-Irish-County Kerry. Indeed, just about the best and happiest audience I ever spoke to was at the Northern racing town of Downpatrick, where I was assured that the crowd would contain a heavy sprinkling of those actively involved in 'the struggle' on either side. Such thoughts show one observable truth. That wherever Irishmen gather to talk about horses, they make the world, however temporarily, a more pleasant place.

Gowran Park, 10 miles east of Kilkenny and some 65 miles south-west of Dublin is typical of the Irish racing heartland. There is no great ceremony pervading the place (even though a spanking new grandstand has recently replaced the old model), but the large, undulating mile-and-a-half circuit is set in beautiful rolling countryside where everyone knows their horses. This is so much the case that Gowran Park's 20 meetings mix flat and jump racing with enviable ease and in the 'bumper' (amateur riders' race) men and women jockeys have mixed without fuss since 1974. Even on an unsung summer evening you can still find some of the game's great professionals like J. P. McManus (Centre Below) and Sean Graham, on his left, who have become legends in their own lifetimes, as punter and bookmaker respectively. Both can win and lose as much as £100,000 a race but still rely on their wits and active racing knowledge to keep them ahead.

4
FRANCE

'Racing buffs will have it that when things returned to claret-swigging normal after the Revolution, some bewhiskered Russian blue-blood named Prince Labanoff walked out on to the springy turf in front of the chateau at Chantilly in the autumn of 1833, and said something along the lines of: "Mon Dieu, let's have a horse race!" The subsequent impromptu contest was won by a Monsieur de Normandie, who was an Anglomane to the point of speaking French with an English accent'.

HISTORY, even if Henry Ford thought it was bunk, has a nasty habit of repeating itself. But for that one niggle at the back of the mind, anyone who makes the 42-kilometre trip north up the N.16 from Paris to Chantilly can only think he has come to racing's promised land. For this surely is racing perfection. First take a beautiful old Roman town (allegedly named after some leg-weary centurion called Cantillius) ringed by forests, lakes, a Versailles-type chateau, and a great turf stretch where Napoleon once paraded his legions. Then add 3,000 racehorses, the neatest betting system in the world, massive prize-money, strong and enlightened control, and you have for the horse world almost as good a time as the Condés had down at the chateau. That's when you remember what happened in 1789.

Now there is no need to go into too much fanciful stuff about tumbrils rumbling down the Piste des Lions, or guillotines in Chantilly's Grande Place, but it's worth remembering that it was because of the excessive grandeur and detachment of the nobles' life-style that the French Revolution came about. Now, with million-dollar yearlings and multi-million-dollar racing stables using the self-same forest rides that once rang with the sounds of the Condés at the chase, it's in no way fanciful to fear that a left-wing government might cast a baleful eye.

But first, let's celebrate the achievements, and at the beginning of the Seventies France was the greatest single example of what could be done in racing by adapting old traditions to present needs. That, after all, was the principle by which the English gentry first developed the thoroughbred racehorse from Arab stallions imported from the Middle East and in France's case it was from the

(Preceding Spread) The paddock at Longchamp. Set next to the River Seine at the eastern end of Paris's central Bois de Boulogne, Longchamp is only a couple of kilometres from the Arc de Triomphe, after which its most famous race is named. Run on the first Sunday in October, the Prix de l'Arc de Triomphe is Europe's richest race and regularly provides the season's ultimate showdown. At Longchamp, there is an arena with a style and importance to match its name.

Chantilly, 25 miles north of Paris, is France's most historic track and training centre. It was here, in 1834, that the first organised race meeting was held and two years later saw the first running of the French Derby, Le Prix du Jockey Club. While some of the spectators look as if they have been around since the first Prix du Jockey Club, many of the buildings the runners pass were present long before. The 18th century pile (Bottom Right), called Les Grandes Ecuries, is quite literally a chateau for the horse. Inside, there is stabling for some 250 equine inhabitants, all built by order of the Prince de Conde who lived in the actual Chateau de Chantilly across the lake at the eastern end of the course. The eccentric prince, of royal Bourbon blood, was so convinced that he would be reincarnated as a horse that the vast stables were built to ensure that his next, four-footed, existence would be in the style to which he had been accustomed in his first life. Today Les Grandes Ecuries are still used by ordinary riding horses as well as, one imagines, by several squadrons of whinnying ghosts from the past.

![Street scene showing the café tabac des chasses à courre with storefront signs reading "LA CHASSE A COURRE" and "cafe tabac des chasses a courre", with thatched umbrellas, a moped, and pedestrians walking past.](image)

English model that they began their racing at Chantilly, as such terms as 'le lad', 'la boxe' and even 'le outsider' testify, along with such out-posts as Le Restaurant Jockey Club and l'Hotel Epsom.

Maybe the story of the actual origins has lost little in the telling, but don't forget this is the town whose chateau had the same architect (Mansart) and landscaper (Le Notre) as Louis XIV's Versailles, and the chateau has its own exotic fripperies, like a whole room given over to monkey motifs, and little temples and ornamental fountains all around the gardens. And if that doesn't convince you it was a world of make-believe, remember the tale of poor Monsieur Vatel the chef who, in 1671, laid on a 5,000-man banquet for his master to entertain the King, but ordered two plates too few for the beef. He did the only decent thing and committed suicide.

Thus racing buffs will have it that when things returned to claret-swilling normal after the Re-

volution, some bewhiskered Russian blue-blood named Prince Labanoff walked out on to the springy turf in front of the chateau in the autumn of 1833, and said something along the lines of: 'Mon Dieu, let's have a horse race'! The subsequent impromptu contest was won by a Monsieur de Normandie, who was an Anglomane to the point of speaking French with an English accent.

Oh to have been an Anglais in those days! For, lacking any racing expertise, the French turned to the country which had already been doing it for nearly 200 years. By 1845 there were more than 200 horses and 20 trainers at Chantilly, all from across the Channel, and by the 1890s Roger Longrigg quotes some griper as complaining: 'All, or nearly all, the jockeys are English'. Those dizzy, expatriate times have gone for ever, but you can still find the odd grizzled, be-bereted veteran who puts down his Pernod and breaks into sing-song cockney to tell you how he and a dozen other

kids were brought out as the annual English draft of apprentices. In those days, most of the trainers carried English names. They have nearly all gone now, although the Head family is in its third generation of being (eponymously) at the top of the training and riding tree. Old man Willie fought in the British cavalry during the First World War before becoming a highly successful trainer, a role his son Alec has filled with great distinction for 30 years and now Alec's daughter, Criquette, is also training, while his son, Freddie, has been three times champion jockey, and has accomplished the surely unrepeatable feat of winning the Prix de l'Arc de Triomphe for each of these three training generations of his family.

Mind you, back in those early 1830s and 40s, it was probably sensible to box clever with the best-known of all Anglais–Lord Henry Seymour, who tended to such anti-social habits as handing round exploding cigars and slipping purgatives into the tea. There were other rather more serious problems, of course, most notably the foreign occupations after the Franco-Prussian War in 1871, and during the two world wars this century, and although a French horse, Gladiateur, did win the English Derby, and indeed the Triple Crown, in 1865, he was trained much of the time in England; and after Gladiateur it was not until 1914 that Durbar II became the next French-based horse to win the Derby. Genealogists might note that Durbar's official trainer carried the good old Parisian name of Thomas Murphy.

It therefore took some time for French racing to throw off the British colonial cloak, and while such fine horses as Ksar and his son, Tourbillon, began to put the French breeding industry together after the ravages of 1914-18, it was not until after the Second World War, with five Derby winners between 1947 and 1956, that the French horses really proved themselves. Yet all that had gone before could not compare in significance with the present-day prosperity, which has a lot to do with a new betting idea first tried on January 18, 1952.

This was a 1-2-3 forecast bet which, in a country which had no football pools, could offer a huge return for a tiny stake, and which was often so unpredictable that people would mix up all sorts of numbers, such as their children's birth-dates, to try a permutation for the big money. With the sale of tickets through the 6,000 Pari-Mutuel offices in the corners of cafés around the country, as well as on the racetrack, the Tiercé became a national passion, with whole magazines being devoted to the pros and cons of the runners in that Sunday's race. And any sociologist who hasn't sat sipping a 'cassis blanc' of a Sunday morning while France wrangles over its Tiercé bets before the midday deadline, has missed a major source of material, as well as the most pleasant place yet invented to contemplate an afternoon's activities, as the French say 'aux courses'.

But whatever way you define these pluses, they have a long way to go to match the flood of filthy lucre that the Tiercé has provided. Pari-Mutuel betting had been ticking over in France since bookmakers were banned at the turn of the

Chantilly, like all racing places, starts early. But being Chantilly, it does it with more style than anywhere else in the world, with little cafés like this. In the summer, work for the 1,000 lads, 60 jockeys, 200 apprentices and 90-odd trainers can start as early as 4.45am in order to beat the heat of the day and get a first crack at the turf gallops. Before 7am lads and jockeys can be back in the cafés after the 'premier lot' (the first batch of horses to exercise) to take coffee or something stronger. Two more 'lots' and maybe the occasional 'boisson' (drink) will follow before all Chantilly's 3,000 horses have been exercised, fed and bedded and the yards swept. Then those who are not going racing are free till 'evening stables', the cleaning, checking, grooming and feeding routine every yard has built into its afternoon schedule. It makes for a long day and the years can leave their mark on a stable lad.

century, but it was not until the Tiercé arrived that the real potential was appreciated. By 1975, Tiercé betting alone (and this is confined to one race on Sundays and occasional feast days) accounted for almost half the total turnover of £150 million, and by 1981 the turnover of a Tiercé day was up to eight times the normal average. From all this, the Government was taking four million francs in tax, even if racing still got a billion back from the 21-billion total.

When you go to Chantilly, you can see this boom translated into fact. The town of the Condés, which housed 930 horses in 1950, and 1,370 in 1960, reached a peak of 3,440 in 1975, double the number at either Newmarket, England or Belmont, USA. Well that's what the figures tell you, but the real beauty of Chantilly is that you could probably hide away 10,000 horses there, and most people would still consider the place no more, no less, than the ultimately chic dormitory town, the house on the forest's edge, the train to the Gare du Nord.

This double life is never better felt than if you take a seat at the café opposite Chantilly station at 7.30 of a weekday morning. To the outside eye, the scene is all about big, sleek Peugeots whirling up for the Paris train, and crumple-eyed commuters whizzing up to the counter for Le Figaro, leaving a tang of after-shave behind with the small change. But push on past the corner to the tables within and you will find Chantilly's other world already a quarter of the way through its day – trainers and their assistants looking big and rugged in heavy rubber boots compared with the jockeys, neat leathery little manikins, one jodphured leg crossed over another as they sip a café noir and study the day's runners in the Sport Complet.

Here you may find big, friendly, bespectacled Jacko Cunnington. Even, if the bridge game hasn't gone on too late, his famous owner, Omar Sharif. There is ace trainer Francois Boutin, not 50 yet but the hair turned almost white in tribute to the professionalism that hides behind that film-star elegance. His then jockey, Philippe Paquet, possessor of heart-throb accent and style plus fellow rider Henri Samani, for long a central part of the racing family and, when I was there for some months in the mid-Sixties, already the owner of the smartest suede jackets outside a bôutique window.

At Longchamp the stars of the show include the Aga Khan, 1981's leading owner in France, England and Ireland, and the late Francois Mathet, an inveterate umbrella carrier and the greatest trainer of the postwar era (Bottom Far Left). Yves St. Martin (Right), was apprenticed to Mathet and 13 times Cravache d'Or (champion jockey). Alec Head with his daughter Criquette (Top Near Left), are both trainers of Arc de Triomphe winners and members of France's most remarkable Anglo-French family. Alec Head's son Freddie, with dark glasses (Top Far Left), has ridden Arc winners for his father, sister and grandfather Willy Head. With him is Gary Moore, who rode Alec Head's 1981 winner, Gold River. Phillipe Paquet (Bottom Near Left) is Moore's brother-in-law, a former French champion, who joined Gary riding in Hong Kong.

In summer, the days have started long before this station-side breakfast break. The heat of the later morning, and the competition for first use of the precious strips of grass marked off for galloping that day, mean that there's nothing unusual about a string of horses pulling out of the stable by 5.15am. In the interests of consciousness, that means getting a large café au lait down you in the Bar des Jockeys opposite Les Aigles, the biggest training ground, by 5am, and if you are an advanced student of this most charismatic of racing centres, you knock back a calvados with it, too. It might not do much for your riding, but it does wonders for the voice.

If you are doing this every day of your life, you tend to become immune to the romance of Napoleon marching his legions (hence Les Aigles), or the entrancing beauty as the dew lifts off the Les Aigles turf, or the mist clears from the chateau lake. With a much stronger trade-union element, the Chantilly stable lads have been more militant than their Newmarket conterparts, and the 1979 running of the French Oaks (the Prix de Diane) was actually stopped by a cordon of striking lads blocking the course. But of a morning there is the usual self-sufficient mixture of hangover grumbles, good-natured abuse and Don Juan-type tales, along with a mixture of petting and threats to the horses they ride. But I do remember one lad who used to stay above most of the joking with the slow smile of a man who has seen behind the curtain. 'Ah, Max', the others would say, with an accepting dip of the head, 'Il a fait Sea Bird'. (He looked after Sea Bird.)

As a matter of fact, Sea Bird II, whose six-length Arc de Triomphe defeat of Reliance, Diatome, Meadow Court, Anilin and Tom Rolfe, remains the outstanding performance in the lifetime of most European observers was something of a pig in the morning. 'Pas de bouche', Max used to say to us open-mouthed acolytes. He would then spin out tales of how he, Max, had personally coaxed through the mornings this wonder horse whose method of locomotion in the slower paces was to twist his head round almost to your boot while 'dishing' his off-fore violently to the right. 'Il etait fou', Max would say, putting an impressive finger to his head. 'Mais au travail…un machine'.

What a place it was, and what an even more amazing place it has become. Seventy-five stables, five different training areas besides the original racecourse ground, 84 hectares of sand, 116 hectares of turf, not to mention 40 kilometres of roads and tracks through and around the great beech forests of the Condés, where the red deer still roam.

What remarkable horses and men have stamped it, too. Alec Head, with his English hat and riding mack, and those gifts of organisation that sat so lightly on his shoulders that there's a memory of him tweaking the nose of his brilliant filly, Pistol Packer, as if she were a child's pony. Angel Penna, joking about the sheep he used to keep with Allez France. (The first one died, and the replacement had the bad habit of chewing the great mare's ankles while she slept.) Then Penna watching Yves St Martin loose Allez France's long, flowing stride in a final pre-Arc work-out up the Piste des Lions, and St Martin's beautifully-weighted three-word comment: 'elle est prete'. (She

is ready.) Most vivid of all, perhaps, the distant, brooding presence of Francois Mathet, in his own far corner of Les Aigles, hands behind back, head thrust forward in his frowning Napoleon stance, watching his 200-strong troop file endlessly by. That's so many horses that for one individual to be training them all seems quite absurd, until you see a lad shake his head ruefully and say: 'Il connait tous'. (He knows everything.)

As in Adam all die, so in racing most empires change, and the proof of Chantilly's vitality has been the way new names have come forward to replace the old. Maybe you can no longer look down a race-field to see the colours of Stern or Strassburger, the orange of Boussac or the hoops of Volterra. The glory days of Countess Batthyany came and went, even the dark blue Wildenstein silks have left the stage they dominated for almost a decade. But Stavros Niarchos is back in the big league, Mahmoud Fustok has built a new showpiece stable on the southern side of Les Aigles, and all the while the remarkable Head family steadily

---

Come August, the whole French racing scene shifts to Deauville, that ultimate watering hole just down the Normandy coast from Le Havre. The place was first made famous by Charles, Duc de Morny, half-brother of Napoleon III, who saw it as the nearest resort to Paris, only 125 miles separating the two. To amuse the patrons, the horses make the four-hour trek from Chantilly and Maisons Laffite to set up temporary shop in the ivy-clad stables, and at times take to the sea themselves. If, at Deauville as elsewhere in France, no race day can begin before lunch there are nevertheless still plenty of shirt-sleeved 'turfistes' on hand afterwards to watch the horses file out on to the track. But for all its style, a race day at Deauville can still leave you wondering which way you are facing.

adds to its laurels, and the 'new' Aga Khan (if anyone holding a title for 20 years can still be classified as new) has completed such a successful re-structuring of his racing resources that he seems set to outpoint even the tremendous achievements of his father and grandfather.

It's worth studying the Aga Khan's operation, because he represents a unique blend of the old owner-breeder tradition with present-day business acumen. In his disarmingly intimate way, he will talk about how he 'knew absolutely nothing when Daddy (Aly Khan) died in 1959', and of how if he took on the horses and the studs (and there were eight of them at that stage) the whole racing empire would have to make financial sense.

Sitting opposite the Alfred Munnings portrait of the 'old' Aga Khan's 1936 Derby winner, Mahmoud, you begin to appreciate the enormity of the inheritance. The 'old' Aga had four other Derby winners, and was 13 times leading owner in Britain, while Aly Khan, who moved the centre of racing operations to France, was the leading owner in Britain, France and Ireland in the year of his untimely death. But listening to the present Imam outlining his operation, and watching him sift through computer print-outs on the possible matings for his 172 brood mares, and then walking round the extraordinary new training stable at Aiglemont, is to know that he is very much his own man.

The tones may be soft, but the decisions and the culling (four of the studs were sold after Aly's death) have to be steely, and if Karim will never have his father's horsy badinage, there are a growing number of men who have him to thank for what, remarkably, has become a self-financing operation. The sale of Blushing Groom to America in 1977 funded the purchase of the Dupré stock which included the subsequent French Derby winner, Top Ville, whose sale in turn paid for most of the Boussac bloodstock purchase. Such mergers would sound like a case for the Monopolies Commission if you didn't know there were all sorts of other teams, and the cream of the yearling market, pitched in against him. Even so, the 1981 position when he ended up leading owner in both Britain and France, and just failed to complete the Derby double with Shergar and Akarad, is pretty amazing for our supposedly contracting corner of the 20th century.

In simple terms, the Aga Khan's outfit is the biggest single-owner operation in the world. There are four studs in Kildare and Normandy, 40 horses in English training stables and more than 100 in the new complex at Aiglemont under the wing of Francois Mathet. Despite the presence of all sorts of brilliant assistants like Ghislain Drion and Margarette Lang, you couldn't conceive of one man coping with quite so many destinies if it were not for the ultra-modern glass-fronted building up above the stable compound. For that is the headquarters of the Aga's main work, the affairs of the Ismaili Muslims of which he is spiritual leader, and that means not just a few hundred quadrupeds, but more than 10 million souls.

None the less, this is something of a horse mountain, and it is the rationale of Harvard rather than the Hay Barn that has got the Aga on top of it. In the early days, this brought some scoffing as he appeared at the races with a computer file under his arm, especially as he hadn't endeared himself to the regulars by moving his horses from the care of his father's friend, Alec Head, to the more forbidding Mathet. Even now, there was a certain incongruity in the sight of him looking over his yearlings at Saint Crespin (Normandy) one April afternoon while a secretary solemnly recorded even my most banal 'nice-sort' comments.

Yet when you challenge him about over complication, the reply comes back–polite, quick and uncomfortably direct. 'Well, how much do you remember?' he asked, ignoring the fact that after the sort of lunch I had had I would have been muttering 'good sort' if they had led out a wildebeeste for me to look out. 'I don't mind admitting that I can't retain everything in my head', he went on. 'And what's the point of being too proud to use modern methods? I am trying to run a clean and successful operation for everybody's sake'. Seeing as how we were there to make a film about Normandy in apple-blossom time, and had been sunk without trace by an unseasonal blizzard, we were hardly in the business of lecturing the Aga Khan on time and motion.

The truth is that a big-scale racing set-up is all about reports and communication, as anyone who has been to Robert Sangster's records-room bunker in the Isle of Man will appreciate. What's more, if you want to have a big outfit to breed as well as race, and continue to have some time for other activities, you couldn't really beat France in the Seventies. Naturally you are going to need other outlets and bases. Alec Head and his astute partner, Roland de Chambure, have now got a place in Kentucky at which to keep their mares visiting American stallions–you have to try and perm the best blood available. But as a base, France offers brilliant prize money (with more than a billion francs to be won, over 60 per cent of horses pay their way), really hefty breeders' incentives and, best of all for the busy man, most major tracks within an hour of Paris.

Naturally, with more than 270 courses all around the country, France has one of the most far-flung racing businesses of any nation, but at the top level everything is centered on Chantilly or Paris's other nearby training centre at Maisons Laffitte. And with great respect to such important one-offs as the Grand Prix de Vichy, all important flat racing is in the Paris area except for some pre-season stuff at Cagnes-sur-Mer in January and February, and a mid-term break at Deauville in August.

So if we think trainers have it pretty good as regards facilities in Chantilly (and we do), we English positively resent the civilised way they conduct their travelling arrangements. If the 'patron' had started at 5am, he could have seen all his three lots of horses go out to exercise by 10.30, had time to do all his office work, then have a nice lunch and still leave time to drive the 40 minutes to Longchamp for the first race. There's a simple comparison. In England, a trainer thinks he's being hard done-by if he has to leave for the races before breakfast; at Chantilly, it's before lunch.

It's a racing gourmet's Mecca all right, but not without its pitfalls, as witness the sorry end of the only ride I will ever take in the Royal car. It was an idyllic Longchamp Thursday afternoon in mid-May, and after the Queen's colt, Charlton, had run third in La Coupe, Lord Porchester, the Royal racing manager, offered me a lift to the airport. Maybe Her Majesty wasn't there, but no one would have guessed it from the style of the limousine and its phalanx of motor-cycle outriders which carved a path through the rush-hour traffic around the Arc de Triomphe and out towards Le Bourget. Yet no sooner had I started to think that I could die a happy man than I realised with sweating, lip-biting certainty that death was right at hand. I had eaten a bad oyster for lunch. Somehow they stopped in time, and I scrambled over Lord Porchester's immaculate Savile Row suit to be horribly sick all over the Boulevard Peripherique. Royal cars haven't seen me since.

Such upper-crust mischances shouldn't cloud the fact that Paris is the world's best bet for the ordinary racegoer. Not only does he have five beautiful tracks within an hour of the city centre (Longchamp and Saint Cloud within 10 minutes), but the massive betting money returned has kept entrance fees down as well as prize-money up. Five or 10 francs is a standard charge and the cash has been so well spent on the customer's behalf that in at least two cases he has facilities unmatched anywhere in Europe.

Not at Chantilly, perhaps, which has hopelessly too little room for the big crowds it expects for its two classics, the Prix de Diane (French Oaks) and the Prix du Jockey Club (French Derby), but which could perhaps be forgiven anything else for its remarkable chateau-side setting. Maisons Laffitte, out to the west of Paris, is far better since its face-lift, but is still nicer to look at from the road than to look out of from the stand. But once you get to Saint Cloud you are talking about style, and at Longchamp and Evry you are getting into improvements of quite mind-boggling proportions.

After all, Longchamp has the prime city-centre site of any racecourse in the world. Imagine a race-track in New York's Central Park or London's Kensington Gardens. It has such a view of Paris across the Bois de Boulogne, with the Eiffel Tower in the distance, that even regular racegoers sometimes have to pinch themselves to believe it. And it has the finest stand in Europe. More remarkably still, don't forget that this stand was actually built farther down the track, and then shunted into position on rails once it was ready. Admittedly, the average speed was about 1.5mm an hour, but it still conjures up the most magnificent possibilities.

If a building as vast as the main stand at Longchamp can be pushed along by rail, where will it end? The Empire State Building, the Houses of Parliament, Harrods?

In some ways, the course at Evry is even more amazing. Just beyond Orly Airport on the Autoroute du Sud, it is 30 kilometres from Paris and, opened in 1974, it is the newest major course in Europe. Seven years after the opening day, the track, with its grandstand, all-round viewing area and paddock behind, its variety of refreshment areas and its computerised Pari-Mutuel windows could still claim the impressive distinction that the worst complaint was that it was so far from Chantilly. And that was only an hour's run, and just 30km, from Paris.

It is a significant, however that for all their attractions Evry, Longchamp and the rest of the Paris tracks draw disappointingly few of the capital city's five million inhabitants. Despite easy access, low entry charges and marvellous facilities, there are still only moderate crowds on a weekday, and even such a major event as the Arc de Triomphe, with 35,000 in 1981, is something of a disappointment since Longchamp can take 80,000, and almost a third of that attendance was made up of trilby-hatted English on package tours. The Epsom Derby claims to have almost half a million people scattered across the Downs, but if you had 10,000 Frenchmen among them, the shock would lead to questions in Parliament.

British racing has an attendance problem, too, but it's reasons are far more obvious – it's much more expensive, less well-endowed and much less centralised. Indeed, the British racing game is in many ways the poor, disorganised relation, Britain getting some £20 million where France gets £100 million, of a comparable total betting turnover of £2½ thousand million. Besides massive prize money and luxury racecourses, this means that in England necessary welfare services such as the care of injured jockeys and the training of apprentices have to be done by hard-working, but inevitably under-financed and unco-ordinated, charity work. At Chantilly, there is a modern 71-bed hospital for jockeys and stable staff, a 280-desk apprentice school and three other centres for lads and apprentices, part of a nationwide pattern all funded and administered by racing's overall governing body, the Société d'Encouragement (pour l'amelioration des races de chevaux en France).

When you have walked around the university-campus-style apprentice school at Chantilly, and compared it with the tiny, makeshift little effort at Goodwood, it would seem absurd to suggest that British racing may yet turn out to be healthier than its infinitely richer and clearer-structured sister. We talk in riddles, perhaps, but your best clue is to compare the racing coverage in the national newspapers on an ordinary day. In Britain, there will be full cards from two, even three, meetings around the country, and at least two

articles about them. In France, just the Paris card and the briefest of summaries. Then there's televison coverage. In Britain, three meetings, and up to 10 races, screened live every Saturday. In France, just the Tiercé race on Sunday. It's as if the ordinary public don't bother about racing except for their beloved Tiercé betting, and anyone who has had the misfortune to have had such gentle blandishments as, 'allez le six!' (go on the six) bellowed in his ear will know that very often the bet is on the number, not the name.

While everything was booming financially, such comments sounded like a purist's quibbles, and jealous ones at that. But what if the four billion francs that the Government gets out of racing, began to lose pace with inflation? If another form

of betting offered equal public inducements, far greater Government race take-out and much smaller capital cost? And if a Left-wing faction took power threatening wealth tax and assorted fiscal horrors to clip the wings of the sort of investors that racing needs, and with which Chantilly abounds? Well, all those things happened to France in 1981, betting increasing by five per cent compared with 13 per cent inflation

Normandy's half-timbered style provides an unmistakeable backdrop as the Deauville runners gallop past and later return to the world's most Norman weighing room. For years Deauville has kept up the tradition, started in the 1860s, of being the place where 'Le Tout Paris' goes in August. But the rival attraction of the Riviera and other Mediterranean enticements, plus the costs associated with putting on a racing operation for just six weeks, has made the future of these scenes far from secure.

and with 30 per cent increase in Loto (the lucky numbers game with a weekly televised draw), which is smiled on by the Government, since the take-out is almost 50 per cent. And don't forget that the Mitterrand Government which arrived that May brought along enough huffing and puffing about fleecing the rich that several 'high rollers' planned to quit Chantilly, and fashionable pessimists were almost as keen to talk of leaving as white men of 'taking the gap' once a black government took control in Zimbabwe.

There's nothing new in such pressures on horse racing, but the trick in beating them is to project the game as such an immensely popular, throughly honourable pursuit that for a Government to attack it would be political madness. So suddenly, for French racing, lack of popular involvement looks suspiciously like an Achilles Heel and, what's worse, such apathy is of quite long-standing.

If you were to poll a group of Frenchmen on the most famous racehorse of the 1970s, you can bet your life they wouldn't say Allez France or Youth, but Bellino II, the hero of the more proletarian, but well-supported, trotting world, and back in 1968 I remember listening to the sports news on the evening of the French Derby, when the big race's only mention was that there had been a 'bon Tiercé a Chantilly, le 17, le 4 et le 13'.

No doubt Louis Romanet and other bright-eyed young men in the Société d'Encouragement will start beating the oppressed-minority-drum for racing, but if that is to be effective, they have to be sure that the house will bear close inspection. As we have seen, this certainly works regarding facilities and transport for the ordinary racegoer. The huge prize money, right down to fourth place, also makes the average finish far more competitive than you see in Britain, where riders on the fifth, sixth and seventh horses are often about as positive as a possum in the final furlong. But considering the favourable circumstances, neither the horses not the people swept the European board in the Seventies as one might have expected, and the reason is probably just that conditions look so easy.

This eternal truth was nowhere more evident than with the riders, for the centralisation around Paris means that all the top jockeys will be riding at one meeting each day. Although this sounds good, it also means that the opportunity for the young apprentice to ride against the stars is far more limited, and therefore his graduation, and the

Longchamp, the champions and the cognoscenti. Arc de Triomphe winners like Allez France and Yves St. Martin (Top Centre), Star Appeal and Greville Starkey (Middle Centre), Three Troikas and Freddie Head (Bottom Centre) are watched by the world's most cosmopolitan crowd. Indeed, the cross-channel invasion from Britain has become so strong that the main bar beside the paddock was renamed Le Bar des Anglais. Enough to make a local racegoer hide his head, we have come a long way since Gladiateur, immortalised in a statue at the course, won the 1865 Epsom Derby for France and was called the Avenger of Waterloo.

necessary challenge to the establishment, is a much slower process. If an apprentice gets 'hot' in England, he will immediately find himself, albeit at a 'second' meeting, under the full media spotlight, and opposed by several of the leading riders. If a French apprentice rides a double at Fontainebleau or Croisé Laroche, he will have been opposed only by second-raters, and no one will know about it except the most studious.

So although the contract rider for a big stable has to face all the usual slings and arrows of keeping his trainer's and owner's confidence, he doesn't get the pressure from beneath that he would have in Britain, nor, for that matter, the pressure from his rivals he would have in the United States, where a beaten horse's trainer will sometimes have alternative jockeys' agents bad-mouthing the incumbent before he's even reached the scales.

France, nonetheless, hasn't done too badly for a country that gave Britain 200 years' start and now, 150 years later, finds herself by far the richest and, with 264 individual race-tracks, infinitely the largest racing state in Europe. What's more, those riches extend to much more than money, as an anyone will know who has dropped by one of the many little tracks in the French heartland. It is unlikely to be all flat racing, but none the worse for that. One day, when I rode in a steeplechase at Fontainebleau, there was also an amateurs' flat race, an apprentices' flat race, a hurdle race, a ladies' race and two trotting races. I didn't ride the winner,

but at least I got a smacking kiss from one of the lady jockeys right outside the weighing-room.

Much more organised, but still considered almost slums by the Parisian heroes, are the circuits at Vichy, Lyons, and Marseille. And Cagnes-sur-Mer, on the Riviera, actually holds the centre of the stage in January and February. The Cagnes track has one of the most beautiful sites in the world, and to ride out there on a clear, crisp January morning, with the Mediterranean just across the road to the south, and the snow-capped Alpes Maritimes on the northern skyline, is an unforgettable experience for any racing man.

Cagnes is almost as well appointed as Evry, and the public seem more enthusiastic, warmer blooded perhaps–certainly keener to believe that the whole game is an enormous plot to which they were about to find the key. As I went out to ride one day, a huge Algerian gentleman leaned over the rail and said: 'pas le tour!' (don't pull it), and an apparently charming little jockey, who became very friendly with us all, turned out to be the Mafia's go-between in one of the worst Tiercé scandals French racing (albeit, jump racing on this occasion) has ever suffered. No fewer than 15 jockeys were separately bribed in a field of 22.

An established Paris rider will also find that the interpretation of the rules gives him an easier life than he would have across the Channel. Although there is not much difference in the actual wording, the practice in England is to allow jockeys to bunch

much tighter, and go through narrower gaps. In France, what might seem trifling interference can cause suspension, and so rather than take the risk, jockeys pull out much wider to make their challenge in the straight. This may well make for fewer disputes in running, but it also takes away from the necessary cut and thrust that should be central to a jockey's being, and it is with no prejudice whatever that I say this has become

evident when you watch French jockeys ride on English racecourses.

In all such comments, there has to be a shining exception made for Yves St Martin, a prince among jockeys of any era. Son of a Bordeaux jailer, and supposedly weighing only two-and-a-half-pounds at birth, he impressed Francois Mathet enough to be first jockey, and indeed champion of France, before he was 21. Since then he has taken the title 14 times, and won two Arc de Triomphes, five French Derbys and numerous major races abroad. And always with the style that he has made his own, match-winning cool ('toujours le suis tres froid au depart', he says, with no false modesty) and brilliant, almost revolutionary, balance.

For in his way, Yves St Martin changed the face of European racing. Where the American Tod Sloan at the turn of the century had shown the advantages of riding with short enough leathers to lift your seat out of the saddle, so in the early Sixties St Martin was the trail-blazer of riding even shorter, and shifting the point of balance from above the girth up to the point of the shoulder where, in fact, a horse carries it easiest. The taller, leaner Lester Piggott has become even more synonymous with this style, but he rode his first Derby winner four years before St Martin had his first success of any kind, and coincidence though it may be, it was not until Yves had burst upon the scene that the Piggott leathers were pulled up, and the most famous posterior in racing took on its skywards tilt.

At that time, I spent two long summers in France, and again and again would be drawn down to the start just to watch the way St Martin left the stalls, and within a stride would be perched up in the mane, with the horse seemingly galloping free beneath him. He was then, and has remained, the best-balanced rider I have ever seen. He is also an altogether charming man of whom French racing is justifiably proud. Yet he and Piggott have to be held responsible for some of the least effective sights you will see on a racecourse. Their imitators pull the leathers up as short – sometimes they even get part of the balance right – but when it comes to lowering themselves to propel a horse at the finish, they begin to look like someone trying to learn riding the monocycle. Such a description would be very unfair on Yves's great rival, Freddie Head, four times champion of France and four times winner of the Arc de Triomphe. But while Head on his home ground is impressive both for his strength and his timing, even he has more than once looked so insecure arounö the helter-skelter of Tattenham Corner that Mill Reef's jockey, Geoff Lewis, stuttered out the immortal line: 'If F-F-F-Freddie keeps on like this, the g-g-gypsies will be asking for d-d-danger money.'

Eccentricity of style will eventually wash through, particularly as more jockeys, like Phillippe Paquet in Hong Kong, pit themselves against top riders in other countries. But what makes France a fine place for a jockey, also gives him a problem. It tends to make him mentally fat, and there has never been such a thing as a top jockey who was fat.

As those who know and love the fast-talking Johnny Campo in America will appreciate, the same comment cannot be made about trainers, 'The Fat Man' crowning his career by saddling the 1981 Kentucky Derby winner, Pleasant Colony. But while the Boutins, Heads and Mathets could probably train a llama to sing the blues, the suspicion that life is perhaps a shade too easy for the average Paris trainer doesn't go away. Of course, it's understandable that they should concentrate on the rich pickings at home, but judging them on their achievements across the Channel doesn't help the cause. For in Britain during 1981, with no restrictions on entry, Vayraan in the Champion Stakes, was the only French-trained winner.* Whereas British trainers, facing barriers in all but the top races, won 11 events and over half a million pounds in French prize money.

That's when you remember that for all its mist-shrouded beauty, Chantilly can be a crowded training centre. Great shouts of, 'Merde, merde!' one morning showed that another trainer had got on the grass cantering ground before us, and his 40 two-year-olds soon trampled the so-called 'turf' into something like a rainy-day car park.

But despite what many English professionals might disparagingly say, I don't think that the most serious criticism of the French racing scene should be laid entirely at the trainers' door. It is often alleged that French-trained horses are running on something stronger than hay, oats and water. In short that, by British standards, they are being doped. It's a situation which has had two major flashpoints – in 1976, when Boutin's Trepan was disqualified from major victories at Ascot and Sandown after his dope test showed positive, and in 1981, when Mathet's Vayraan was found positive after the Champion Stakes. In both those years, far wider allegations were made on the medication issue, and in 1981 two leading French trainers were suspended by the Société d'Encouragement.

Now once you get into the medication scene on either side of the Atlantic many people, especially the British, tend to don the white sheet as if anyone who gave a horse something peppier than a lump of suger was the biggest crook since William Palmer. The truth is that the racehorse is a finely-tuned machine, and the area between what is treatment and what is 'assistance' is a very grey one which can only be defined if the authorities are very clear in their parameters. The rules will be honoured only if the testing procedure can comprehensively screen all samples. Despite an agreement in 1980 that Britain and France would have the same standard whereby any 'non-normal nutrient' in the blood would lead to automatic disqualification, it soon became clear that France was having trouble with her side of the bargain. One trainer was stood down, but rumours continued of all sorts of interesting 'parcels' flying in from the States and, more disturbing than gossip, a report from one observer that ridiculed any claims of parity between the British screening system and the French.

Once it becomes apparent that the testing net is not effective, all hell can break loose, with vets believing that certain treatments will not show up. So by the time Vayraan (trained by the most anti-doping of all trainers) had his positive test in the same week as another French trainer was suspended for 'irregularities', the situation was so confused that Jean Lyon said dryly:' It looks as if the agreement on anti-doping procedures is working about as well as the Common Market'. With only 22 miles of water between the two countries, it is absurd for Britain and France not to operate the same system, and the sooner a central testing bureau is set up, and all trainers and vets are made clearly aware of its implications, the better for the game, and for the breed.

In fact, French bloodstock did not have the good time during the Seventies that many had predicted, and by 1980 their thoroughbred birth-rate had fallen to 3,000 (down 1,200 in five years), such promising sires as Lyphard, Caro, Val de L'Orne and Blushing Groom had been sold to America, and Baron Guy de Rothschild, the breeders' president, was complaining bitterly about unfair taxation. It can be seen that French breeders want doubts about the medication background of their classic winners about as much as Noah wanted rain.

Yet overall, France has got together a magnificent blend of past and present. And if its very grandeur now puts it under threat, that's a penalty it will have to learn to live with. Perhaps it should remember the message of Les Grandes Ecuries, that huge chateau-type building put up at Chantilly in 1730 by the Prince de Condé in the belief that he was going to be re-incarnated as a horse, and therefore might as well live in the style to which he was accustomed. Looking at the blue-blooded nags all round Chantilly nowadays, who is to say that Condé's dream did not come true? And if that piece of madness can survive 250 years, why shouldn't a semi-insane sport like horse racing continue for a year or two longer?

---

*Vayraan failed the dope test but was controversially allowed to keep the race after a seven-month enquiry showed that he had produced his own steroids.

Clairefontaine is Deauville's little sister but lacks nothing in charm or decoration. Situated some four kilometres from the main resort, it has a smaller, less pretentious racetrack encompassing jump racing and trotting as well as the flat. The steeplechase course can be seen inside the flat race rail. Fourteen days racing in all take place at Clairefontaine through July and August, and the track caters for crowds of around 5,000, about half that of the bigger Deauville establishment.

5
WEST GERMANY

'Where else in Europe would you see all varieties of pet pooches being led around (and sometimes watering) every corner of the racecourse? And if the stiffest Newmarket shirts could somehow relax their canine ban on English Two Thousand Guineas day, they would surely burst a button at the Gelsenkirchen-Horst sight of a dozen kids having a kickabout on the members' lawn as the runners for the big Classic filed past'.

SPORT LOVES to avoid politics, but there was all too literally no escape for German racing when the roof fell in on the Third Reich in 1945. Not only did the eventual division of Germany hive off to the East Hoppelgarten, the leading racing centre, and Gradiz, the National Stud, but scores of priceless bloodlines vanished in the fighting. Most macabre of all was the fate of Gradiz's top stallion, Alchimist, a German Derby winner. As his grooms fled westwards from the Russian invading force, they briefly left Alchimist in the little town of Torgos. When they returned, the ravenous troops had eaten him. As that student of German racing, David Conolly-Smith, points out, by modern standards the horse was worth millions, so "this must have been the most expensive meal of all time."

In the best romantic tradition, this un-scheduled military feast was not the end of the story. For Alchimist's son, Birkhahn, brought him posthumous honour in the 1948 German Derby, and after five years in the Eastern bloc, Birkhahn came over to the West, where *his* son, Priamos, was an outstanding racehorse, travelling to France to win the Prix Dollar and Prix Jacques le Marois. In addition, Birkhahn became the maternal grandsire

(Preceding Spread) When racing gets it right it combines, entrancingly, timeless natural elegance and modern-day comforts. That's the mixture when you breakfast on the course at Baden-Baden, Germany's oldest and most beautiful track, set on the edge of the Black Forest in the southern part of the country. Baden-Baden was one of the great spa towns of the 19th Century and racing came to it in the 1850s as naturally as casinos and lovely women. The horrors of two world wars have caused understandable setbacks and the best German horses still tend to be a little behind the French, English and Irish. Nevertheless, when it comes to style and atmosphere, the big Baden-Baden Festival at the end of August can match any meeting in the world.

German racing may have its problems but a day at Gelsenkirchen-Horst, 40 miles from Dusseldorf, depicted on the right hand page, for the 2,000 Guineas (Henckel-Rennen) shows how they get many things right. There is, remarkably, far more of a family atmosphere than is found at equivalent British or French tracks. Where else would you have little dogs also having their day and children outnumbering form students among the spectators? The considerable air of easy-going friendliness even extends into the jockeys' room where the East German refugee, Lutz Mader, on the left, sits with valet Michael Schuirtz and fellow jockey George Bocskai. Bocskai won the Henckel-Rennen on Tombos (Bottom Left). He rode for the remarkable Heinz Jentsch (Top Left), 21 times champion trainer in a sport which has survived the ravages of war; witness the Ruhr valley industrial background at Gelsenkirchen-Horst. But while a leading figure of German racing such as Hans Heinrich von Loeper (Middle Left) has been important to the revival of German racing, the pictures from Baden-Baden, on the left hand page, show that it is still vulnerable to attacks from outside. Jockey Mick Miller and trainer Geoff Huffer, for example, receive their trophies after their Newmarket horse Tina's Pet had won an important sprint. Moreover, among the jockeys who have settled down to ride very successfully in Germany are the former British apprentices Steve Eccles (Bottom Left) and David Richardson (Bottom Right).

of the brilliant 1970 German Derby winner, Alpenkonig, who now stands alongside Priamos (or at any rate in the next-door paddock) at the leading stud, Gestut Schlenderhan, and the two of them have played a major part in the drive to put Germany back into the European big league.

It was clear that West Germany was not far from such stature at the end of the Seventies. In 1975, the German-trained Star Appeal trounced Europe's best in both Britain's Eclipse Stakes and France's Prix de l'Arc de Triomphe, and in 1980 the German champion, Nebos, was only two lengths off Detroit at the finish of the Arc after looking distinctly unlucky. But if things have come a long way from the stage as late as 1955, when there were just 520 thoroughbred mares left (two-thirds of the number registered 100 years earlier), the overall standard still looks vulnerable to foreign attack, and in 1981 English-trained horses alone took three races, seven places and a £131,000-odd slice out of the German cake.

Depending on your point of view, you can argue that this state of affairs shows how well the German racing industry has put itself together after the war, or how far it still lags behind the major powers. What is indisputable is that the method adopted has been a protectionist one, with all the Classics and many other races being limited to German-bred horses. This has certainly meant the establishment of some fine family lines, but it has also involved Germany's missing out the big American connection that has been the great feature in Britain, France and Ireland in recent years. There is no point in sending an American-bred yearling to race in Germany if it can't run in the Classics, and until a new Nebos actually wins the Arc, not enough interest will be taken in German Bloodlines to prick the pockets of the big stallion syndicates.

Yet much progress has been made, and as anyone who has met him can testify, much of the credit is due to the drive and foresight of the Director General, Herr Van Loeper. With no apology for this most terrible of puns, it can be said that German racing has been in very good Hans. In organisational terms, this has been most marked with the development of a very healthy prize-money structure, the average in 1981 being 9,454 Deutsch Marks (£2,333) a race.

On the training front it is also clear that the likes of Heinz Jentzsch and Theo Greiper have little to learn from other countries, the Eclipse and Arc de Triomphe victories with Star Appeal in 1980 providing ample evidence of Greiper's expertise. But interestingly enough, half of Greiper's staff are from England, as indeed is Star Appeal's lad, Fred Townend. For, as France did some 10 years later, German racing took the British as a model when their first modern-style meeting was arranged at Bad Doperan on August 22, 1822, by the Anglophile Baron Von Biel.

The sport caught on so quickly that there were 20 racecourses in Germany by 1830, and more than 50 by mid-century. Not for the first time are you left wondering how within 100 years two countries with such shared enthusiasms could twice set at each other's throats in the bloodiest conflicts history has ever seen.

What's more, you cannot talk to any senior German racing personnel without also realising that the Iron Curtain which split the country in 1947 also delivered a terrible blow to the thoroughbred racing industry. Hoppelgarten, the principal racing and training centre, and Gradiz, the German National Stud, found themselves in the Communist sector, and that, in horse-racing terms, was very much the wrong side of the Curtain. For the thoroughbred remains, as it began, a luxury animal hardly suited to economically straitened socialist régimes.

These historical legacies are all around. At Gelsenkirchen-Horst, 30 miles from Dusseldorf, where the German Two Thousand Guineas is run, you hardly dare ask about the extent of allied bombing, and at Cologne's racecourse in the heart of the Ruhr you look in disbelief at the way the grandstand, racetrack and surrounding training centre survived the destruction of 1945.

The racing which has emerged from the ashes does not have an Australian-type hold on the media, or the status of a number one spectator sport attraction as in the United States. Indeed, after that 1982 Two Thousand Guineas, you were pushed to find any mention at all in the major newspapers, and although there was a healthy crowd that afternoon, the average attendance is down below 3,000.

But while the horses and the jockeys (of which more later) may lack a little international class, there is one distinctive feature in which German racing heads the European racing league. More than in any other country, a visit to the races seems a family day out. Perhaps you don't get the smartest set or the heavy "players," but you see about as many wives as husbands, not to mention children and, above all, dogs.

Where else in Europe would you see all varieties of pet pooches being led around (and sometimes watering) every corner of the racecourse? And if the stiffest Newmarket shirts could somehow relax their canine ban on English Two Thousand Guineas day, they would surely burst a button at the Gelsenkirchenhorst sight of a dozen kids having a kickabout on the members' lawn as the runners for the big Classic filed past.

This lack of heavy protocol extends to the training grounds, for when next morning we wandered mistakenly into the Cologne stable of the Two Thousand Guineas' winner, Tombos, at 7am, his trainer, Heinz Jentzsch, and his jockey, George Bocskai, were already slaving away, very much in their working clothes.

Jentzsch's 15 German Derbys and 17 trainers' championships are credentials enough, and across

the track his great rival, Heinrich Bellow, developed Nebos to be the German Horse of the Year in 1980, as well as finishing fifth in the Arc de Triomphe. Bollow, a beaming little hedgehog of a man, also boasts the rare distinction of having now trained 1,000 winners, after having ridden a similar total of firsts. Britain's great Harry Wragg is the only other man we know to have achieved the double, so claimants better write in quick with their claims to join the most exclusive club in the world.

Yet as Heinrich Bollow watched horses splatter through the rain puddles on the training track, and then entertained us to the sort of breakfast that accounted for the 20 kilos he put on in the year he quit riding, he more than once referred to the outstanding facilities at Hoppelgarten. Then, in the immaculate little suburban house, out came the scrapbooks lovingly recording every winner ridden and trained, with the Hoppelgarten entries significantly breaking off in 1944, and the winners resuming at Dusseldorf, Cologne, Munich and other West German tracks from 1946.

"Hoppelgarten was my home–I was born and raised there," said Heinrich. "But there was obviously no future for us, so we had to come to where the horses were." A least for him and his wife, also born in Hoppelgarten, the trip across was made before the Iron Curtain rang down. For Lutz Mader, Bollow's young jockey also Hoppelgarten-raised, the problems were more difficult. Indeed his first attempt at swimming out to the green pastures of the West ended in imprisonment, and it was only after a year behind bars that the East Germans allowed their diminutive captive to continue his career on capitalist horses.

Paradoxically, the great economic miracle to which Mader escaped has in many ways passed racing by, and it is significant that the two biggest studs and stables, the Gestuts Rottgen and Schlenderhahn, date back to an earlier age, Rottgen to the 1920s, and Schlenderhahn to 1869. Moreover, while both of them are immensely impressive to visit, their future is clouded by the fact that both owners are gallant but elderly ladies.

Different training systems near Cologne. Theo Greiper and his English head lad Fred Townrow (Top Left) at the remarkable training grounds of the Gestüt Röttgen, where they handle over 50 horses for Mrs. Maria Mehl Mühlens. Built between the wars, the Gestüt Röttgen has as impressive a set of buildings as any operation in the world; among the bright ideas in a stable that turned out the 1975 Arc de Triomphe winner, Star Appeal, is the mechanical muck sack (Centre Top) which can take the waste of six boxes before being shunted smoothly down to the dung heap. Training, by contrast, on Cologne racecourse itself does not look quite so modern on a soaking morning (Bottom) but it is where Heinz Jentsch has for long topped the German lists. It is also where Heinz Bollow (Top Right) has produced an endless stream of winners including the Preis von Europa hero Nebos, achieving in the process the rare distinction of riding a thousand winners as jockey and then notching up more than four figures as a trainer.

At Rottgen, just 15 kilometres from Cologne and now beginning to be flanked by the factories and depots of the new order, the sense of being a fortress against modernism is accentuated by an impressive Victorian-style gate-house, 12 kilometres of outside wall and a fairy-tale schloss in the centre. This truly amazing set-up, including 48 mares for breeding and 53 horses in training under Theo Greiper, was originally financed by the success of the famous 747 perfume. Today there is still plenty of the product available if you use the guest bathroom to freshen up before meeting Mrs Maria Mehl-Mülhens, widow of the recent owner.

An hour's drive north-west is the great establishment of Schlenderhahn, which can boast as big a stud, if not such a resplendent training establishment as Rottgen, and an even longer and more glittering history. Schlenderhahn was founded in the same year (1869) as the German Derby, a race which its horses have now won no fewer than 16 times. From the start, the stud has been owned by the Oppenheim family, and since 1952, a period which has seen the emergence of the three present stallions, Alpenkonig, Lombard and Priamos, has been in the care of Baroness Gabrielle von Oppenheim.

In 1953, the Baroness took on a one-armed ex-cavalry officer, Ewald Meyer zu Dute, as stud manager, and the eight owner and ten breeder championships in the following 20 years showed she had made the right choice. But as Meyer zu Dute sticks his riding crop under his stump and points out horses representing the stud's famous bloodlines, you can't help thinking of the traumas that he, and it, must have seen. "Obviously a lot was lost," he says. "But we have tried to build up, and the German horse is becoming good again."

The old soldier's enthusiasm for a British involvement is reflected in a couple of Schlenderhahn's products being regularly sent to race in England, and the connection is nowhere shown more strongly than on the jockey front, with such men as David Richardson and Steve Eccles going right to the top in Germany.

As even their best friends in England could not pretend that either of these two nice men would have been a Piggott or Eddery if they had continued their careers in Britain, the Richardson-Eccles success story in Germany raises a query about the local riders which also occurs if you study the jockey bookings for any important German Sunday. Again and again you will find that local connections have thought it worthwhile to fly in some British knight of the pigskin to ride their horse in a big race.

Such habits hardly add to the confidence of local riders, who doubtless often wish that the protectionism applied to German horses was extended to those in the saddle. But open competition is usually the best way to improve standards, and whatever it may be like for the poor old German jocks, my experience of one

such Sunday trip from Gatwick confirms that it is not too bad a deal for the British raiders.

I don't pretend to know what the financial arrangements were to tempt Messrs Lindley, Mercer and Lewis from their beds, but if you are planning a racing day-out in a small plane you can't have much better companions, especially if they ride winners, thereby making the return trips from Germany an absurd champagne-filled parody of other long airborne slogs home in very different circumstances nearly four decades before. Memory is always selective, and there is no reason why some of it should not be golden, which is perhaps why this trip was to Baden Baden.

Amid the social turmoils at the turn of the century, the odds against the three great July-August bolt-holes of the leisured classes, Goodwood, Deauville and Baden Baden, surviving intact, must have been hundreds to one. Yet here we are heading for the second millenium with only Deauville, so long the leader of the three as the ultimate racing lotus land, under any sort of threat. Maybe Voltaire wasn't so far wrong when he said: "The superfluous is very necessary."

Superfluous or not, to fly over the Black Forest and to touch down at a little airstrip outside the town is not something to miss. The racetrack is well organised, too, and if you think the lederhosen-clad brass band look as if they have been put there specially for tourists, you are the sort of person who believes that those wild whispy men in kilts you see at breakfast at the Station Hotel, Inverness, are just there for Scottish trade. Maybe they are, but have a closer look and ask yourself who was there first.

The same criteria can be applied to the monster sausages (Bratwurst) barbecued at the back of the stands, but if the racing fitted much of a conventional pattern, it did at least have one challenge to accepted wisdom. In the two-year-old race, the jockeys were not permitted to carry whips more than a foot long, making our familiar men look as if they had snapped theirs in half on the way to the paddock. This is part of a general German drive to protect their two-year-olds against exploitation, no horse of that age group being allowed to run before the first of June, or then compete more than eight times. Having travelled over with three of the most skilful but sympathetic users of the full-length whip British-style, I had to be much swayed by their views that the foreshortened German "cravache" had only disadvantages. "It's too short to wave properly," said Joe Mercer, "and if a horse does need a crack you can't give him one right on the quarters as you should. Most of their boys end up hitting them down the flank, which is the worst place of all, because it hurts them and makes them curl up."

But two other factors have to be considered. One is that all jockeys are not, and will not be, as skilful and sympathetic as Mercer and Lindley, and the second that public support, on which all

present day racing depends, might be seriously jeopardized if a campaign could be mounted against the Sport of Kings on the grounds that it depended on men beating horses in public. As a former jockey, I personally favour Mercer's view that judicious use of the whip is an aid to both steering and impulsion that improve the general conduct of the race, and therefore the integrity of the game. Yet the animal-welfare lobby is a powerful and growing force worldwide, and only a fool would ignore it's influence.

At present there are very different attitudes around the world. In Australia and America such phrases as "hit right out" and "whipping furiously" are accepted as part of a jockey's duties. Indeed, one trainer in Italy insisted on sending for an English jockey because the local boys dare not put down their whips in the straight for fear of being attacked for not trying, and at the Iron Curtain racing championships in Prague, there was enough belabouring to give an ironic twist to the Russians' expressed aim to produce a "Ferro Concrete Horse."

Yet in Germany we have these shorter whips on two-year-olds, and in Scandinavia there is now a rule that permits a jockey to take his hand off the rein to hit a horse only three times in a race. Britain has its usual compromise. The authorities

took a big stand in 1980 with ludicrously punitive punishments handed out to two over-belligerent Irish jump jockeys, but allowed Lester Piggott to resort in extremis to what can best be called machine-gun tactics. These are diabolically effective as Roberto's and The Minstrel's Derby victories so famously testify, but consist in the last strides of getting in the maximum number of blows in the minimum time.

Of course, any ban on whips would need reciprocal agreements in other countries, but however much we professionals might complain that many horses would be just lobbing round wondering why no one gives them a hurry-up swat, it's difficult to argue that all its effect would be bad. Would it be such a terrible thing if jockeys had to balance more with their legs than their arms, if the racecourse test depended much more on which horse was keenest rather than which one was driven hardest? If that was the price we had to pay for public support, would it really be intolerable? Some enterprising firm should get itself some wonderful controversial publicity by sponsoring a big race with a no-whips condition. That way we could all look at the problem in reality.

But these worries are a luxury compared with the real needs of German racing. Greater public interest, a better government deal and new outside investment. It is easy to write down, infinitely harder to achieve. With practically any other country you would call it impossible. Not in Germany. Not yet.

No doubt Piggott's unique genius would find a way of making horses run faster even if jockeys had to ride back to front, but without his wand he might at last give way to some younger men. When that happens it will take away not only Britain's brightest star, but the greatest one-man side-show that racing has ever seen. Racing has always been part theatre, but with Piggott around you sometimes almost expect the curtain to fall across the steaming smiles in the victory circle.

Schlenderhahn is the oldest and greatest of German studs. Founded in 1869 by Baron Eduard von Oppenheim in the palatial grounds of his schloss between Cologne and Bonn, Schlenderhahn has produced no fewer than 16 German Derby winners. Among the stallions are the 1978 champion Alpenkonig (Bottom Left) and Priamos. Since 1953, the stud has been managed for Baroness Gabrielle von Oppenheim by Ewald Meyer zu Düte, who has made light of his war injuries to steer the stud to eight owners' and ten breeders' championships during his reign. As always with stud management, success depends on control of the present (Top Left) and understanding of the past (Top Right).

6
ITALY

'Italy's case has been one of decline from a formerly high standard set, most of all, by the remarkable Federico Tesio. Tesio bred two of the outstanding horses of the century in Nearco and Ribot. What's more, he did it from the equivalent of a standing start because he did not open what was to become the Dormello-Olgiata stud until 1898. By then English breeding had a lengthy history. Yet, by 1966, it was estimated that the Dormello bloodlines were present in over 60 per cent of the leading horses in England and Ireland and over 35 per cent of the Stakes winners in North America.'

ITALY IS a land of many delights but our first visit wasn't so hot. Lord Oaksey and I got accosted in Milan's 'men only' sauna. The second time was better, Rome, no accosting and the Brits won the Derby.

Let's make it quite clear that the two occasions were years apart and, sadly, only on the first of them was I an active rider, Oaksey and I being part of the British team which raced against the Italians at San Siro. We didn't win, but after I finished second on some brute all too aptly named Missile, there was a puzzling sort of compliment when the leading Italian apprentice insisted on buying my whip. Fifteen years later, both the whip and the apprentice had disappeared, and our role was to report on an English raid on the 1981 Italian Derby.

If you are going to be a day tripper, it's best to get the odds stacked in your favour, and that second Sunday in May we did our best, the team including jockeys Hide, Carson and Starkey who were riding fancied Italian horses in the Derby, and John Matthias, who was to partner Glint of Gold, the English-trained odds-on favourite. Old 'Glint' had sensibly been sent on ahead, which was just as well because there were delays and plane-changes, and we arrived sweating at the Hippodromo Capannelle after the first race had started.

By then, Matthias and trainer Ian Balding had met up with Glint of Gold in what we were promised were the racecourse stables, but which, with their Moorish towers and dusty open court-yards, were so obviously a set for Spaghetti Westerns that any moment you expected to hear and see Clint Eastwood come squinting round the corner under his hat.

Mr Eastwood stayed away, which was wise of him, as Mick Weedy and Bill Jennings, who had travelled with Glint of Gold, were rarely beaten in their earlier days in the stable lads' boxing championships, and if they don't exactly say 'Wogs begin at Calais', there is a certain tightening of the face-muscles when they travel abroad which spells danger to anyone who dares to interfere.

There have been great names in Italy's racing past – Nearco, Ribot, Molvedo – and the first Derby Italiano was run 100 years ago. But the great bloodstock boom of the 1970s passed Italy by, and with the thought that this was partly caused by inward-looking protectionist policies, the 1981

race was opened up to horses bred and trained outside Italy. With 90 million lira to beckon them, it's amazing that no other animals trekked south with Glint of Gold who, despite admirable qualities of grit and stamina, had so far shown himself some way short of wonder-horse level.

To be truthful, the Derby hardly had the nation-stopping significance of Epsom or Churchill Downs. Despite a futuristic-looking glass capsule, in which the jockeys passed the scales, most of the buildings looked in need of attention, and at only 10,000 the crowd made less noise before the race than the dozen flags atop the judge's box which flapped and whistled like an old Indiaman beating through Biscay.

A considerable number of people seemed to have conned their way into the paddock, but though one of the Italian horses appeared to be in an advanced stage of mental breakdown, Glint of Gold stayed calm throughout. If his racing or reproductive powers ever desert him, there's obviously a place for him in the police force. Since Ian Balding has long put maximum emphasis on important things like the Kingsclere football team, Matthias, Weedy and Jennings also looked quite unmoved by such a minor event as an Italian classic race, and Glint of Gold passed out of the parade as the only horse not in need of a deodorant.

It was then that by far the most serious piece of running took place, not by Glint of Gold in the race, which he duly collected in his usual, hard-slugging way, with Starkey second and Carson third, but by Mick Weedy, who hared across the infield like an Ovett to make sure no misbegotten foreigner touched his horse before it entered the stalls. Not for nothing does his broomhandle carry the inscription, 'Glint of Mick'.

Another great feat of athletics got Weedy back across the Capannelle to lead Glint of Gold to a presentation ceremony which, because owner Paul Mellon was back home in Virginia, ended up with

Ian Balding being weighed down with four trophies. Quite how good the opposition was, or indeed what Glint of Gold had beaten, was hard to tell, since modesty or fear of kidnap makes practically every Italian owner race under the name of either stud, 'Razza', or stable, 'Scuderia'. Feminists can make of it what they will, but the only recorded kidnap victims were Carnauba (a filly) and Maria Sacco (a lady jockey).

No body-snatching went on that Sunday, but there was a slight chill in the air as Glint of Gold was led off to the compulsory dope test. For the previous October, 'Glint', Mick and the rest of the team had flown down to Milan and collected Italy's richest two-year-old race, the Gran Criterium. There were then allegations, later proved to be unfounded, about irregularities uncovered in the dope test, and the winning money did not come through until after some public prompting the following spring. As Ian Balding shouldered his way through to insist that a separate blood sample was taken this time for his own analysis, it was easy to remember that he had once played full-back in the Varsity rugby match.

Now Glint of Gold is no Mill Reef (good thing, too, in some ways, for his smaller, sharper dad had a nasty habit of biting chunks out of the unwary), but he was tough and honest, as he showed when running on gallantly to be second, albeit at 10 lengths, to the astonishing Shergar in the Epsom Derby. Yet the ease with which he could account for his Italian rivals in Rome and for his German opposition in Cologne's Preis von Europa in October, 1981, points to the gulf those two countries have to cross to get on a par with the top horses in Britain, France and Ireland.

'Italy's case has been one of decline from a formerly high standard set, most of all, by the remarkable Federico Tesio. Tesio bred two of the outstanding horses of the century in Neano and Ribot. What's more, he did it from the equivalent

of a standing start because he did not open what was to become the Dormello–Olgiata stud until 1898. By then English breeding had a lengthy history. Yet, by 1966, it was estimated that the Dormello bloodlines were present in over 60 per cent of the leading horses in England and Ireland and over 35 per cent of the Stakes winners in North America. It is a record, together with the actual champions he produced, that give Tesio a claim to be the greatest thoroughbred breeder of all time.

But Federico Tesio was an inspirational genius; he talked of 'listening to the stars'. Since his death, in May 1954, two months before Ribot began the astonishing career which was to end with two successive victories in the Prix de l'Arc de Triomphe, Italian racing has never looked like recovering.

Significantly, one of the features of Tesio's success was his willingness to test his horses far afield, his first breakthrough coming when Scopa and Apelle won in France, Germany, and England in 1923 and 1925. Now, overseas challenges by Italian horses are an increasing rarity.

The recession has been marked by the drop in the thoroughbred foal rate from over 1,200 to below a thousand during the seventies, a decade which also saw major Classic successes for Italian-owned horses trained in England: Carlo Vittadini's Derby win with Grundy, in 1975, was complemented by Carlo d'Alessio's dual Two Thousand Guineas triumphs with Bolkonski in 1975 and Wollow in 1976.

Today, Luca Cumani, scion of a famous Italian racing house, and himself now training at Newmarket, nevertheless will not accept that things are all that black. 'Of course, there are problems when the economy is such a mess', says Luca. 'Yet Italy has a tremendous amount of racing (3,700 starts in 1980, compared to 2,886 in Britain), Carlo D'Alessio's Scuderia Ciefedi is still a vast operation (running over 80 horses in Italy compared to just 15 in England), and you have far

more chance of winning a couple of races and making it pay. But it remains basically Second Division racing, so what you are not going to get is the real jackpot of winning a Classic and increasing a horse's value by millions of pounds.

Cumani, tall, elegant and a former crack amateur rider has the distinction of also being something of an opera buff. So he might have added that blaming Italy for not producing a second Tesio is like decrying Germany for lacking another Wagner. If geniuses do not grow on trees, they are also pretty rare birds around the racetrack.

(Preceding Spread) John Matthias standing in the glass-sided jockeys' tunnel at Rome's Capannele racecourse, before riding Paul Mellon's Glint of Gold to win the 1981 Derby Italiano, might be a symbol of Italian racing's problems. This was the year the Italian Derby was reopened to overseas horses and the British-trained Glint of Gold's easy success suggested that the local animals were a long way short of the great Italian champions of the past, Nearco, Tenerani, Ribot and Molvedo. The big bloodstock boom of the Seventies passed Italy by and the country's severe economic ills have not helped the health of racing there much either.

Italy's Capannele racecourse was established just south-west of Rome in 1881 and the Derby Italiano three years later. The British still get involved and as the jockeys walk to the paddock Matthias is joined by three other British riders (to Matthias's left, Edward Hide, Willie Carson and Greville Starkey). In the Derby, no one can match Glint of Gold's finish and trainer Ian Balding, holding the trophy, is entitled to look on with delight at a colt which is the epitome of the international racehorse. By the 1971 American-bred Arc de Triomphe winner, Mill Reef, whom Balding trained to triumph carrying the same black and gold colours of Paul Mellon, Glint of Gold, had a career of 10 wins from 17 starts, six of the victories coming overseas. In France Glint of Gold took both the Grand Prix de Paris and the Grand Prix de Saint Cloud, in Germany the Preis von Europa and the Grosser Preis von Baden, and in Italy the Grand Criterium as well as the Derby Italiano. Few horses deserved their after-work drink more, even if few racing parties looked more furtive as they stole away (Brough Scott is in the Mafia glasses).

A WORLD OF
BREEDING

(Preceding Spead) Looking like an equine heaven, Calumet Farm, Kentucky, has a white-railed and bluegrass tradition stretching back half a century. It also has the knack of producing great horses, with five in the Hall of Fame and such as Triple Crown champion Citation for its offspring to follow.

In the three centuries since the British first started to import the Arabian stallions which were to be the founding fathers of the thoroughbred racehorse, their progeny have spread far and wide to contrasting corners of the globe. The result is that whether the offspring are at Diospusztai Menes (4), near Tatabanya in the central Hungarian plain or at the Woodcote Stud (5) at Epsom, just 15 miles from London, the animal is the same. In the case of stallions that can mean a creature of explosive power, as in the picture of Sallust (2) at the Irish National Stud. To handle the breed calls for many qualities. The experience of a man, for example, such as Jassion Fohrind (3) in Normandy; or the horsemanship of Pat Cronin who, in an unusual practice nowadays, rides out the stallion Brigadier Gerard (6) every day at Newmarket's Egerton Stud; and the stamina to foot it beside a stallion, more usual, as does Pat White with Averof (1) and his two Alsatians at the Ashley Heath Stud just outside Newmarket. After this latter picture was taken Averof travelled much further afield, going to Australia and then on to South Africa as a further testament to the global spread of this, the noblest breed.

1	2	3
	4	
5	6	

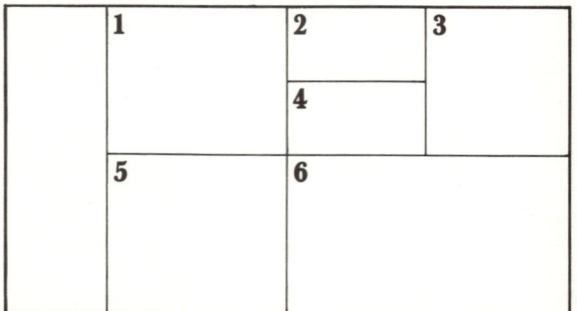

The statue of the famous sire Bull Lea (**7**) looks out over the graveyard at Calumet Farm, Kentucky. In its very presence, there is posed one of the eternal questions of racing, puzzling to even wise old stud hands like Clay Arnold (**1**): will the great racehorse make a great sire? After six seasons at stud, for example, Claiborne's Secretariat (**3**) had still to pass on his brilliant racing ability. At least he is able to live on in an area which, with other such Lexington studs as Greentree (**4**) and Spendthrift (**6**) must be paradise for horses. And even if a Calumet foal has a formidable reputation to live up to, he will not lack for attention and care as witness a foal being checked at Claiborne (**2**). Come the sunset, there is once more the miracle of impending birth (**5**) to be contemplated.

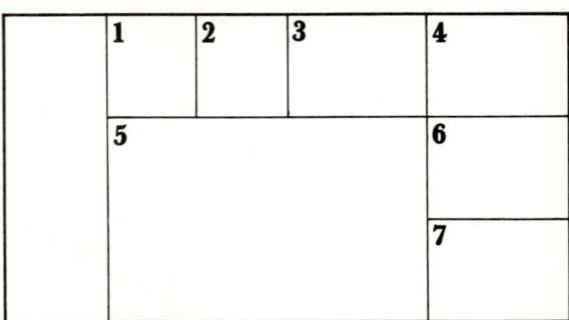

1	2	3	4
5			6
			7

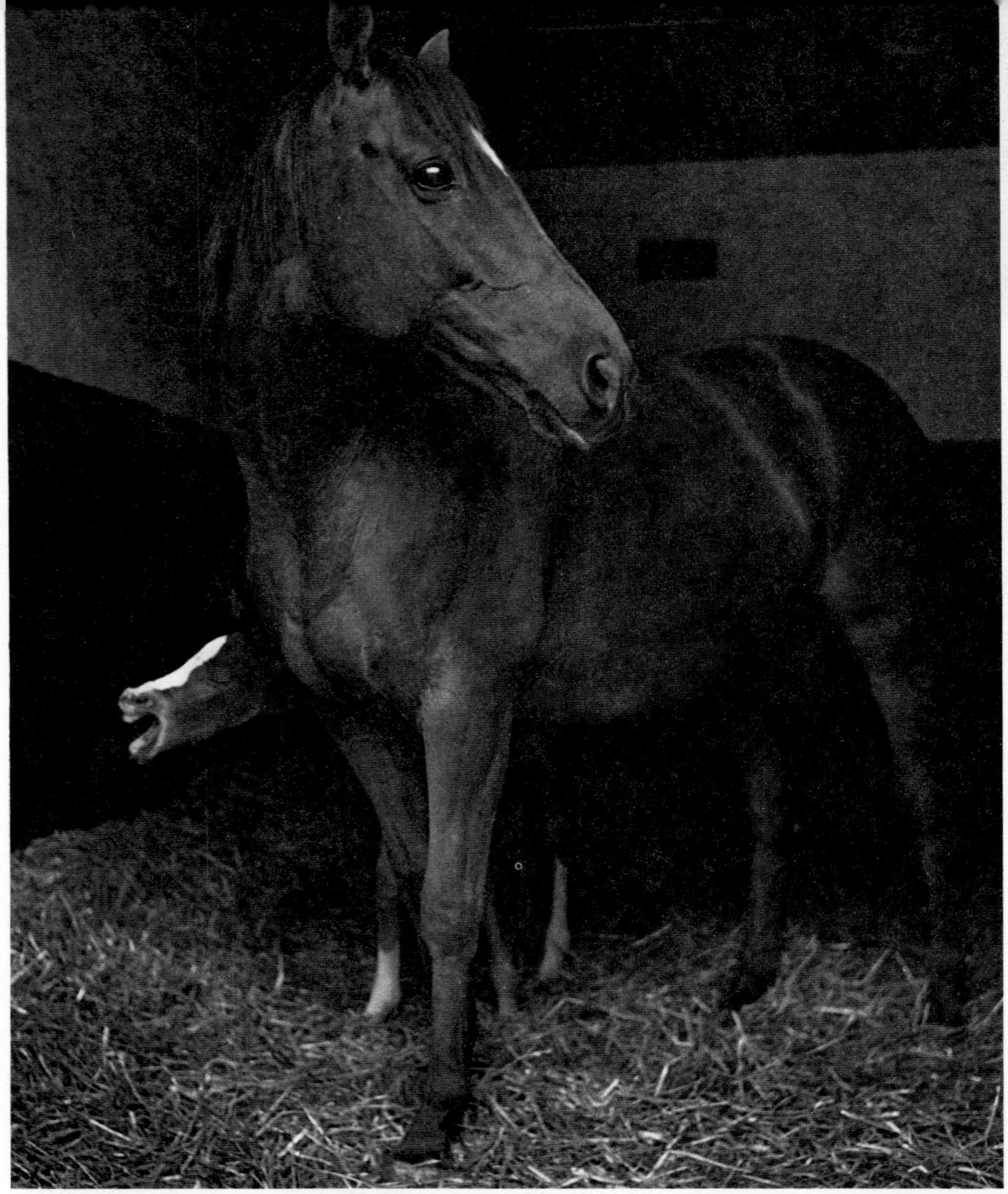

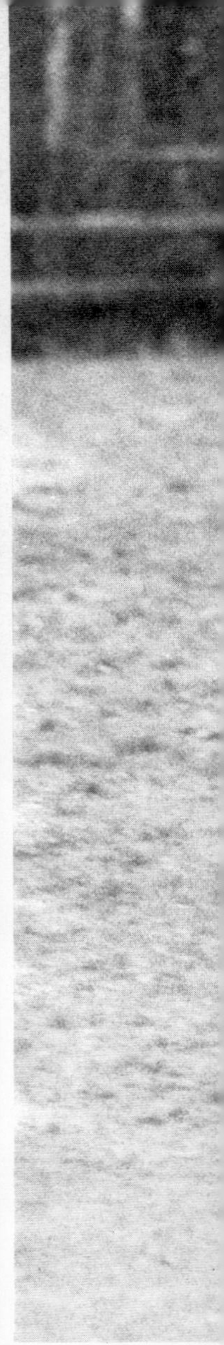

From their very first yawning, faltering, hiding-behind-mother-days (**1**) thoroughbred foals should be handled – with care, as former jump jockey Tommy Stack demonstrates (**5**) at the Longfield Stud he manages in Cashel, County Tipperary. Part of their charm is their cheek (**4**) but once let out in a field, it becomes plain that they are running machines, even if to begin with it is by mother's side at the Egerton Stud, Newmarket (**2**). Soon enough, they are enacting their own day-dreams of Derby glory, like the bonny fellow (**3**) at King Edward's Place Stud, near Swindon. Without head collars, as pictured, catching racing foals would be like trying to snare sunbeams.

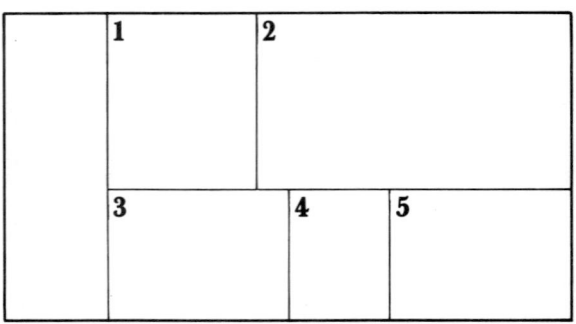

1	2	
3	4	5

Born to run. *This little colt* (**5**) *is on his feet, beside his mother Escorial, within minutes of his birth at the Queen's stud at Sandringham. But while it is natural for all foals to gallop free* (**2,3,4**)*, the chances of any of the 20,000 born annually turning into a champion are extremely remote. Not even a prayer or two from nuns in Tipperary* (**1**) *or a personal message from French maestro Alec Head* (**6**) *can guarantee a winner.*

	1	2	3
			4
	5	6		

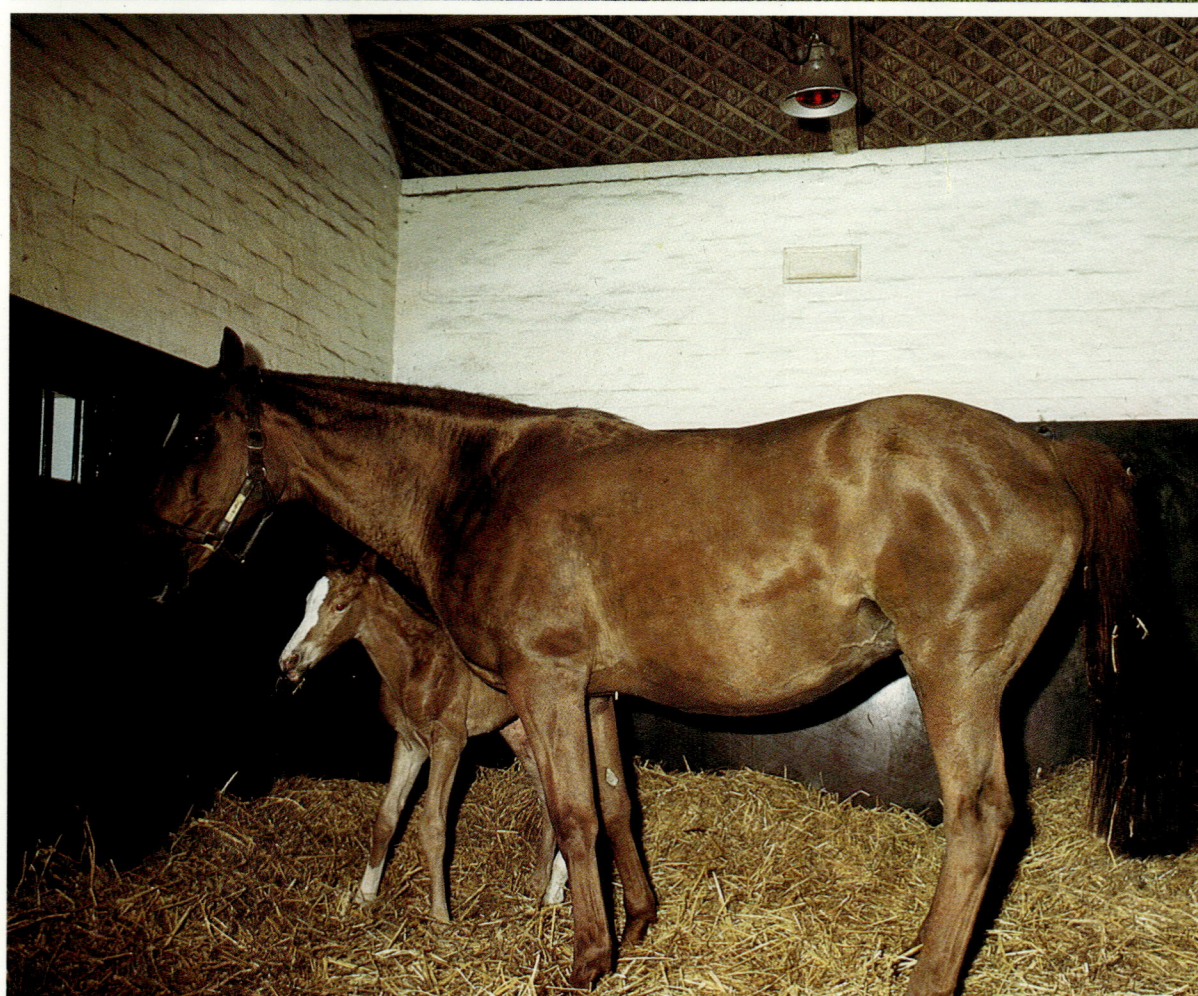

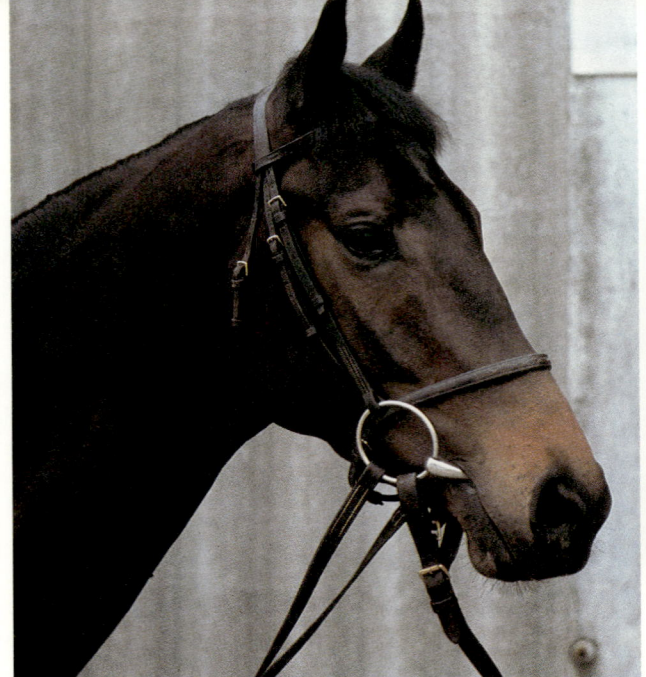

The champion's progress. The neatly coiffured head of To-Agori-Mou (1), Britain's top miler in 1981, contrasts with the sweaty tousle of the 1979 champion, Kris (2), after winning Royal Ascot's St. James's Palace Stakes, and the distended nostrils of Derby winner Mill Reef (5), as he is held after a racecourse workout. All were at a peak of fitness, an ideal epitomised in the picture of a gleaming Beldale Ball (9), as his trainer Colin Hayes holds him among the lucerne and gum trees of Lindsay Park, South Australia. It was just one week after Beldale Ball had given Hayes his first Melbourne Cup winner.

A year or two into stud life and horses like Bustino (6) in England and Best Turn (7) in Kentucky begin to show the curled sultan's lip and bullish crest of the stallion in his prime. Racing is over and gentle exercise, like the lunging of Home Guard (3) at the Longfield Stud in Tipperary or the cantering freedom of Secretariat (4) at Claiborne, reveal nature's most expensive animals at their most magnificent. Elsewhere bridles on a path (8) remind us of more sombre things. That in the end even these galloping symbols of vibrant life will be nothing but memories and a name in a pedigree.

1	2	3	4
5	6	9	
7	8		

Thoroughbred breeding is an odd mixture of beauty, big business, history and mysticism. As the 1978 Derby winner Shirley Heights is lunged (**4**) in the stately grounds of the Royal Stud at Sandringham in Norfolk, he appears to be watched by the statue of Persimmon. Persimmon won the 1896 running of Epsom's Blue Riband in the colours of the then Prince of Wales. Shirley Heights is himself a son of the 1971 Derby winner Mill Reef, seen here held (**7**) by his groom at the National Stud.

In 1983, Mill Reef's stud fee was £40,000, the highest in the country, but even that figure pales by comparison with the prices that an American breeder will have to pay in Kentucky, reflected in the stallion board at Gainesway (**3**). The board boasts 45 sultans, among them the Arc de Triomphe winner Vaguely Noble. His 1983 stud fee was $100,000.

Nice work, if you can get it. But there are some whose job is always to be denied. Witness the picture (**5**) of the 'teasing' stallion at work at Darby Dan Farm before 'himself,' the Derby winner Roberto (**6**), steps forward to perform the marriage rites. Darby Dan Farm is another Kentucky establishment but such is the interchange of bloodstock that the foal conceived may well be born in the rolling tranquillity of Coolmore (**2**) in the County Tipperary or the beech avenue quiet of the Haras d'Etreham in Normandy (**8**).

Another year on and those same Normandy foals will be exercising, military style (**1**), in preparation for shipping to Newmarket for the October yearling sales. After that will come the discipline of the racing stable, the litmus test which will establish if they are worth all the money that has been spent.

1		2
3	4	8
5	6	7

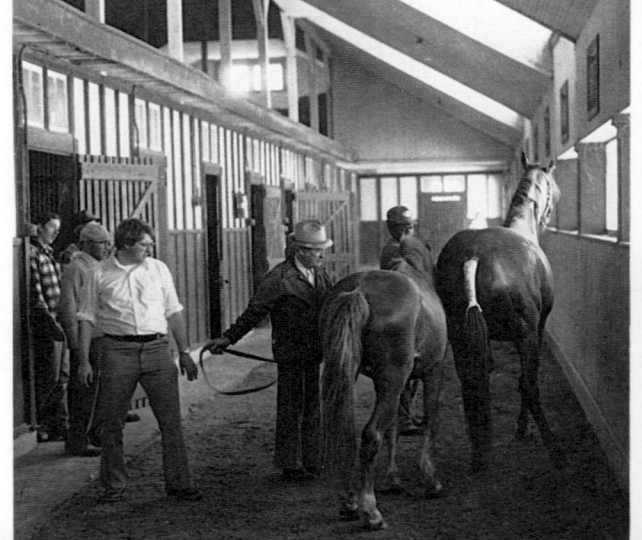

7
USA

'That sense of belonging is a fine American institution naturally fostered by race meetings lasting two or, as at Aqueduct, three months, when racing will go on six days a week, and the officials, horsemen, punters and track workers all have to get along together. The belonging is also there when you talk to Ray Rogers at Santa Anita, David Stevenson at Aqueduct, Tommy Trotter at Arlington, but nowhere does it compare with the feeling at Ellis Park. Mind you, the riverside track has two pretty unfair advantages – country community and the love of a woman'.

IF YOU start by visiting a country's Camelot you are in danger of disenchantment later on. That's true of this view of the United States, and anyone who has been to the spot will appreciate the problem when I write that the first view I had of any part of the American racing scene was Paul Mellon's Rokeby Farm, Virginia, from the air.

Yet what a memory it is. 'Come to the office at midday, and we can go down to the farm for lunch', Mellon had said so quietly that this innocent first-time visitor to Washington DC imagined that Middleburg must be much closer to the Capitol than the 100 miles shown on the map. The car took us over the Potomac river and past the Arlington Cemetery, before turning left into National Airport, and in five unostentatious, fuss-free minutes we were flying away from the endless hassles that ensnare ordinary folk, and within the quarter-hour the private Gulfstream jet (with what looked remarkably like a Picasso on the cabin wall) was circling the beech woods and rolling green fields of the Mellon homeland.

Some say that Paul Mellon even has the grass around the landing strip mown to look as if the trim is only 'natural'. Be that as it may, a visit to Rokeby Farm which he began to develop after the war must be the proof that, if handled with taste, money need not be vulgar, power obtrusive or works of art either selfish or dusty. On the farm, which stretches over 2,000 acres of lush pasture land, there are, besides the concrete runway and somehow almost concealed between the paddocks, some of the most modern aids to horse-husbandry communications and surveillance. But they are there with style.

The horse barns may have special non-slip floors and spy cameras, but they are almost as well sited as Azay-Le-Rideau. The office may have the latest computers and telexes, but it is set in an old school-house straight from the story books of old Virginia. The post-and-rail fencing may not have any obtruding chips or nails, but they forswear the usual bold, white stud fashion for a more uneven elegance, like the perfect Savile Row suit. Why, even the guard on the driveway, armed

like Mars though he must have been, still had a sentry box which could almost have done duty as a rather recherché shepherd's hut.

But forget the style, we were there because of the horses, or one horse to be exact – Mill Reef, the brilliant little bay who in 1971 became the first horse to win the Epsom Derby, Ascot's King George and Longchamp's Arc de Triomphe in one season, and whose dam, Milan Mill, was still gracing the Rokeby paddocks in which she had reared our hero. Mill Reef's only defeat as a three-year-old was by Brigadier Gerard, and the projected re-match in the 1972 was already being modestly billed as the Race of the Century. So the possible agreement of Mill Reef's owner, Paul Mellon, to participate in a film leading up to this cataclysmic event was a prize for us beyond the price of rubies.

Well, Mill Reef got sick and then broke his leg, so the Race of the Century never happened, but the film did. Entitled 'Something to Brighten the Morning', it suffered somewhat from over-indulgence on our part, yet it did provide some unique footage of the beauties of the thorough-bred world in England, France and the USA.

At least it corrected (even over-corrected in some ways) those who pretend the real beauties of thoroughbred racing remain in Europe. Paul Mellon, a scion of a great Philadelphian steel and banking family, and himself one of the major philanthropists and sporting art collectors of our time, was breeding to race for himself, but it's good to report that the more obviously commercially orientated American stud farms have not lost sight of the aesthetic possibilities inherent when green grass, tranquility and thoroughbreds meet.

In 1980 the leading statistics (for the seventh year running) of E. P. Taylor's Windfields farms in Ontario and Maryland reached the level of 304 races worth over three million dollars, making it appear almost like a horse-racing factory. Would that other factories were as beautiful, a comment that applies equally to such great outfits at Lexington, Kentucky, as Spendthrift, Gainesway, Harbor View and Claiborne. And it's no coincidence that Mahmoud Fustok's Buckram Oak Farm, the latest addition to that magic land, promises to be as beautiful as it is modernly functional.

Yet it's not just the bias lingering on those filming trips in the spring and fall of 1972 that makes Rokeby seem the loveliest of all. For you would have to be stony of heart not to feel that the images you see all around are Mr Mellon's living contribution to his unrivalled collection of English sporting art, which he has accumulated since he became a dedicated anglophile during his racing and foxhunting vacations from Cambridge University. When we were at Rokeby, much of the collection was gathered in The Red House, only two stones' throws from the farm office. It was not all Stubbs, Sartorious and Herrings in that treasure chest, either, for on the second floor there was a

whole corner devoted to Degas, with a selection of little wax models of ballerinas and girls bathing so exquisite that you stood open-mouthed and near to tears of wonderment. As if realising the likely impact, someone had put a leather bench opposite them, and while this throughbred Odyssey has got some tremendous outdoor visual memories, nothing bettered that moment in deepest equestrian Virgina surrounded by those masterpieces from 19th century Paris.

Mind you, there was one horrific moment when tears looked like being shed for quite different reasons. Our enthusiastic assistant began rigging up the big floodlights to film the models, and the imagination still boggles at the thought of trying to explain things to Mr Mellon if we had turned on the lights and reduced those priceless flowerings of Degas' genius to a few pools of wax.

Astonishingly, no such disasters occurred then, nor when the cameras whirled on Milan Mill and her new foal, on gallant old Fort Marcy, Washington International winner in 1967 and 1970. Nor even when attempts at getting the great Quadrangle to show how a stallion could move paid off with an impromptu attack on the world speed record round his paddock. Nonetheless, there must have been some sighs of relief as we hitched a lift on the Gulfstream to New York to see the Rokeby racing team in training at Belmont, that sweeping horse city just off Sunrise Highway in the suburban delights of Long Island.

At that stage, there were some 30 horses in the Rokeby barn, under the stewardship of Elliott Burch, and with all their riders sporting the grey Rokeby cap cover, and even some of the 'hot walkers' having the name emblazoned in gold on the grey T-shirts, there was a considerable lessening of the culture shock experienced by anyone used to seeing the throughbred trained English and French fashion, where a stable takes at least a third of its strength out in one great cavalry-type promenade through woods and walkways, and then gives them long steady Indian-file canters before any serious work is done.

Until the horses reached the track, the American system had seemed as good and in many instances better, than the European system. It was not just at Rokeby that there was space and peace throughout the stud area, the buildings and veterinary care of the highest standard, the paddocks magnificently spacious and often far more undulating (and therefore balance-teaching) than we get at Newmarket or in Normandy. And the ordinary black stud hand has just as much 'Irish' horse wisdom as the genuine article. I still recall the real affection with which one Rokeby groom looked out at 20 of that season's yearlings galloping around the paddock, and said: 'Ah remembah Mill Reef – he used to suck his lip'.

Better still than this nursery attention were the schooldays for the yearlings in the fall. Instead of

being sent to the great establishments to be broken in at the same time as the 'real' work of training the older generation goes on, and often getting at the end of the queue with tired and impatient handlers as a result, the American yearlings at Rokeby, and at countless little training farms around the nation, are the number one priority, with their own schedule and even workers (often girls) who come in specially to ensure that the horses are fully and quietly broken.

Significantly, leading trainers in Britain are now following this example. Men like Guy Harwood, who has most of his yearlings backed and broken by the renowned Roy Trigg before they come to the training stable proper. But even they arrive some time before the horses in America do. There they are not allowed into a racetrack training barn before January 1, and then only if a run is in the offing. So some of the classically-bred two-year-olds might not get to the training barns proper until August.

However, that's about as far as preference for the American system of training racehorses will run in these pages. For in the years since that first June Belmont morning watching the massive Kentucky Derby winner, Canonero, hacking off round the track with his exercise boy riding bare-back South American style, nothing has happened to alter my opinion that it's a system that demands the most comprehensive re-appraisal. Journeying around this largest of all racing nations, from Saratoga to Santa Anita, from Ellis Park on the Ohio River to Turf Paradise down in Phoenix in the desert state of Arizona, makes you appreciate that the pressure and competition often throws up horses, men and organisation unmatched anywhere in the world. But the conviction hardens that the training system, dirt-track, of course, speed-orientated and always left-handed, has brought in a quite unacceptable degree of side-effects.

(Preceding Spread) If America is not the greatest racing nation on earth, then it is certainly the biggest and it is one in which public relations figures prominently. An example is the presentation here of the 1977 Volante Handicap at Santa Anita, California, in which everybody lines up, including the great trainer Charlie (The Bald Eagle) Whittingham, on the right, and the smallest but winningmost jockey Bill Shoemaker, in the centre. It pays off: 60,000 thoroughbreds run almost 70,000 races for $450 million on North America's 100 tracks (87 in the USA), betting tops $7 billion and attendance figures over 55 million. By any calculation it makes it the No.1 spectator sport in the land.

A study in concentration. Paul Mellon (left) and his trainer Mack Miller at the Keeneland Sales, Kentucky, where the 1981 average exceeded $200,000. As a member of the Pittsburgh steel and banking family, Mellon has built an international reputation as a philanthropist and art collector. His special interest has been English sporting pictures and nobody who has visited his stud at Rokeby Farm fails to notice that his thoroughbreds in their Virgina setting make living pictures any collector would treasure. They run fast too. Mellon's silks have been aboard some of the biggest winners both sides of the Atlantic, horses like Mill Reef, Damascus and Fort Marcy.

Such a condemnation from a mere scribbler, even one who was a not unsuccessful professional rider, is so presumptuous that in March of '81 I flew back to see the one man in the world who was in a position to make a truly authoritative comparison. Angel Penna has been at the highest level of his profession in Argentina, Venezeula and the United States, and in seven years in France before returning to the USA in 1979, he gathered a whole collection of top races, and has twice taken Europe's richest prize, the Prix de l'Arc de Triomphe.

Those sort of credentials are apt to breed mystique, and we British writers soon built up an image of a weatherbeaten, hook-nosed South American magician given to such fractured English words of wisdom as 'Thees feelee she eesah my freind'. Certainly Penna has an almost tangible charisma. He has a habit, as he did that morning at Belmont outside the green barns of owner Ogden Phipps, of standing to await you a quarter-mile off. And as he stands, legs planted astride, head stuck warmly forward in greeting, you have the urge to run towards him, just as his beloved fillies do for the sugar lumps in his pocket. For all that, Angel has not got all this way without having solid practical views in addition to his undoubted gypsy touch.

It was a Sunday morning, and racing was at Aqueduct that afternoon, so Belmont wasn't busy. Yet out on the training track there was the usual mixture of organisation out of seeming chaos that is typical of the American scene. Organisation because each horse tends to go through three different hands walking in the barn, working against the clock with a jockey or exercise boy, and then being led away by a 'hot walker' for a cool-down. Chaos by European standards because on that one circular five-furlong track, there were some 50 horses from assorted stables all doing different things and sometimes actually going in different directions. It's not surprising that most people insist on having their horses led by a pony – if one of them ran across the track there could be the greatest pile-up since the Ben Hur chariot race.

Penna, tweed-jacketed, also wore a cap atop that dark, Argentinian face which, like the boxer dogs he loves so much, varies in expression between an almost menacing broodiness when

Belmont Park, eight miles south of Manhattan in New York's Jamaica district, is America's most famous racetrack and encourages its spectators to watch both outside and in. With an average attendance figure of 17,000, its facilities may be watched by some other US tracks but they are enough to make a European's binoculars twitch. Among the attractions are vast resting galleries, TV viewing, extensive restaurants and even a full-scale office for the Daily Racing Form's Joe Hirsch, dean of American racing writers (Near Right). But in the end, they all come to see a star and with races like the Woodward Stakes and horses like its 1979 winner Affirmed (pictured with a muddy but triumphant Laffit Pincay in the saddle), Belmont has kept its place as a great theatre of the sport.

solemn, to a smile as warm as the sun. He was now looking solemn; his best filly, Relaxing, was out on the track. After a warm-up, she did almost three circuits, with the last five furlongs in even time (12 seconds to the furlong), the stopwatch in Penna's hand checking out the progress at the quarter-mile poles.

Relaxing, who had become one of the best older fillies in the USA after starting her career more modestly in England, had been spinning along, but was still under some restraint compared with many others, who looked as if race-time had come six hours early. Penna surveyed the scene with one of his great shrugs and said: 'In European training there is training...here no training...here they givva speed. If a horse havva speed they give more speed. If he doesn't have speed they try to put speed. Look atta horse like Nijinsky [Vincent O'Brien's 1970 Triple Crown hero] in England. He wassa speed...he wassa all speed. But then [and here he did a mime of stretching Plasticine with his hand] you stretcha that speed. Here no, here it eesa too tough'.

Harsh words, perhaps, but in the way of master craftsmen the world over, Angel Penna does not set around whingeing about problems – he gets on and surmounts them. His 1980 figures of 45 races won from only 145 starts gave him an astonishing 31.7 per cent success rate, by far the best in the States, just as it used to be in France. 'Look', he said back in his office taking down a series of large, hardback files, 'I have here a record of the last twenty years. It is day-by-day of each horse. I tell you something, I never change the system in my life. It is always the same...OK, give more stamina there, give more speed here, but I never change my base. Just because I see a guy work three eights in thirty-three, I don't want to be the same. It is very hard to win in Argentina, many many horses, not many races. You have to be very fit'.

The great man was in full glorious flow: 'The big thing when I come to Europe, they tell me that because I come from America I never make it in Europe. The English people they know nothing about America, the only thing they know they read in the book. Over here they know nothing about England. But for me it all comes back to one place, my beginning in Argentina. So in England nobody have a stop-watch. In France I never use a watch in my life. Here it is watch even for eat [huge throaty chuckle]. But really every country is the same, the horses is the

<hr />

British runners load at Gatwick for the 7,000-mile haul to Chicago and the first running of the Arlington Million. After travelling to the airport by horsebox, they are walked a few yards across the tarmac (Top Left) to get into separate containers which are then stowed into the body of the plane, as in the case of Madam Gay (Top Centre). Once in Chicago, she and other British hopes, such as Bel Bolide (pictured with lad David Quinn) had to spend three days in a specially-built quarantine barn while blood samples were tested for various equine diseases. Despite this unusual schedule horses seem to take such a journey and the enforced idleness in their stride and although a minor accident prevented Bel Bolide from actually running, Madam Gay put up the performance of her life to finish a close third to John Henry (nearside) and The Bart (sequence). So close was the finish that most onlookers thought that Eddie Delahoussaye had kept The Bart ahead on the far side but the photo-finish – third picture showed that Bill Shoemaker's precision, timing and John Henry's guts had combined to snatch this first-ever million dollar prize right on the wire. In the victory ceremony Shoemaker was dwarfed by owner Jack Rubin and the Governor of Illinois (with trophy), by his own wife Cindy and by Joe Joyce, president of Arlington Park. But they all knew that Shoemaker had once again shown he was the master.

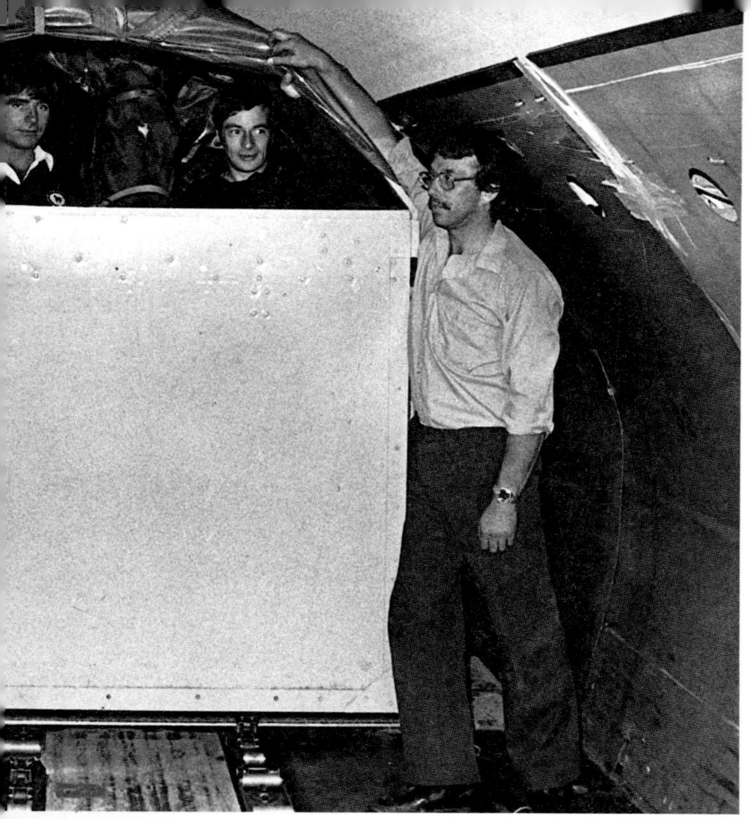

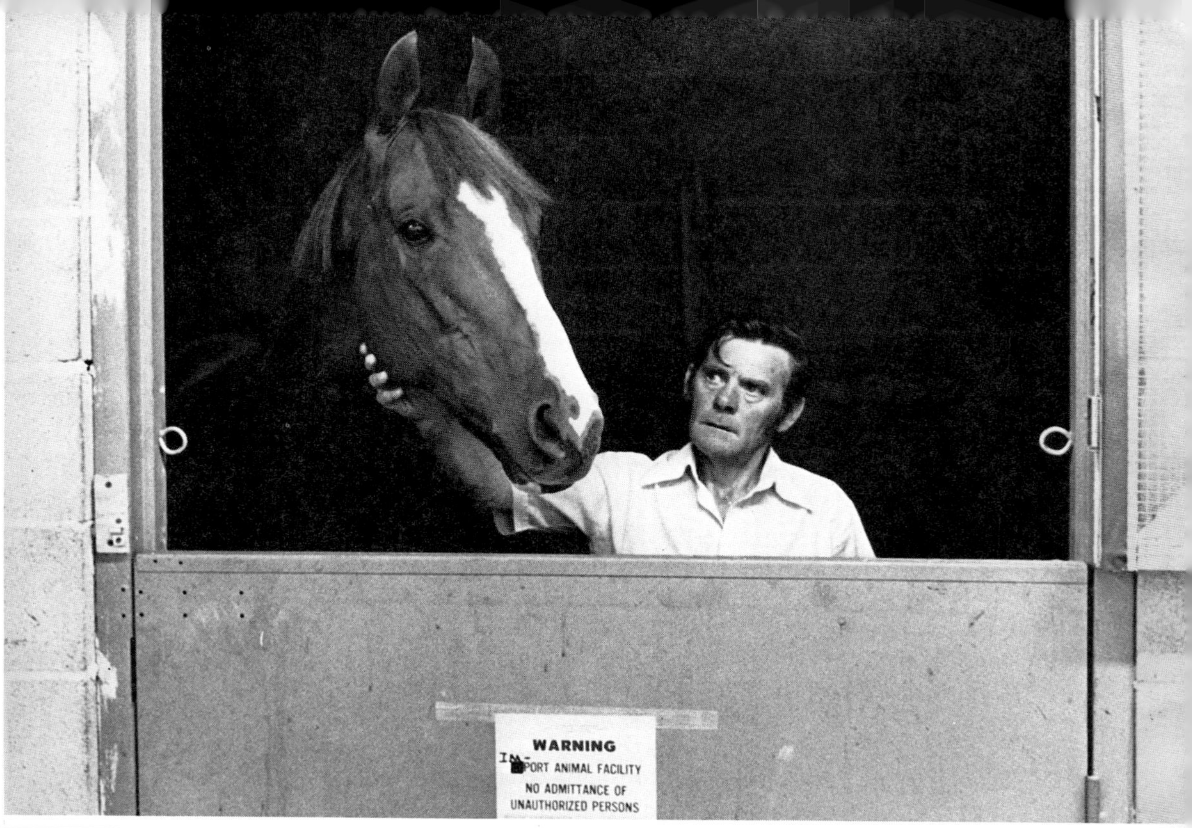

WARNING
IM-
PORT ANIMAL FACILITY
NO ADMITTANCE OF
UNAUTHORIZED PERSONS

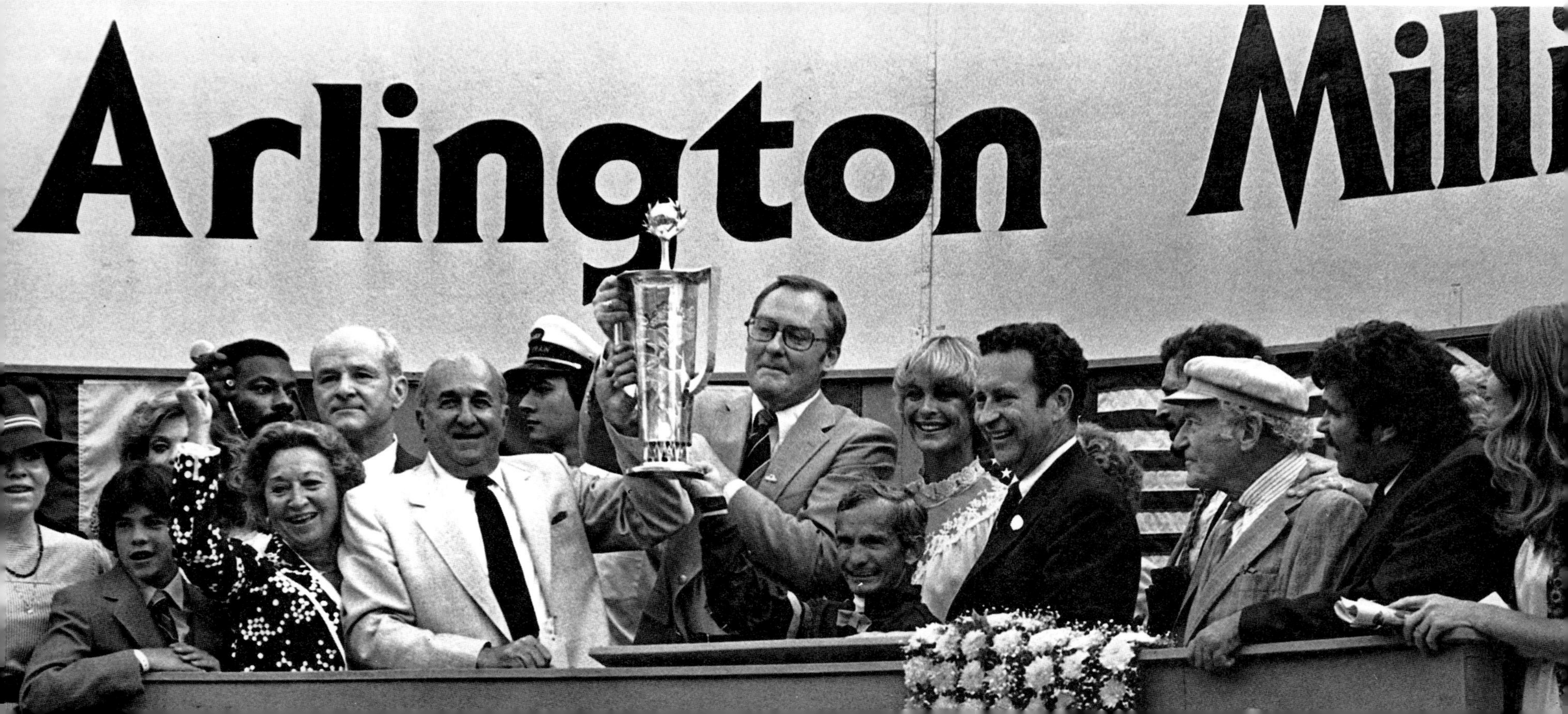

Arlington Milli

same, the people is the same, they even look the same. If you are in the business and you can do it, it's like accounting, you just get adjusted to some law here, or something there, but then it is the same, two and two is four.'

For all his fractured English, the only man to have been a leader of the training profession in two hemispheres and three continents is clear and concise in his comparisons. For instance, on injuries: 'In Argentina, fifty per cent of the horses have a back problem, for the boys they ride without saddles. In France we get some tendon trouble, but the only fractures we get are on the pasterns from racing downhill. In America, we get many fractures. All horses have ankle and knee problems, but the vets they have so much work they are unbelievable surgeons. Here you break a knee, they make an operation, they take bone off and three days later it is all right.'

Or this on the types of horse suitable for dirt-track racing: 'The old European families they have these big, flat feet, and almost certainly they cannot run on the sand. It is easier for them to run in California because the sand isn't so deep, but it is so hard that they don't last so long.' And these timeless thoughts about preparing a horse for the biggest tests: 'If you ask all the trainers in the world how many times they are happy with their horse, they always have something, a pain here, a pain there. That's why, when you have a horse in unbelievable condition you run a good race. But how many times do you have him one hundred per cent? And a big race is like an exam – it is only one time. You run a handicapper, and maybe you win with eighty per cent but, with good horses, it is one hundred per cent or they beat you.'

It is when Penna gets into personal and professional preferences that the transatlantic perspective becomes clearest. Europe, and for him France in particular, having the training facilities and the style. But America is where the action is: 'In Chantilly, you have everything, the best training facilities I have seen anywhere in the world. You go to the races at two o'clock and afterwards you eat in Paris, the centre of the world. But the racing is spoilt, everyone is spoilt. In France, and in England, if a horse wins ten races and loses two, everyone asks why you lost the two. Well, here a champion wins twenty races but nobody asks why he lost the other twenty races he ran in. It is much healthier, and look [now he's drawing with

Spring in Kentucky. Runners race past the dogwood blossom at Keeneland in Bourdon County, an area which still holds the style as well as the names – Paris, Versailles, Louisville – of its first French settlers. The racetrack, built in 1936 as a link in a racing chain going back to 1787, sticks rigidly to its traditions: 45 racing days spread over two meetings, Spring and Fall, with no running commentary. In Keeneland, so the saying goes, they have 'racing as it used to be'. It is certainly different and with its tight one-sixteenth-of-a-mile oval, set against one of the prettiest backdrops in American racing, Keeneland is the ultimate track for the connoisseur.

a red Biro], it is much easier for a trainer. If you have a horse you run him in a claimer* for $30,000 and you lose. So you run him in a $25,000 claimer. If you lose, for $15,000; if you lose again, for $10,000. And finally you win. We have a claimer here for $100,000 dollars to $1,500 dollars. If your horse he no die, he win. That's why in America there are twenty-five thousand trainers. In England, seven hundred trainers, five hundred of them starving. In America, not many starve'.

The problem for American racing is that most trainers get their bread by operating rather a different system than the patient touch that serves Penna so well as he tilts for top races. While he took just 145 starts to collect $1,400,000 in prize-money, mostly in the rarified atmosphere of the East Coast, down in Chester, West Virginia, Dale Baird, numerically the most successful trainer of the 1980s, took no fewer than 1,964 starts and a remarkable 306 victories to amass less than half Penna's money total. If you are racing on a tight dirt track like Dale's base at Waterford Park, you

*A claimer is a race, similar to a British selling race but without an auction afterwards, in which any runner can be 'claimed' for the advertised price. This limits the quality of runners.

just cannot achieve these sort of figures without giving horses some help. And with the advent of 'permissive medication' over the past 10 years in all bar New York, Montana, Vermont and Idaho of the 24 states which allow horse racing, it is now true that most horses in most races could not survive without either butazolidin (for soreness) or lasix (for burst blood vessels).

In the exalted world of the Pennas, the Whittinghams and the Barreras, where you aim to bring top horses to their peak, you don't get any evidence of drug abuse, or even perhaps much worry about it. 'If you takka an aspirin every day, or you have bute every day, you kill the potential', says Angel. 'Anyway, Spectacular Bid he run with bute every time, and in the Kentucky Derby last year every horse run with bute. Nobody care about that'. But that is a view from the top. From the bottom, or even from the side, it doesn't look quite so easy, and a visit to Arlington Park for the inaugural running of the Arlington Million produced two impressive pieces of evidence.

The first was the state of the track. With 3,000 horses on the strength, Arlington Park, set in Chicago's leafy north-western suburbs, is the

largest racing centre in the Middle West, and with a 121-day meeting between early May and the end of September, it has the longest continuous operation on the continent. It has a fine 50-year tradition, and since it was recently taken under the wing of Madison Square Garden, it became progressive enough to mount in August, 1981, the world's first million-dollar thoroughbred race. All that, but the track was lousy.

Of course you can't legislate for unseasonal monsoons which were hitting Arlington when we

The camera lies. Keeneland (Top Left) is actually left-handed like the other 104 tracks in North America, even if this fish-eye lens shot may suggest the opposite. But Keeneland does have some distinctions. Set six miles out of Lexington, in the heart of Kentucky's Bluegrass Country, its stands and stabling are used for the record-breaking Keeneland Sales. In July, 1982, 297 yearlings were sold at these sales for more than $100 million. The following year, the yearlings on sale were to include the first crop of the progeny of Spectacular Bid, numbered 4, who prepared for the Kentucky Derby by winning this Bluegrass Stakes at Keeneland. As Spectacular Bid was led away (Bottom Far Right) it was not only those closest to him that foresaw him winning the Triple Crown and inspiring the sort of adulation normally confined to pop stars.

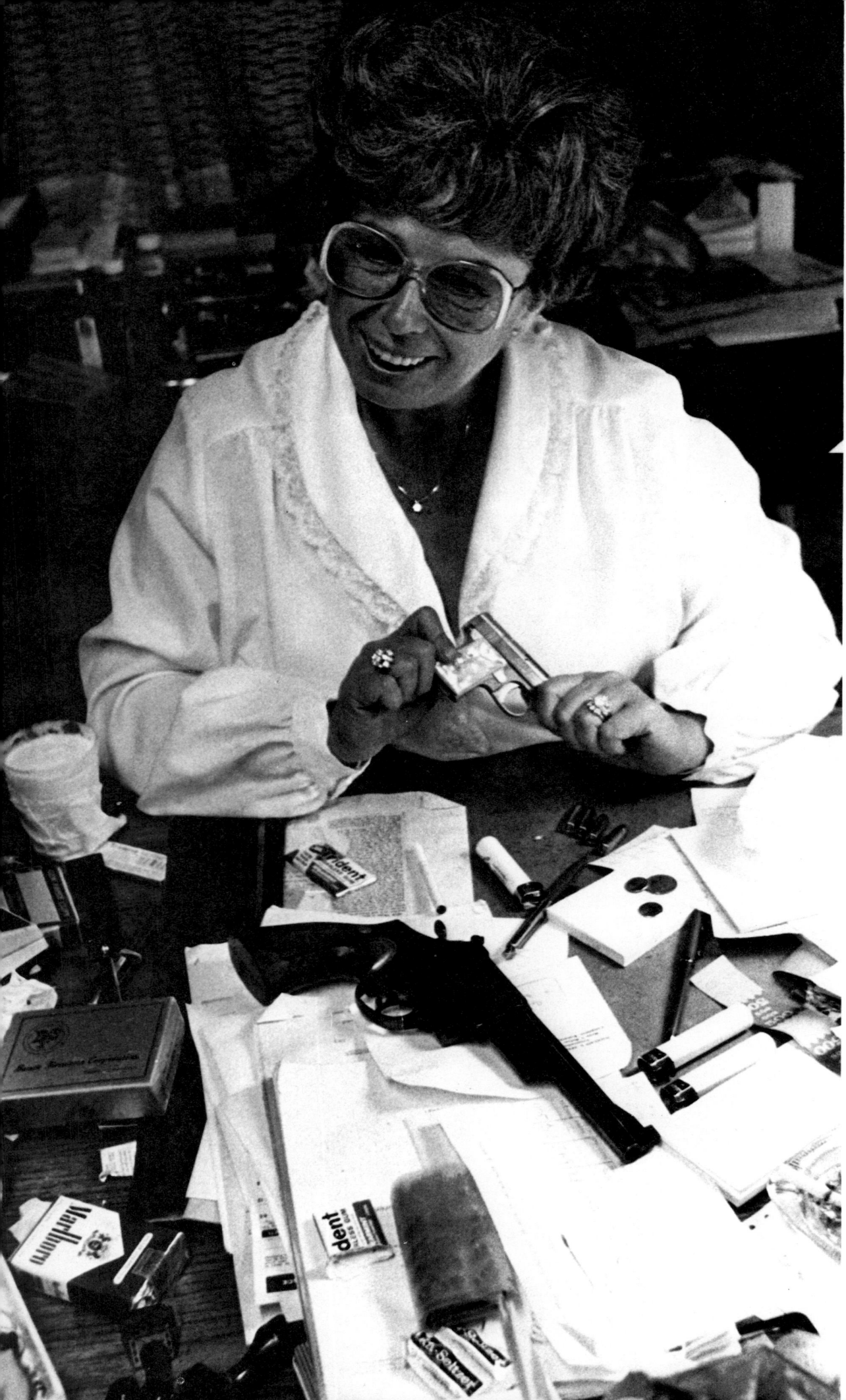

hitched in at the back of the British runners' horse-plane, and it's also true that even some American trainers were fighting shy of the hard-based slop which was both the racing and the training track, but nine races a day still went on, including a $500,000 two-year-old event in conditions that rough-and-ready British trainers wouldn't normally canter in. And if you looked at the medication lists published daily, you would find that at least eighty per cent of all the horses running would be aided by either butazolidin or lasix, both proscribed drugs in Britain and France.

If this was disturbing, even more was the evidence of an old acquaintance, Bobby Elliott, formerly champion apprentice in Britain and then working at Arlington after a long spell in Hong Kong: 'This is all pretty organised here, you should go to some of the bull rings [the little tracks five furlongs round]. Nobody can afford to wait for horses to get right there, so they just give them some more bute and run them, as if they were motor-bikes. One day I had four rides, and three of them never even finished.'

Anyone who thinks that putting forward these two subjective British opinions is just a holier-than-thou exercise, should have been in the cool elegance of Saratoga's national racing museum for the 1980 Jockey Club Round Table Conference. This is normally not much more than a genteel talking shop for the leaders of America's racing life, but when a grey-suited lawyer named James J. Hickey started outlining the clauses of a bill to be set before Congress, you could feel an almost mushroom-cloud threat hanging in the air.

The bill is called the Corrupt Horse Racing Practices Act, a title which, Mr Hickey pointed out, just about insures its passage by name alone. 'How can you vote against corruption?' asked Joe Hirsch, the craggy-faced dean of American racing writers. 'It's like voting against motherhood.' But in a land where three-quarters of the 60,000 thoroughbreds are now supported by drugs outlawed in Europe, and where only three of the 24 states which permit racing subscribe to a no-medication rule, the withdrawals symptoms would be horrific. Joe Joyce, the dynamic head of Arlington Park before he moved on to run General Instruments, summed up the feelings of most horsemen you could find when he said: 'As written, this bill aims at the death of American racing.'

What was worse from the horsemen's point of view, was that the Jockey Club also attacked their assumption that drugs were the only way to keep the show on the road. Its president, Nick Brady, produced some telling statistics to show that the average number of starts 'pre-medication' in 1969 was 10.1, compared with 9.5 ten years later, thereby suggesting that any assistance from drugs was

When you say Ellis Park you say – Ruth F. Adkins, executive vice-president, treasurer, general manager, hutchmother and taskmaster-in-chief. Her office is not a place to horse around.

James C. Ellis PARK

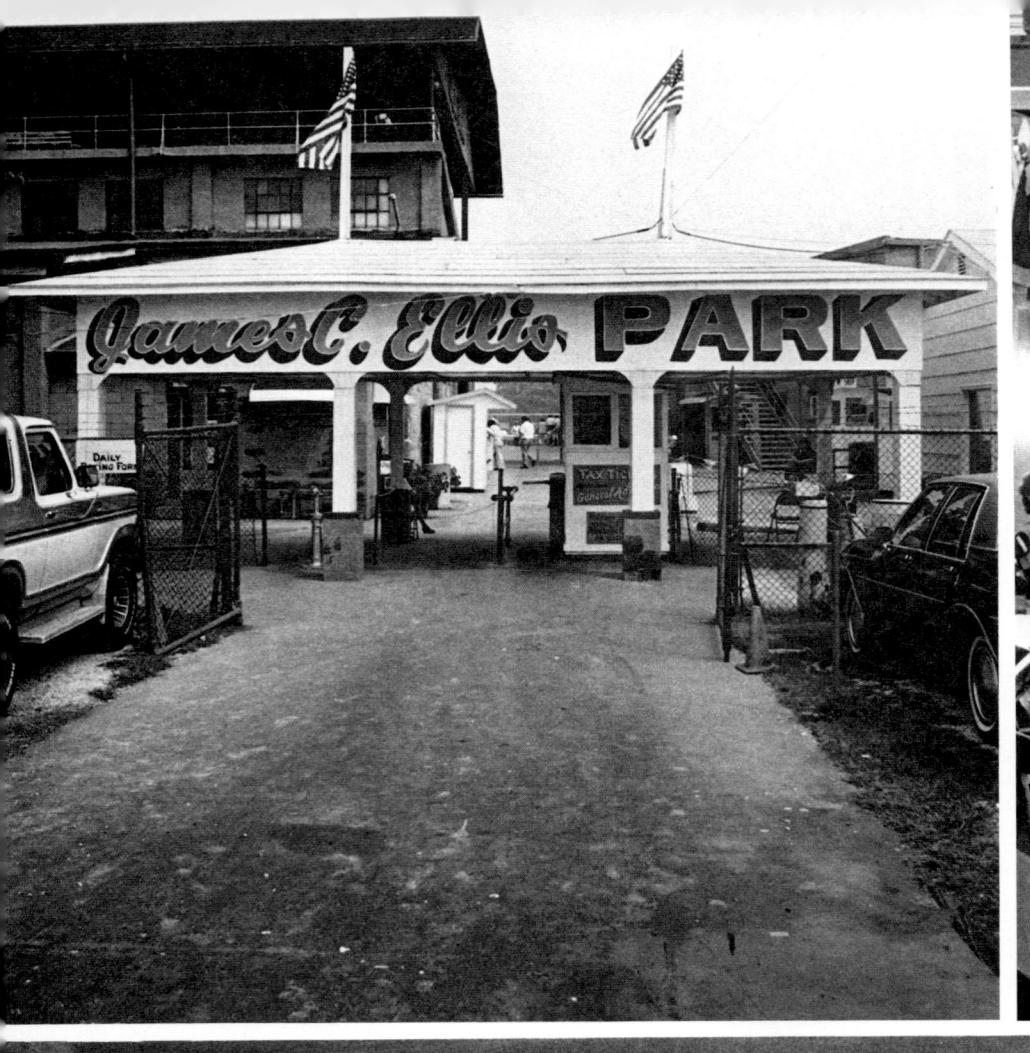

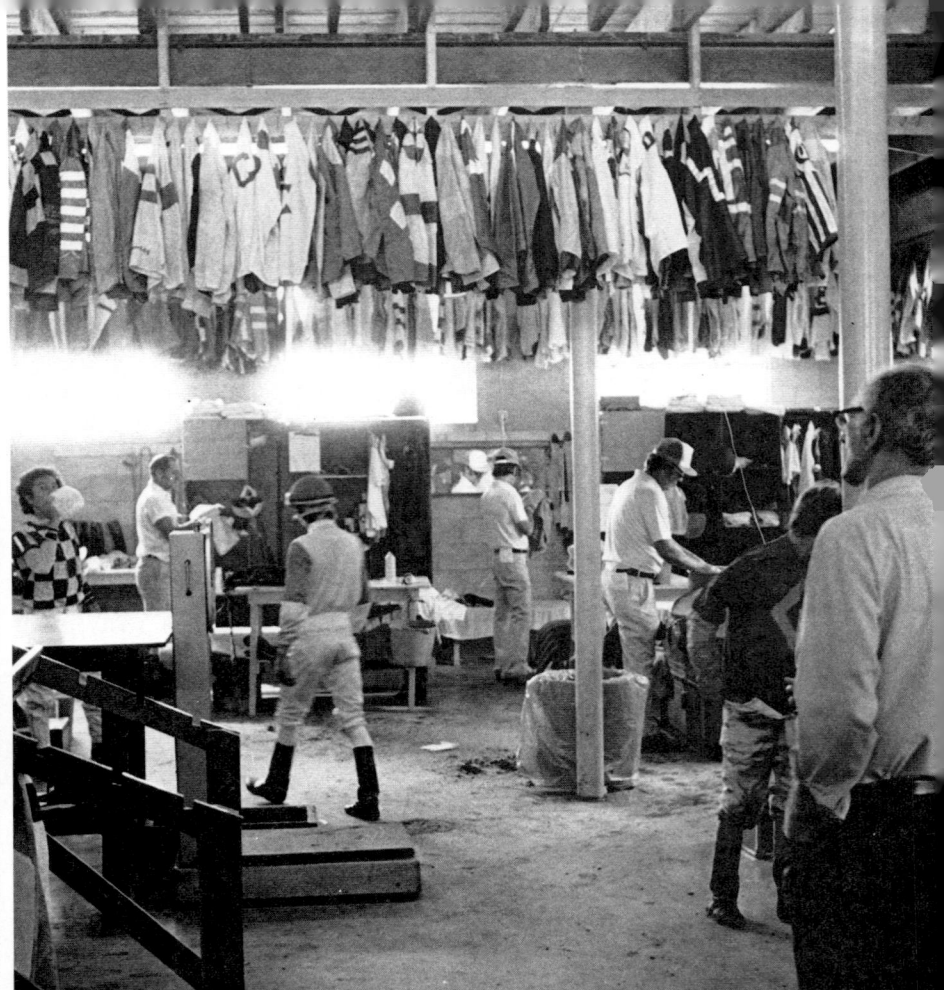

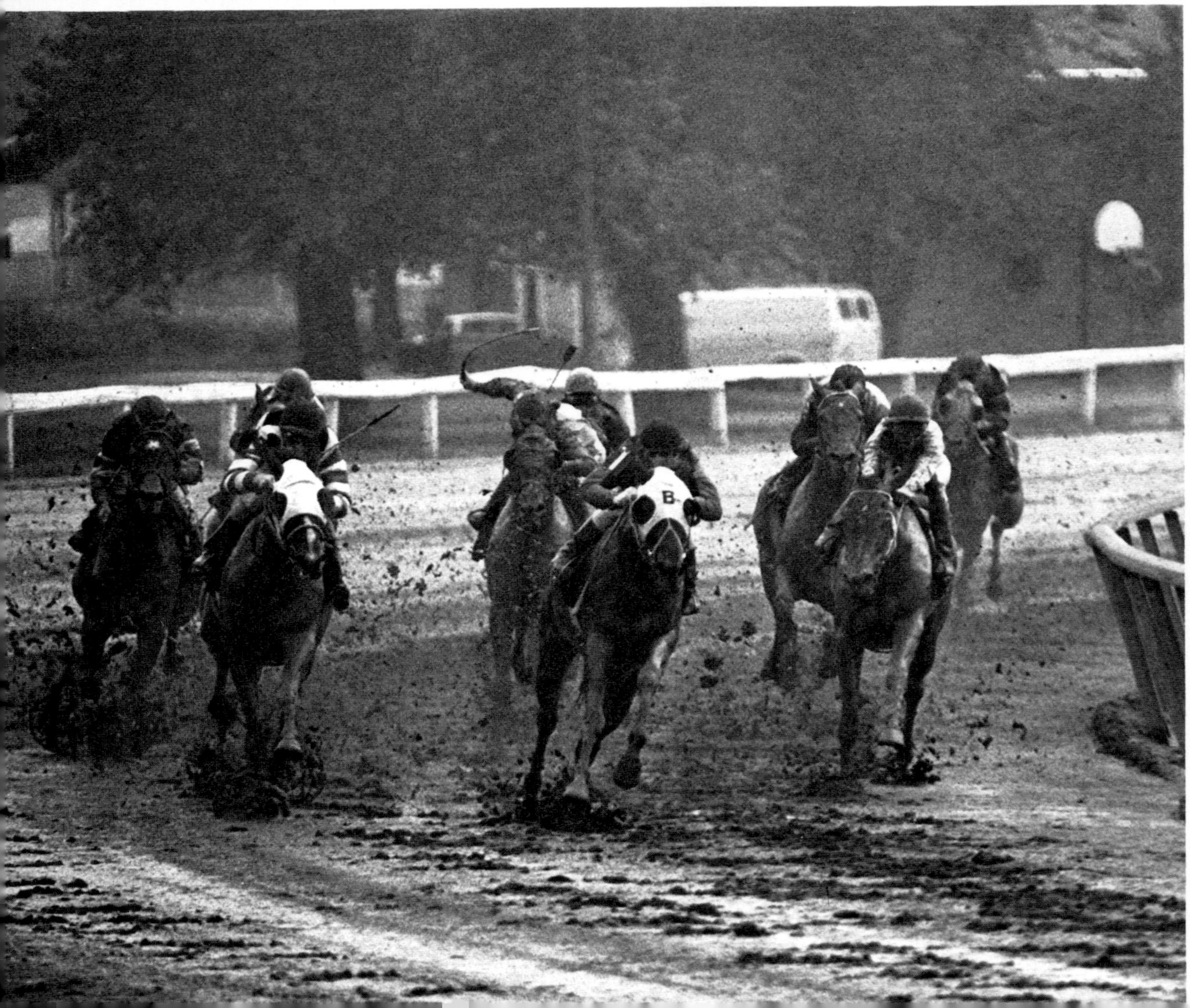

ROOKIE

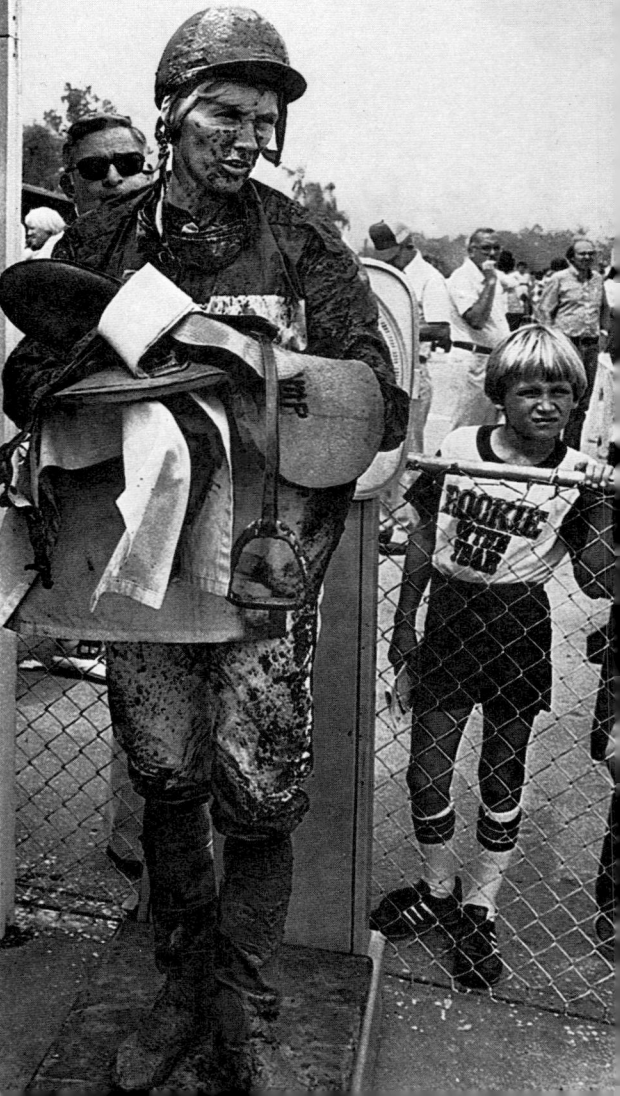

essentially short-term: 'Our position is no-medication; none until laboratory-testing procedures have reached a level where violators of carefully controlled medication programmes can be detected'.

Brady's words had an almost Kennedyesque ring about them, but a visit a year later to a symposium at the University of Arizona's remarkable racing degree course at Tucson didn't reveal many signs either of major clean-ups or of imminent catastrophe, although a trip up to Phoenix on the Sunday did produce horsemen admitting that the imposition of the famous 'Hay, Oats and Water' no-medication rule at the beautifully appointed Turf Paradise track hadn't produced anything like the decrease in runners originally expected. (For unworthy scoffers at the name, slap in the middle of the desert as it is, I can confirm that inside the normal dirt track Turf Paradise has got the brightest of bright green turf tracks, laid down on a sand base at some $400,000 cost, and after only three years it stands up to an amazing amount of wear.)

To this observer, the extraordinary thing about the discussions among the distinguished team that Gary Amundsen had brought to Tucson was, that while they worried about the possible effects of the Corrupt Horse Racing Practices Act and crowed about the continued record-breaking demand from overseas for American bloodstock, no one ever put two and two together. They did not suggest, for instance, that splendid though these overseas earnings and prestige might be (Keeneland Sales drew 39,469,000 dollars from abroad for its 1981 July yearling sale alone, 44 per cent of the total), present American training and racing conditions put such a strain on a young horse that the millionaires buying the top-class stock at the yearling sales will have them trained in Europe.

At the time of the Round Table conference, one leading American owner had 25 horses based in Britain, of which only two were non-operational. Of 35 in the States, only five were racing fit. At the top level, such statistics counter-balance all the fantastic prize-money on offer, and the breeders' prizes for locally-trained horses, as a look at the new stallions for America in 1982 reflects. The first four in value, Storm Bird, Nureyev, Northern Baby and Northjet, standing at accumulated fees of £405,000 a service, were all bred in the States, but raced in Europe before returning to Kentucky to take the syndication money and endure the rigours of being breeding machines.

Ellis Park is just in Kentucky's Henderson County although it is on the northern (Indiana) side of the Ohio River, just three miles from the university town of Evansville. At the track, even if the accommodation for jockeys is not quite Hilton Hotel standard, a weary head can still find a few moments of peace. Out on the track, a summer thunderstorm may make things testing but its just what's needed for the only soya bean crop to grace a racing infield (Top Right). Neither can mud lessen the delight of winning jockey Dianne Divine, whose steady success made the small spectator's T-shirt something of an insult.

The stud values available for the top performers in Europe are mind-blowing. In 1981, Robert Sangster's Storm Bird, a brilliant two-year-old but producer of just one moderate performance at age three, was syndicated to Ashford Farms, Kentucky, for $30 million, the equivalent of the British prize-money for the whole season. With that sort of jackpot to play for, would you risk your young blue-bloods in a training system with its emphasis on speed, and on dirt tracks, and always round to the left?

Yet if excessive strain blights one system, the huge cash lure looks like warping the other. Like Shakespeare's soldier, the classically-bred European horse 'seeks the bubble reputation', and once he's got it, few can resist cashing in quickly. Result—if the American horse gets through the system, he has to be a much tougher, more proven, machine. What sort of horses must Secretariat, Seattle Slew and Spectacular Bid have been, and who could conceive of a three-part series like the dramatic Triple Crown battles of Affirmed and Alydar in 1978?

Of those immortals, Seattle Slew was the least busy with just 17 starts in three racing seasons. After him came Secretariat with 21 (in only two years on the track), while Affirmed had 29 and Spectactular Bid 30 races in their respective three-season careers. Compare this with our side of the Atlantic. Brigadier Gerard has been the busiest super star of recent times with 18 starts in three seasons. Mill Reef had 14 races over the same period while Nijinsky had 13. But Troy and Shergar had only 8 starts in just two seasons in the public eye.

So the greatest attraction of American racing remains the attitude that a racehorse is for racing. It just astonishes me that with 100 tracks across the continent, they can't think of any shape other than a left-handed oval. What's wrong with going right-handed for heaven's sake? Plenty of horses prefer it that way, and if it is good enough for Longchamp and Ascot, why not for the Land of the Free? In these days of minority causes, our next campaign should be: 'End Discrimination Against Right-Handed Horses'.

At the very least, you could spin a few races round the other way, just as the French do at Maisons-Laffitte. Better still, with such comparative riches around, what about some really extensive investigation into an improved racing, and above all training, surface such as the Dormit Woodchip track now doing service in Holland

Behind the scenes at Ellis Park. The barn of the leading trainer Theo Foley does not depart from the basic need to keep men happy and horses contented. And while top horse Tiger Lure (Left) may not be renowned the world over, he has still won over $200,000 and reduced the six-furlong record at Latonia to 1 minute 08.4 seconds. Work rider Larry Miller (Top Right) is also evidence that life at Ellis Park is far from the breadline – he collects $600 a week during the season.

and used by many trainers in Britain. After all, American racing has some of the most forceful, ingenious people running the show, and if you doubt that, you should drive down through the cornfields of Indiana and have a look at the security arrangements at Ellis Park. Don't peer too closely, though, because the hardware includes a pearl-handled ·22 pistol cunningly concealed in the racing manager's cleavage.

If this makes you think that Ruth F. Adkins, she of the bouffant grey hair, butterfly spectacles and loaded silk blouse, is no lady to tangle with, you have got yourself an affirmative. But although some people tried to tell us Ellis Park was out in the sticks, the fact that it is a long way from being Hicksville says much about American racing, and even more about Ruth Adkins and her team.

Geographically, Ellis Park lies on a northern loop of the great Ohio river four miles south of the old settler town of Evansville at the very bottom of Indiana. By an almost British piece of boundary quirkiness, Ellis Park claims to be in Kentucky, which is no bad thing since horse racing is outlawed in Indiana, and therefore track-starved Hoosiers (don't say we don't pick up the lingo) travel up to 200 miles across the state to what was once the Kentucky-owned Green River Island but thanks to the fact that the Ohio shifted course, is now firmly attached to mainland Indiana.

Ellis Park makes no mighty claims to be Belmont, Aqueduct, Santa Anita or even Arlington Park. Indeed, it was lucky to be born at all, James C. Ellis buying the 200-acre site in 1924 only after the initial founding in 1922 had gone into receivership. Yet in a 59-day meeting between July 2 to Labor Day (September 7 in 1981), Ellis Park took more than a quarter of a million people through the turnstiles, and $30 million through the betting windows, and studying its problems brought the pluses and minuses of American racing into sharper focus than all the trips to the major tracks put together.

For a start, their problems are similar, but as the likes of Ellis Park are on a much smaller margin, they are much closer to the hangman's noose, and that concentrates the mind wonderfully. Take the perennial problem of Government-and-race-

America's most famous racing day, the Kentucky Derby, occurs the first Saturday in May at Churchill Downs in Louisville, Kentucky. Those twin towers look across at the nation's most throbbing infield, packed with 90-odd thousand people out of a total attendance of almost 150,000. Some study form, some horticulture, most become experts on mint juleps, a dangerous, mint-decorated liquor mix, but all of them can say they were there. In 1979 that meant seeing Spectacular Bid (Centre) win the Kentucky Derby and go down in racing history.

course share of the handle, which in New York the likes of Ogden Phipps and chief executive Joseph P. Hefferman were able actually to improve in the horseman's favour along the old argument that excessive taxation was killing the goose that laid the golden eggs. Well, in New York the whole plant is so magnificent that the question is one of degree, but when Ruth Adkins says: 'At the end of nineteen-eighty we were in a position where we either had to do something or close the shop', you can look out towards the Ohio river on the the other side of the Ellis Park back-stretch and fully appreciate the deal.

You can also realise that people like Ruth Adkins are among the fundamental strengths of the American system. Independent, bold and above all realistic, Ruth has worked her way from being a common-or-garden secretary to running not only the strange and special world of a racetrack but, as farm manager to James C. Ellis Estates, she also organises major production plants of those two other familiar Kentucky trademarks, Bourbon and tobacco. When she comes to lobby her case it is not – as in Britain we suffer most of all – in the semi-apologetic role of some gentleman bemoaning the passing of more leisured, less expensive, days. It is to demand a fair deal for her track and her racing family.

That sense of belonging is a fine American institution naturally fostered by race meetings lasting two or, as at Aqueduct, three months, when racing will go on six days a week, and the officials, horsemen, punters and track workers all have to get along together. The belonging is also there when you talk to Ray Rogers at Santa Anita, David Stevenson at Aqueduct, Tommy Trotter at Arlington, but nowhere does it compare with the feeling at Ellis Park. Mind you, the riverside track has two pretty unfair advantages – country community and the love of a woman.

Not for nothing did Ellis Park's resident feature writer, Erik Von Fuhrmann (he's a Professor of Literature in real life) describe Ruth Adkins as 'the Den mother'. Others may have bigger flocks. At Aqueduct, there are 3,000 horses, and a total head-

count of some 5,000 personnel on the track, but none can be better tended than Ellis Park's. Why, on the first night she even introduced us to a tall, open-faced man who turned out to be the new padre, the priest of the back-stretch with a little chapel converted from one of the stables. Maybe the Three Wise Men and the Shepherds were about, too, if we had only known where to look.

Ruth took us to her little office by the front gate and there, surrounded by mementoes of 33 years' involvement, protected by a massive colt revolver on her desk (not to mention that little pearl-handled number in its cosy hiding place), she expounded a policy of management that could save a racing nation–ours, not hers. 'I think the

racing industry for a while forgot about the people', she said in a voice as pure Kentucky as the Bourbon she had poured for us. 'Everyone was so involved in the problems of the business that they forgot about the person who makes the business go, that is the person who comes through this gate.'

Easy cliches, you might think, but the great thing about Ellis Park, and indeed about many tracks around the States, is that you can see how they have thought about the customer. At this supposed Midwestern 'gaff' there was computer-ised Tote, air-conditioned clubhouse, closed-circuit colour TV, gourmet food and all sorts of package inducements to spend your evenings sampling the varied delights of Henderson

County's Ramada Inn or Evansville's Executive Inn, and your days at Ellis Park. More than that, newspapers and posters carry the track's new slogan of the punter's yell, 'C'mon, C'mon' across the Tri-State (Indiana, Kentucky and Illinois), and

At Churchill Downs horses (and tractors) don't allow the rain to have the last word. The dirt track surface is based on a sandy loam found in this northern end of Kentucky. It gives a good running surface in dry conditions but when it's wet the horses need a complete spring clean afterwards and jockeys use up to four pairs of goggles in a race, pulling down the top pair once they get completely clogged up. The clogging on the track is lessened by "floating out" after each race: six tractors pull 20-foot wide wooden floats round the Churchill Downs 1¼-mile circuit and literally squeeze the water off the track.

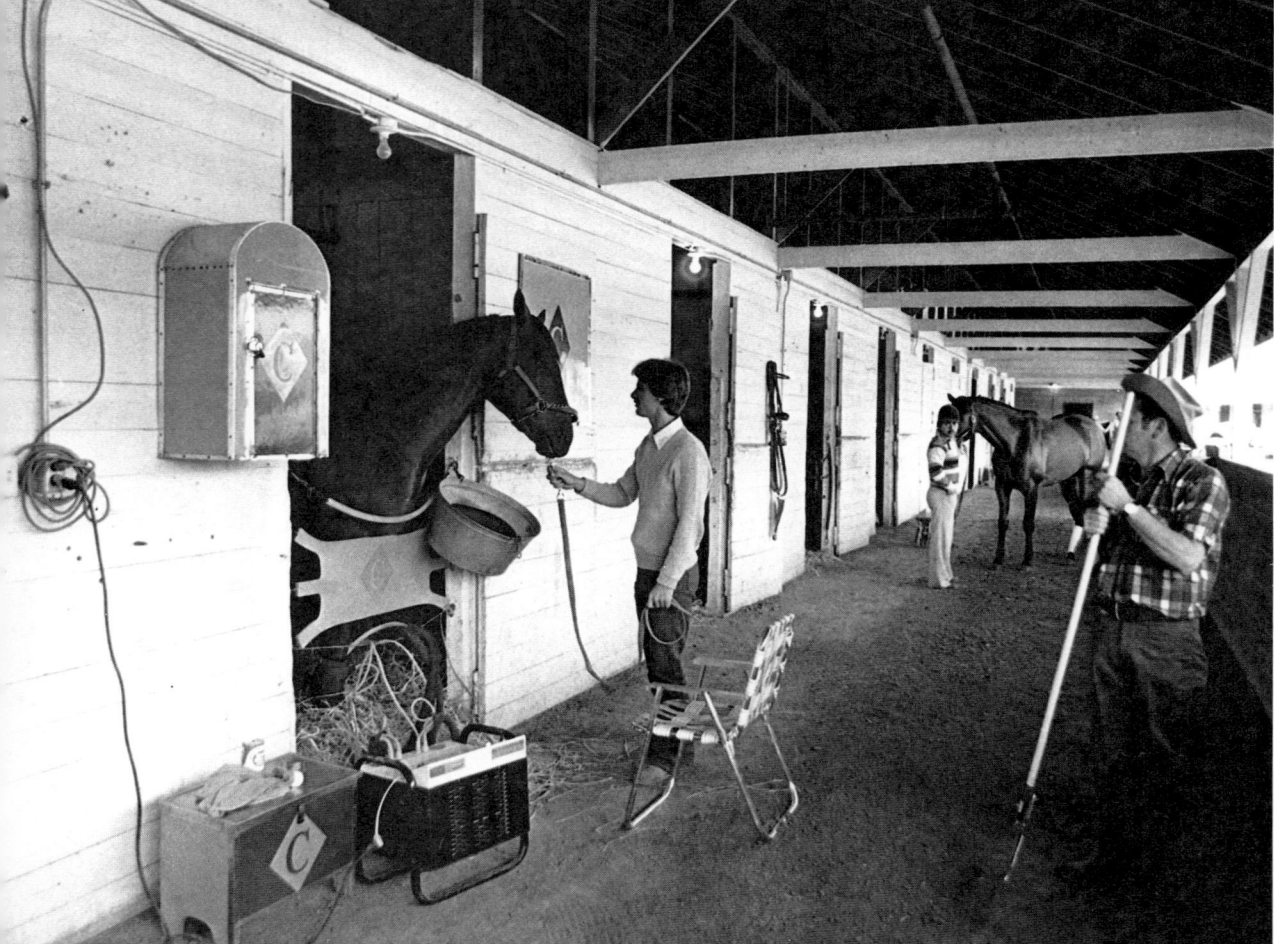

Ruth Adkins says with that old Kentucky chuckle: 'I hand out free tickets promiscuously. I pay the state fifteen cents a ticket, which keeps them happy, but it also helps to promote my business.'

The idea that you have got to promote to survive is into racing minds at the highest level. Why, we even saw the dawn training routine 'Breakfast at Belmont', or the same thing among the elm trees in up-state New York, 'Saratoga Sunrise', where keen race fans eat their ham and eggs while watching their favourite horses work-out. And it was the New York Racing Association who dreamt up the evocative TV and newspaper commercial: 'Come and see the World's Fastest Creature, the Thoroughbred Racehorse' – a slogan which wins top marks for effect, but hardly for accuracy. What about the poor old cheetah, which over a couple of furlongs could give 20 lengths' start and a beating to any horse ever bred?

The true vastness of the whole American racing business had finally hit me that cool March morning some six months earlier in 1981, when the visit to Angel Penna and New York's Aqueduct coincided with Daily Racing Form's Annual Review of the Year. This 80-page statistical treasure chest included a whole page listing every one of North America's 100 race-tracks (87 US, 11 Canada, 2 Mexico) from Ak Sar Ben to Yakima Meadows, and had begun by clubbing you over the head with the news that the 1980 attendance total had reached 55,437,392 spread over 7,443 fixtures and 68,243 races, pretty hard to take if you have been trying to cope with a busy British year in 1980 comprising just 4,140,358 total attendance over 898 fixtures and 5,629 races.

The most trumpeted statistic of all was that the total betting handle had passed the $7 billion mark, but since our little island pulls £2 billion ($4 million) that wasn't half as impressive as how they siphoned the money off from the bettors and how, with new gimmicks like the Pick Six (accumulator bet) they could actually increase their turnover against the economy's downward trend. When we sweltered down the Saratoga backstretch in August, the turnover was registering a 10 per cent boost, and when we stumbled red-eyed from a missed Los Angeles connection into Santa Anita's Oaktree meeting in the fall, the figures for this Pick Six-fevered plant were up no less than 17 per cent.

Such a success was not that easy to get. After all, Ellis Park itself was 6.5 per cent down in turnover in 1980, but turned things around with a media attack to get the public through the gates in a way quite undreamed of in Britain or France and with a victory over local government about an issue in which now only Britain and Ireland stand anachronistically aloof – Sunday racing. The more you look at it from the outside, the more absurd our attitude seems. There we are, a highly industrialised nation with only two days of leisure, yet we ban race-going on one of them despite the

fact that (in Britain at any rate) we have a far smaller church-going percentage than on mainland Europe, where they have always had Sunday as a race-day fun day, as well as the Lord's Day.

Nowadays, it's fashionable in Britain to mutter that it would be impossible to get the necessary legislation through Parliament, and that the overtime rates demanded by the unions would make Sunday racing financially impossible. Such protests may stand up indoors, but they look pretty shaky when exposed to the elements further afield. At Ellis Park, with closure looming, something drastic had to be done. We don't think Mrs Adkins actually drew her pistol from its holster, but she sure as hell made people realise her track's problems, and got them to allow her to experiment with Sunday racing.

'With the public, and indeed with the horsemen once they realised it meant more money, it has been a great success', said Ruth at the end of her 'meet' lasting 59 days. 'The problem, of course, is my staff, who have been on time-and-a-half, but if they were to insist upon double time they would sink the whole ship. At the moment we are staying afloat, and attracting a whole new family audience on Sundays.' This reaction to racing on the Sabbath was shared by David Stevenson in his computerised bunker at the nerve-centre of Aqueduct's enormous racing plant, which has just about everything going for it except that it is about three feet from the end of the runways of Kennedy Airport. The compact, bespectacled Stevenson, one of the few ex-jockeys to make it into the highest echelons of racecourse management, says:

'We have had Sunday racing in New York for the past seven years, and the trend is very clear. You get

(Left) Backstage scenes at Churchill Downs as the tension builds before the Kentucky Derby on the first Saturday in May. Already the Louisville weather can be hot enough to make a wash a pleasure, while in the cool of the barn the Hollywood Derby winner Flying Paster has electrical treatment to eliminate soreness before carrying California's hopes in the USA's most famous classic. He finished out of the numbers.

(Right) Some people call racing 'the great triviality'. But not these 'horse players' at Churchill Downs. The pari-mutuel windows (bookmakers were banned in 1939) offer bets to win, place (first two), show (first three), Exacta (name the first two), and Daily Double (first two races). Units can be as low as $1 but a single bet of $50,000 'to show' has been recorded. Luckily it did. The record turnover for a single day was $10.3 million, for Derby Day in 1978.

a slightly bigger attendance, but a little less handle than on a Saturday. You have got more of a watching audience than a serious betting one, because it is a new audience, more of a family day out, and that can't be bad.'

Another thing that can't be bad despite one of the longest-running corruption charges since the Trial of Warren Hastings, is the standard of American jockeys. Because the rhythm of the actual races is so different, there has been a tendency for the European and American race fans to ridicule one another's riders. I have heard Cordero booed at Longchamp for having trouble going (ponyless) to the start, and Lester Piggot was roundly condemned for 'riding like a bum' in 1968, despite winning the 17th running of the Washington DC International.

But the series of International Jockeys' Championships which began at the Meadowlands' amazing modern plant in New Jersey in 1979, and which has seen two very popular Britain versus America team contests in England, has opened eyes all round to one of the truths that Piggott likes to mutter in his laconic but perceptive way: 'Everyone has to get used to their own tracks, and wherever you go in the world you will find that the top boys are good, and very hard to beat.'

There has also been the personal experience of Steve Cauthen, who started his career as the all-time American sensation, winning 487 races and a first-ever $6 million dollars in his first full year of 1977. Then, with Affirmed's Triple Crown also behind him, he switched to the British scene, where within three seasons he had settled into the highest class once again. 'Of course there were a lot of things that were different', says Steve with his natural Kentucky charm. 'Most of all, the tracks. One would be left-handed, another right, another straight, some uphill, some downhill, even [Windsor] a figure of eight. Your riders have been reared on them; I had to learn. And the pace of a race is much slower than at home, so I have made some adjustments, but a horse is still a horse.'

However Cauthen may like to play down any changes he has had to make, watching those three seasons has illuminated the different things needed on either side of the Atlantic. When he arrived, he was extraordinarily sharp and streamlined but seemed, as at first sight Cordero and Shoemaker did, to have difficulty both in holding horses early, and in punching them out at the finish. Now Cauthen looks more upright, but consider-

Far from the madding crowd, an early morning session on Saratoga's training track has a rural feel about it, even if the professional observers still miss few tricks and the temporary wooden stables are in some cases dressed up into a showpiece. But there are also workouts on the track itself and these are scrutinised by the most pampered training spectators in the world. They are the fans who have come to sample Saratoga Sunrise: a breakfast plus commentary on the morning gallops. All delicious stuff but whether or not it helps forecast the afternoon racing (Right) is another question.

ably more poised at the beginning of a race, and has far more muscular, pumping drive in a finish.

The difference is hardly surprising. With the pace that American races are run (three world records set in 1980), and with a pony-rider to lead you to the start, brakes are the least of your worries. Add to that the uniform flatness of the tracks, and you have a horse running much freer under you than the bedraggled, routed cavalrymen that the runners resembled as they struggled up Salisbury's undulating straight on the first typically boggy day that Cauthen raced in Britain in 1978.

Not that the likes of Laffit Pincay and Chris McCarron lack much when it comes to vim. You don't have 1,964 rides and 405 wins in a single year, as McCarron did in 1980, without being able to push a bit. And, although Lester Piggott once said provocatively: 'America is the easiest place in the world to ride–you just have to stand on the horse', anyone who has watched Velasquez or Shoemaker threading a way through the mayhem of a horse race will appreciate that they are not short on finesse. And Piggott ought to watch out, because Patricia Cooksey actually rode more winners than he did in 1980. Maybe her successes were gained in such un-Ascot-type places as River Downs and Beulah Park, and admittedly all the girls we've seen so far have been lacking in fire-power, if not skill, yet in America at least the monstrous regiment of women is on the march.

Moreover when American jockeys, of either gender, go to war they are both better protected and under greater threat because of the presence of an agent by their side. Men like Lenny Goodman,

Steve Cauthen's original Svengali; Tony Matos, for long the cool back-up to the extravagantly gifted Angel Cordero; and Victor Galardi, the genial bulky presence behind Jorge Velasquez. All of them capable of swatting the half-chance at 50 paces and incongruously addicted to the first-person singular, it's more than a double take when you first hear Victor Galardi say: 'I ride five good horses tomorrow afternoon'.

Thus protected, all the jockeys have to do most of the time is climb on board the horses the agent has booked for them. By contrast some English riders can become one-man juggling acts grappling with their possible engagements. But no contract can give British-style 'stable jockey' security, particularly when anything less than a star performance will see rival agents clustering round a trainer suggesting none too subtly that their boy could do a better job.

As to corruption, you would probably find quite a few worms if you turned over every stone, but that is true not only in all racing but in all walks of life. The Errico race-fixing allegations sullied the good name of some famous racing personalities, and on a lower level I was pretty shaken by one remarkable and strictly unofficial conversation down one of the seamier corners of the Arlington back-stretch. It was stated, quite matter-of-factly, that a certain stable's success the previous year was due to a jockey who used a battery. 'Oh yes, if he was going to use it on a horse that afternoon', our informant confided, 'he would come and try it in the morning. Sure seemed to make those horses go. He'd have the battery

taped to his fingers with a couple of prongs in the end. Bit difficult getting rid of it after a race. He gave it to me once'.

So there is some wickedness around. So what? The trick is not to let it swamp you and there are quite a few above the tide yet, with the biggest example set by the smallest and oldest of them all, the astonishing man that is Bill Shoemaker. Whether or not it is true that he was incubated in a shoebox, or as was once claimed, actually spent the first 10 years of his life in one, there is no disputing the fact that he rode his 8,000th winner in 1981, his 51st year, or that his achievements during that twelve-month in winning 150 races worth almost $5,900,000 earned him the Eclipse Award as Jockey of the Year.

More than that, this man who has already ridden more winners than anyone in history continued to set an example of winning skill on the track and Arnold Palmer-style humanity off it. Watching him play cards between races in the Santa Anita dressing-room, his legs so short they didn't reach the floor, and listening to him talk with boyish enthusiasms and old-world wisdom, was to realise that the only thing small about Shoemaker was his physical stature.

It was fitting, therefore, that he should have left us with the outstanding memory of the American game. It came, on the outskirts of Chicago, on the last Sunday of August, 1981, when Noah's Ark deluges, a disappointingly small crowd and lack of a major foreign involvement looked like warping the hoped-for impact of the first Arlington Million. Then Shoemaker and a lean, mean, once-unwanted six-year-old gelding called John Henry came up the outside with a speed and drama that caught the breath and landed them in front right on the wire.

So the richest race ever run was won by the world's most successful horse and jockey, John Henry's eight wins from 10 races in 1981 making him Horse of the Year and taking his record career earnings to beyond $3 million. Watching him being hosed down outside the barn afterwards made you realise that no amount of dollars can beat the real thing. Vast racing plants, betting 'handles' and all the myriad worries and wrangles that have made a million-dollar industry out of something that started as a sport, still come a long way second to the raw excitement of a great horse laying it on the line.

Maybe that was not Camelot, but it sure was a long way from disenchantment.

Started in 1934 and laid out beneath the San Gabriel mountains in the leafy suburb of Arcadia, 14 miles from Los Angeles, Santa Anita has made the most of its position and Californian climate. Its 125 race days average over 30,000 spectators each and draw some of the best horses and jockeys in the land. Among the riders is the most successful in the world, Bill Shoemaker, past 50 now, past the record 8,000 winners mark, and selective enough in his mounts that a game of poker with the jockeys' room attendants is a more frequent luxury than the busy days when he rode over 400 winners in a single season. Even so, Shoemaker's corner of Santa Anita, with its rows of saddles, boots and other equipment is still the centre of a multi-million pound business. In 1981 alone, Shoemaker was on the back of over £3 million-worth of victories, making him, at 5ft and 98lbs, small only in size.

8
ARGENTINA

'For sheer spectacle there can be no racecourse in the world to match Gavéa, which looks up at the famous Christ the Redeemer statue from its shoreside home at the southern head of Ipanema Bay. Yet neither the rugged mountain country, the mango swamps of Rio's river-delta airport nor the harsh red earth and speckled vineyards of Sao Paolo, our other Brazilian stopover, give you the "horse-land" feel that comes on seeing the flat, yellow-green miles of pampas that stretch below on the approach to Buenos Aires airport'.

MUHAMMAD ALI is not easily up-staged, but to some extent Gerry Cranham and I pulled it off in the first week of December 1980. 'The Greatest' made a guest appearance on our Saturday afternoon TV show, but he missed out on the unprecendented double of covering races at Nottingham and at San Isidro, in Argentina, in successive days. Could we think he didn't want to?

But we did. Because if the three o'clock at Nottingham was a goodish quality and excitingly-fought hurdle race, even the most ardent PR men for its sponsors, Panama Cigars, could hardly claim it as a global event. But that was just the status achieved by the 6.30 at San Isidro next day, the 81st running of Argentina's most important race, the Gran Premio Internacional Carlos Pellegrini.

Mind you, the South Americans had, at £238,000 total prize money, some £236,00 more than Nottingham to attract contestants with, and it was blue-skied early summer in Buenos Aires, rather different from the damp early dusk that traditionally settles over the great Midland conurbations on wintry afternoons. But forget the excuses, the Carlos Pellegrini was an unforgettable race, and with horses from France, Germany and North America, as well as the leading South American countries, a truly international event.

It was also an unforgettable journey, and as you fly through the night, and the time zones, to touch down in Rio de Janeiro next morning, you have to shake your head at the thought of those first little Spanish galleons battling for weeks across the oceans to make the first European arrival four-and-a-half centuries ago.

For sheer spectacle there can be no racecourse in the world to match Gavéa, which looks up at the famous Christ the Redeemer statue from its shoreside home at the southern head of Ipanema Bay. Yet neither the rugged mountain country, the mango swamps of Rio's river-delta airport nor the harsh red earth and speckled vineyards of Sao Paolo, our other Brazilian stop-over, give you the 'horse-land' feel that comes on seeing the flat, yellow-green miles of pampas that stretch below on the approach to Buenos Aires airport.

The temperature was in the eighties which, if not quite up to Kuala Lumpur standards, still made the air-conditioned cool of the San Isidro members' dining room (Exclusivemento) a sought-after haven once we got to the race track after a quick change in the steamy cupboard laughingly called an hotel room.

We had actually touched down at 12 noon which, if seeming several ages away from the three o'clock at Nottingham the day before, appeared perilously close to the preparations for that after-

(Preceding Spread) The first horses came to Argentina with the Spaniards in the 16th century and the Moorish influence lives on in the country's oldest racetrack Palermo, almost in the heart of Buenos Aires.

Argentina's richest race, the Carlos Pellegrini at San Isidro in December, is part of a long day's journey into night. The 91,000 spectators have come to see 14 races as well as Argentina's surprising contribution to woman's lib, Marina Lescano (Bottom Near Right), the most successful woman jockey in the world. But in 1980 she was unplaced in the big race behind Alberto Pla, on Regidor (Top Far Right), whose connections were celebrating long after the lights were switched on for the later races.

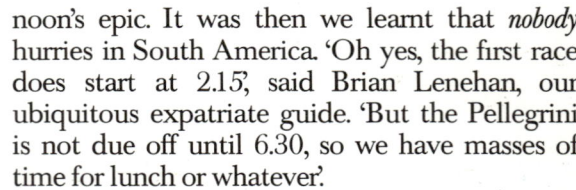

noon's epic. It was then we learnt that *nobody* hurries in South America. 'Oh yes, the first race does start at 2.15', said Brian Lenehan, our ubiquitous expatriate guide. 'But the Pellegrini is not due off until 6.30, so we have masses of time for lunch or whatever'.

In fact we indulged in neither lunch nor whatever, which was just as well because on the 15km drive west out of Buenos Aires to the leafy western suburb of San Isidro, we came across a car short of one wheel but containing the youthful quarterback bulk of American trainer Don Combs, the immaculate bantamweight form of his jockey, Jorge Velasquez, and other camp followers of their contender, Yvonand. Apparently the wheel had lost itself, not been removed by some other hostile vehicle, but that must have been against the run of play to judge by the tactics employed by most drivers. You began to wonder how a strange jockey might fare on the racetrack, but Velasquez gave his

slow Panamanian gunfighter's smile, and just said: 'Ees not bad. I have five rides at Palermo last night, and two winners. Ees no problem'.

Palermo is Argentina's original premier track. Set right in the centre of Buenos Aires, it has a magnificent, slightly fading Spanish turn-of-the-century opulence, with meetings twice a week on its sand course, and staging both the 1,600-metre Polla de Potrillos (their Two Thousand Guineas, and the 2,500-metre Gran Premio Nacional (their Derby), two legs of the Argentinian Quadruple Crown. The other two legs, the Gran Premio Nacional over 10 furlongs, and the Carlos Pellegrini over 2,400 metres, are run where Combs, Velasquez, three-wheeled cars and all were headed, the sweeping 50-hectare parkland of San Isidro racetrack. Like the rest of Argentina, San Isidro has had the odd argument with central authority, and in 1974 the government took it (and Palermo) away from the Jockey Club. And when San Isidro

didn't seem to be paying, it was closed down and not handed back to its original owners until July, 1978. By that time, major rebuilding was needed to get it into shape, but with the resilience of a nation that had then got its inflation *down* to 60 per cent, 40 million dollars were raised, San Isidro was re-opened in December, 1979, and now, a year later, was celebrating the final rehabilitation, the return home of the Carlos Pellegrini.

This day was a big race occasion which, for size and sheer general enjoyment, could stand comparison with anywhere in the world, having half the police presence and, at 91,000, double the crowd of Arc de Triomphe day at Longchamp two months before.

Of course, the Argentinians had a few things going for them. A beautiful shaded-shrub and blue-flowered jacaranda-tree setting, three big stands and, above all, beautiful weather even hotter than that sizzling afternoon when Henbit had struggled

broken-leggedly home in the Epsom Derby six months before. But even if the weather was a bit of luck (it had sluiced down the previous night at Palermo), the attitude, and indeed the glorious prolonging of the day, were something special. For the sun was setting somewhere towards Cordoba when we realised that this 12-race 'Pellegrini' card just has to be the most extended classic day of all. Sure, the Arc and Derby afternoons stretch on a bit, but at least everyone hiccups their way home after nightfall. At San Isidro, they just switch on the floodlights and walk to the start as usual. Why waste energy galloping about? This is South

Palermo races on sand. On the left, the field is led into the straight by Marina Lescano, the first woman to win the 'Quadruple Crown'. The action can be a long way from the spectators on this big wide track (Below) but identification is made easier by numbers on jockeys arms and horses bridles, as well as the usual saddle cloth (Bottom Left).

America and the nights are long and hot....

For the ninth race, the relentless Cranham had the typical idea of lugging all his equipment across to the infield and photographing back towards the lights. The manoeuvre drew plenty of complaints from this quarter, particularly when the scaffolding we climbed up ('Must get a bit of height, give us perspective') began to sway like a giant bamboo in a whirlwind. But to watch the straining limbs and flashing silks of the race-finish, with the stands lit up in the background like three vast shining venus fly traps, made me grudgingly admit he had a point. Anyway, jet lag and the effects of free beer were setting in, so at 10.15 pm, with one race still

is trying to follow the trail blazed by the remarkable Marina Lescano, who at 23 has unquestionably accomplished more than any lady jockey since Lady Godiva. With 69 winners from 460 rides, she actually stood third in the jockeys' table on Pellegrini day, and in the big race she was on the legendary Telescopico, whom she brought through in 1978 to become the first horse to land the coveted Quadruple Crown since Forli back in 1966. (Specialists might note at this point the desirability of such a clear-cut, and therefore sought-after, Quadruple Crown, with classics at one mile, 1¼ miles and one mile 4½ furlongs for the three-year-old generation, and then a race, the

touch, and Marina, little legs clamped high on the withers, clearly gives her horses a freedom and a balance that many men, bigger and more muscular, would envy.

When Marina Lescano and Telescopico won the Pellegrini, it was run over 3,100 metres on the Palermo sand. But neither the 600 metres shorter distance, nor the San Isidro turf, could provide an excuse for the former wonder horse, who had recently made a successful comeback (at Palermo) after an abortive campaign in the top European races during 1979. Indeed, though Telescopico featured in all the magazines, the received wisdom was that he had no chance because of severe

uncontested, we gave it away knowing that another couple of hours would go by before San Isidro would belong only to the relentless beat of the crickets in the summer night.

By then we had seen plenty to impress us both with the strengths of Argentinian racing, and the problems for raiders from the Northern Hemisphere. The local horses in this early summer (July 1 is the Southern Hemisphere birth-date) looked in fine condition overall. So did the punters, who splashed eleven thousand million pesos on the day's racing and seven million dollars (N.B. change of currency) on the Pellegrini alone, and the jockeys not only looked pretty competent, but one or two more than competently pretty.

The first race we watched was won by a neat little girl apprentice called Irene Guimares, who

Pellegrini, against the seniors over 1½ miles. Since the first and third legs are on the Palermo sand, and the second and fourth on the Isidro turf, the horse that takes all the tricks has really proved himself.)

Perhaps a nation that has had two Senora Perons around in the past 20 years is used to dominant females, even if most of them remain housewives. But it was as pleasant to see the lack of ooh-la-la fuss about Argentina's star jocketta as it was to watch the sunny, unpretentious professionalism of the lady herself. Marina is a tiny 4ft 10in, 7st square-butted little figure, and although she did not ride a winner that day you could see that she knew the way to go about it. No woman is going to match a male rival for strength, so she must play on her lightness and

training troubles. So it was infinitely more surprising to see him backed down to favourite than to watch him fade from a good position in the race itself.

The big event certainly didn't lack for buildup. There was hardly room enough in the final parade ring in front of the stands for all 22 runners and their connections, and the nervous preliminaries, with the jockeys crossing themselves, stretched on for 18 minutes after the official 6.30

Although San Isidro's weighing room with its electric print-out scales is one of the most open in the world, the leading jockeys (Above), can still look less than scrutable. Champion Vilmar Sanguinetti, on the left, and Carlo Pellegrini hero Alberto Pla flank Marina Lescano, the girl who broke all barriers to become one of Argentina's top jockeys.

start time. Races apparently don't begin until the Tote-only betting operations end, and when all were finally installed, the loudspeakers gave a great symphonic fanfare before the horses were sent on their journey.

San Isidro has a big, galloping track 3,000 metres in circumference, so the mile-and-a-half (2,400 metres) with only one bend and a three-and-a-half furlong run-in was a perfectly fair test for the Northern Hemisphere horses. Their complete failure (the French horse Perouges, in ninth place, did best) emphasised the problems of such a journey. A horse stuck in Paris, Washington or ice-cold New York, in December, grows a thick coat which has to be clipped off once it hits the Argentinian summer. But the achievement of the French firm, Hipavia, in getting their horses from stable to stable in just 20 hours was remarkable. And would have been even faster but for a four-hour Customs wrangle. All the lads I spoke to thought that their horses had faced an uphill task. 'Eet was quite eempossible for our horse', said Jacques, who was with the French Derby third, Providential. 'He arrive a week ago. We give him three days easy, then one canter. He seem all right, so one piece of work and he run bad'.

Ten thousand miles is an awfully long slog home with a beaten runner, and there were other excuses. The American horse, Yvonand, didn't stay on this galloping track, the French Soleil Noir hadn't run for six months and Pawiment was in his third country in three months. 'His American trip obviously didn't suit him', said his Cologne-based owner, Waldemar Zeithelhack, 'but I still think you could bring a horse down here and win'.

Zeithelhack is no stranger to the impossible, having won the Arc de Triomphe with the 119-1 outsider, Star Appeal, in 1975, and doing successful business on both sides of the Iron Curtain. His leasing of the top-class Polish horse, Pawiment, to win Germany's Preis von Europa and Italy's Gran Premio del Jockey Club, must be the greatest triumph of racing pragmatism in recent years. Pawiment was due the next week to trek all the way back to his fatherland, which had a lot more than the usual snow clouds hanging over its head at that end of 1980, Poland's time of 'Solidarity' and the threat of Soviet intervention.

Politics aside, it is significant that despite all the travelling, the French horse, Perouges, could still finish within 10 lengths of the winner, for although Perouges had won a Grand Prix at both Vichy and Bordeaux in 1980, there would be plenty of European horses who would fancy giving him 10 lengths' start, especially for 500 million pesos. So the argument about how good the Argentinian horses are remains tantalisingly unresolved, and, while times are notoriously misleading, the fact remains that the winner, the three-year-old Regidor, clocked 2min 26.09sec on this fast, but not rock-hard, turf, which would have set a record anywhere in England. As he and his squint-eyed jockey, Alberto Pla, hacked down to receive an ovation from the cheap end of the course (let's try *that* at Ascot and Epsom), it was easy to think that here was a genuinely top-class horse.

Moreover, a million dollars would buy him.

But talk of horseflesh as bargains at a million dollars has two effects. The first is to produce a whispy sense of unreality, the second is a pecuniary sniffing of the air, and it might be said that the second tends to banish the first as the scent increases. Northern Hemisphere noses have been pointed at Argentina ever since the great Forli went to the United States in 1966 and became, as sire of Forego, Thatch and Home Guard, one of the great sires of the Seventies. Telescopico's comparative failure in Europe in 1979 (he was only six lengths behind Derby winner, Troy, in Ascot's King George VI and Queen Elizabeth II stakes), won't have fooled the bloodstock hounds, and if Regidor would be "cheap" at a million dollars, what sort of value would be Mountdrago, only a length behind him but having already run 20 times and won nine, including two legs of Quadruple Crown, in only two seasons?

The argument against the likes of Regidor and Mountdrago is that nobody up North knows anything about their breeding, the names of their sires, Pepenador and Sheet Anchor, sounding more like yachting cottages at Cowes than the sires of two international champions. 'Maybe you don't know them', said the San Isidro racing secretary, Ignacio Pavlovski, 'but they all come from the best bloodlines, and we reckon that our climate can produce fine horses'.

Apparently it has been ever thus, or at least since 1581, when Juan de Garay landed at La Plata, 20 miles from modern Buenos Aires. That was 47 years after the founding Pedro de Mendoza had fled home, leaving five mares and seven stallions to run loose on the pampas, and they had put that time to such good effect that the plains were, according to Roger Longrigg's essential History of Horse Racing, 'already swarming with horses'.

San Isidro scenes. Despite the soaring temperatures, horses tend to sport at least a rug (Above Right) and sometimes a hood (Above Left) but for mere humans (Left) more obvious remedies are required.

Today the herds are mostly of the railed-off planned-procreation type but, among thorough-breds at least, over-production is clearly a problem, the most recent statistics showing a foal population of 7,700, with only 4,500 animals at present in training.

That is the third largest (after the United States and Australia) foal population in the world, and with only four days' racing a week to provide the opportunities around Buenos Aires, the trick is obviously to go for quality. Knowing Pavlovski not just for his tall, welcoming urbanity at San

Isidro, but also for the veterinary prowess that took him to France when Angel Penna was master-minding the Wildenstein racing empire, it was no surprise to find that as a stud manager he was clearly aiming above the Andes.

Santa Maria des Araras, the property of Brazilian banker Julio de St Angelo, was reportedly 'just down the road' from Buenos Aires. Compared with the 1,000-mile run to the tip of Cape Horn, that might be strictly true, but two-and-a half hours is a longish spin to lunch, especially if you have waited two hours for the

taxi, and then endured an eye-shutting flat-to-the-boards trip whose hazards included loose horses on the roadside, and virtually all traffic oncoming.

Santa Maria is an immaculate new Normandy-brick complex just five miles short of the central town of the renowned Capitan Sarmiento region. There is a 40-box courtyard for the mares and foals; a separate stallion unit, two beautifully-designed Moorish bungalows and, when we got there at 2pm, not a soul in sight. Fearless detective work, and an ear cocked for merriment, eventually revealed that not all the barns were for horses,

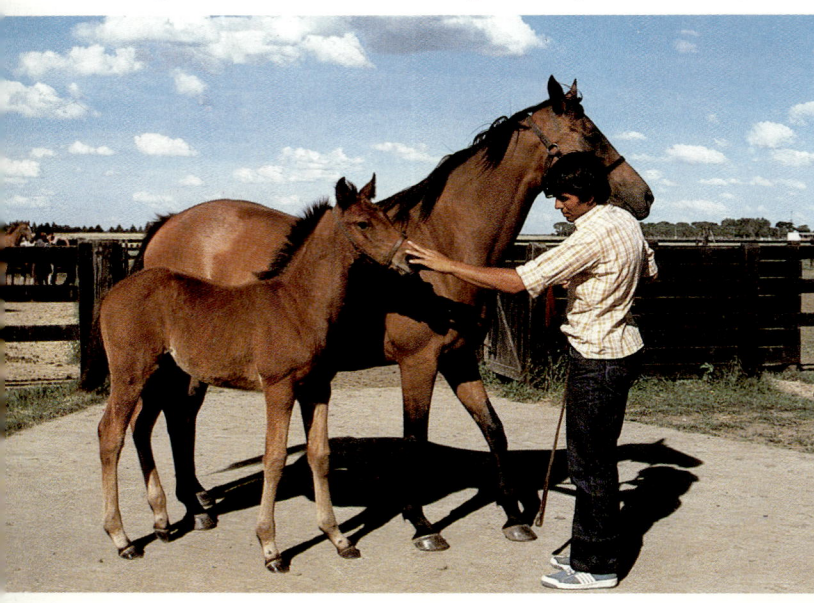

one of them containing no fewer than 27 people at table in battle with enormous glistening chunks of meat barbecued on an open fire.

It must be said that slaking the thirst on plenty of the excellent Vino Tinto which accompanied this offering rendered exact recollection of the tour of this and its neighbouring stud, where the successful young Tan Pronto stands, fairly difficult. As always when owners, friends, potential buyers and assorted hacks come to 'look over the stock', there was a lot of standing about while horses were led past and pedigrees recited. What was different in

this case was the demonstration that unlike the weak-headed creatures in England, Ireland or Kentucky, Argentinian horses and horse persons have little need of shade, and by the time the 5,000th mare and foal were led past, we were panting like dogs in a heatwave.

Santa Maria is a new venture, but stud farms have a full 100 years' history in Argentina. Santiago Luro set up the Haras Ojo de Agua at the end of the 1870s, and in 1907 he imported the Ascot Gold Cup winner, Cyllene, sire of four Epsom heroes himself, and destined to also be a great

influence south of the Equator. So, too, was Diamond Jubilee, Edward VII's man-eating Derby

Argentina established itself as the most fertile production land for horses back in 1581 when Juan de Garay landed at La Plata to find the pampas swarming with horses, the descendants of just five mares and seven stallions abandoned there less than 50 years before. Today in the same beneficial climate, exist as many efficient studs and handlers, like this one at the Santa Maria des Araras. Unfortunately, lack of planning has meant that a boom has become a glut; Argentina now produces over 7,500 thoroughbred foals a year with only space for 4,500 horses in training, the worst over-population in the world.

winner of 1900, and there were some day-dreaming moments to be had looking out for armless octogenarians among the stud's workforce.

But in the wideawake world of finance, it's fascinating to note that Diamond Jubilee and Cyllene cost £31,500 and £25,000 respectively over 70 years ago, yet when the famous Don Yayo Stud wanted to supplement the ageing but successful Con Brio in 1979, they had to pay only 25,000 guineas for Petronisi at Newmarket Sales. If Petronisi, a fair handicapper by Petingo out of an Exbury mare, becomes as successful as Don Yayo hopes, he could yet be Argentina's magic answer to the cost of living. But in reality, where Epsom Derby winners command an automatic £5 million valuation, his price reflects the comparative lack of money in Argentinian racing at this moment. It also emphasises the point, repeated by Regidor's breeder when we visited

his historic Spanish colonial home on the way back to Buenos Aires, that the climate has to make champions out of the lesser scions of the great European and North American families.

The one query we took back from these heartlands was about the handling of some of the horses on the studs. The grooms and gauchos looked pictures of swarthy calm as they vaulted on to the round-up ponies, but some of the animals they went to catch and present looked about as relaxed as frightened guinea pigs when you go to clean the cage. So despite the eye-aching early hour, the trip next morning to see the finished product, the horses in training, at San Isidro was a great relief. It was more than that, a revelation. Four concentric sand tracks and one turf track outside them, 1,000 horses not only coming on and off, but lined up by the hundred in cavalry-line style on the very track where their stable

companions gallop past. All of it done with the minimum of fuss, (not a loose horse was to be seen in three separate morning visits), and every horse save those actually galloping with a jockey up, ridden bareback.

Yes, bareback! The South American reader will just shrug in recognition, the North American may have seen occasional visitors dispensing with saddles, but to the European the idea that you should exercise a whole stable, a whole training centre of volatile thoroughbreds, without any saddle to sit on, or stirrups to put feet in, is inconceivable. Yet it worked. It worked. The basic lads' uniform of T-shirt, jeans and sockless plimsolls was hardly equestrian *haute couture*, but they sat their horses with the unmistakable ease of the natural rider, and their horses repaid them with a doglike obedience that amazed the visiting eye. To British lads, long famed for their horsemanship,

it's an almost insufferable challenge, so there is a case of champagne to the first stable who can get a string of a dozen or more out and back to exercise without a saddle–Ireland, France, indeed all Europe, to be included.

Out on the track, most of the top jockeys would have a saddle to ride fast work–Marina Lescano came past perched neat and high above the withers like a little red-shirted doll–but even they don't bother all the time. Alberto Pla, the cadaverous-looking Pellegrini hero, hacked by with just a stable sheet between his smart grey slacks and his horse's skin, and Vilmar Sanguinetti, the undisputed champion with a 22 per cent strike rate, confirmed that to all of them riding without a saddle was second nature.

Sanguinetti boasted the impressive figures of 217 wins from 913 rides already that season, 100 more than his nearest rival, but he remains delightfully unintimidating because his face is almost permanently creased into a front-tooth grin which makes him a dead ringer for Mickey Mouse. 'I was brought up in Uruguay', he said as he looked across at the assorted pilots thundering past old-print style. 'When you are a boy you just don't have a saddle, so that is how you learn. And in most cases it is better, the horses are quieter and that makes it easier for us.'

Granted that it was an on-the-plant operation set in one great 40-hectare green-hedged arena, it was still an extraordinarily impressive set-up. Not only the behaviour working on the track, but on a large eucalyptus-shaded sand-ride around the perimeter and an extensive eight-hose washing bay where Cranham fired off so many pictures it was a miracle he didn't get a hosepipe up his 500mm lens. There was also a 200-metre swimming pool where one horse was clearly in training to swim the River Plate, as we saw him do four laps and he looked set for the duration. Yet the outward visible signs at a training centre can often emanate from a stable-yard horrifyingly lacking in inward spiritual grace, and so after blowing 3,000 pesos on a glass of milky coffee and a delicious crispy little croissant, we got a lift round the yard of Carlo Ferro, who was third on the trainers' list, and for a few moments it looked as if good old British traditionalism would get a look in at last.

'All very well for these chaps out on the pampas, but you can't really slop around like this in the street', prompted the Colonel Blimp in us all

Who needs a saddle? At San Isidro more than 2,000 racehorses go out of a morning and none of the lads (Above) would dream of using a saddle. Even a crash-helmeted jockey (Left) will expect to ride with only a pad between him and a slippery crash.

as we watched half a dozen horses and riders loaf past the sleeping dogs, broken dustbins and other impediments that make up a side street in downtown San Isidro. And Blimp thought he was going to have a field day when we stumbled through a narrow opening to Ferro's yard–no more than 15 boxes in various stages of horse readiness, a narrow patch of cooch-grass lawn with a pump in the centre and the whole strung with ropes and drying rugs above, like a square-rigger on washday.

But that was the point. It was wash day. The boxes, mostly on wood shavings, were clean. The horses might be stuck into a limited routine, but they were obviously well tended, and the lads might, for all we know, be robbers, thieves, arsonists and child molesters, but in simple dealings with the thoroughbred racehorse they have no peers. Getting a string of racehorses out on to the road and away for exercise can be a major nerve-wracking, horse-wheeling, jockey-slipping performance. All that happens here is that horse walks out of box, lad puts stable cloth on its back, vaults aboard and walks on, taking about as long as it does to read these words. So there is the second and maybe easier chance to win a case of champagne. It goes to the first stable that can produce a string of 12 or more whose lads can vault on board sideways and effortlessly, gaucho style, a sort of Western Roll into the plate, not the absurd jumping up on to the stomach and then wriggling your leg over while the horse gathers speed down the lane, that is the official English method.

Don't let's make this a complete panegyric. 'After all', as habitués are fond of saying, hands spread wide, when taxis, food, drink or whatever has failed to arrive, 'this is South America'. As such, it is in no further away from the basic corruptions, and in December 1980 they had Telescopico's trainer Juan Bianchi on appeal for 'medicinal' irregularities, and Mountdrago's erst-while handler, Nestor Jallay, officially warned off from managing his string at La Plata, but he was still keeping a weather eye on them by means of a startlingly brilliant manoeuvre. At the end of the La Plata training ground there is a big new block of flats climbing towards the sky. As each floor is finished and furnished, so Senor Jallay goes up with it, and he gets a panoramic view of the training track. We understand he always has a telescope with his morning coffee.

There were no signs that Carlo Ferro would have to take up sky-climbing in the near future, except perhaps to oversee all his separate yards at once. For he has five different places like the one we were in. Each has its own head lad, with an overall head lad-assistant trainer who shuttles between them all and supervises feeding, which

Spots before the eyes. Cold showers are no ordeal if you are a racehorse in the sweltering heat of San Isidro.

incidentally happens morning and evening, with the night-watchmen taking all food, hay and water out of each horse's box between two and three in the morning, so that the animals go to work on empty stomachs.

Naturally, with 65 winners in a season, he is going to attract keen labour, but in a place which many in Britain would like to think had an inferior standard of living to our own, the lads get 600 dollars a month basic, with a percentage of winning and (other authorities please note) of any sales of horses from the stable. While good stables will already have planned it with their staff, it has long seemed absurd that when the improvement brought about in a horse by a training team is recognised, not just by the winning of a race but by a profitable sale, there is no official guide on how any profits should be split, if split at all.

Ferro is a gentle, bulky young man with receding hair and a face like a soulful bear. But he has a firm intelligence, and he realises his **advantages**: 'I only get boys from the country.

They can all ride perfectly, so they only have to get used to the stable ways'. He appreciates, too, the 28 per cent take-out from the Tote betting pool which, after six per cent is deducted for costs and expenses, is split 11 per cent in tax to the government, six per cent to prize money and five per cent to further racing development – an exactly even split between government and racing compared with the 9-1 in government's favour under which British racing staggers.

A veterinary graduate, Ferro also claimed that there were more people like him coming into the profession as trainers and as owners, and so he hoped the problems of lack of opportunity for the moderate horses, and the lack of any great export demand, could be solved by some dynamic thinking. All this was being translated as we sat at a restaurant rather significantly called Los Locos Annos (The Crazy Years) looking out across the River Plate, which was almost as brown as the 'Blue' Danube. He was telling us about his resting farm for young and sick horses 70km away

in the country, and how he never ran his horses outside Buenos Aires unless it was as a special favour to help some festival.

We tried to explain to him that some weeks a leading English trainer might take his horses and himself to a different meeting every day. We were sitting indoors in the air-conditioned shade away from the December sun, and facing something twice the size of a telephone directory called a 'pauco' steak. I started to say how sometimes the weather could be a shade rawer in April at Newmarket, but thought better of it. Old pampas proverb: "Jealousy is a dangerous vice."

At the San Isidro training grounds, on the outskirts of Buenos Aires Argentinian horses soon learn to keep their cool. While waiting their turn to work they are lined up on the very edge of the track, approached through leafy avenues. Afterwards they can have a cooling dip in the 200 metre swimming pool. But it is no haphazard affair. Leading figures, like trainer Carlo Ferro (Right) and San Isidro secretary Dr. Ignacio Pavlovski (Top Right), are veterinary college graduates.

9
EASTERN EUROPE

'It was schnapps again with Zoltan's elder brother, Janos, as early as eight next morning. We were in the main reception lounge at the Alag training centre, 30 kilometres from Budapest, a big, panelled hall still looking like the hunting lodge it was obviously modelled on at the turn of the century, antlers facing old hunting and racing prints on the walls. After the schnapps, the talk was of Kincsem and the great horses of the past, and with one of the diplomats who use Alag as a riding club coming in booted and spurred, the feeling that the equestrian torch had been passed intact down the years was irresistible'.

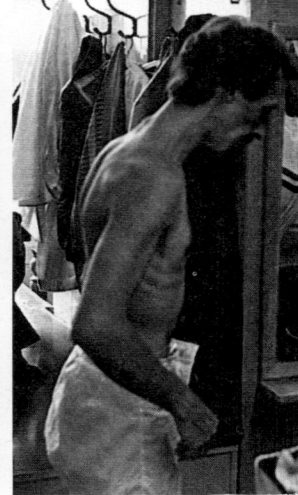

THERE'S A theory that the easiest way round the world is to walk bow-legged and put 'Horseman' on your passport. It's worked pretty well so far, even if, for this Westernised ex-jock, there was the odd twinge of doubt at that most bemusing and challenging of racing events, the International Socialist Race Meeting in Prague. It was not that the hosts were not hospitality itself, or that the jockeys and trainers spoke about their horses in nothing better than the warm boxer's-second way that is the rule elsewhere; nor even that the day ended up quite a few koruna to the bad. It was that by our fat-cat Western standards this was a big race day that could not take place.

Where was the archetypal cigar-chewing owner we feel is a necessary pillar of the game? Where was the big Mercedes without which no champion jockey can be complete? And, most of all, where in this still desperately hard-pressed land were the punters eager to make the racecourse rich by playing the horses with what the wife left over from the housekeeping?

The challenge to all of us this side of the Iron Curtain is that horses, 12,000 people and some balmy Czechoslovak sunshine proved that you could still have racing without these 'essentials'. The state farms owned the horses, the jockeys carried their own kit and looked as if they had come by scooter and since the gambling unit seemed to be 10 korunas (about 15p) and the betting method was the old pick-a-ticket pari-mutuel system, no comrade was going to lose his shirt.

What's more, the preliminaries were specially designed to put racegoers off such dangerous things as gambling on individuals by staging a pre-race parade only a notch or two short of the Olympics in concept. Each nation would have its flag carried by an outrider on a magnificent white stallion, followed by their respective racing

(Preceding Spread). Contradiction in terms. Jockeys from Eastern European countries weigh out at Prague for the Sport of Kings. This was the customary preliminary to one of seven races making up the Socialist Countries International Meeting, with horses and riders representing individual nations of the communist bloc. Their state-run lifestyle may be a far cry from the Hapsburg Empire days but centuries of horsemanship and decades of racing have laid roots that flourish still.

The flags still fly in Eastern Europe as the racing in Prague is preceded by a display of national teams, headed by the Soviet Union. But even though the Russians dominate, pragmatic racing leaders like Hungary's Doctor Feheer (Top Far Right) can still produce an effective thoroughbred operation. When it comes to the racing itself, even in socialist countries there are opportunities for investing your dough, and guidance (Top Third Right). And in the changing room (Top Second Right) emancipation has allowed in lady jockeys, who ask no favours out on the track. But out there, even if the local hero Nicolas (Bottom Far Right) does at least win the Cena Berlin, three out of the seven international events go to the Russians. It makes the victory ceremony, such as that for the Cena Budapest (Centre) slightly repetitious.

German three-year-old called Cil, and in the unsaddling enclosure afterwards it soon became clear that a lot more than the korunas was on the line. A massive piece of plate was handed to the Polish racing supremo, and we all faced inwards while the red-and-white flag of Poland was hauled to the top of the wooden flag-pole, and the strains of the Polish national anthem filled the air. It was the time of the threat of Russian invasion of Poland to quieten the ill-fated Solidarity movement and as the fraternal delegates faced the Polish flag you had to suspect, like Macbeth, that there were 'daggers in men's smiles'.

The theatrical note was maintained before each race when the starter was driven to the stalls in an open coach pulled by four magnificent white horses in the manner made famous for Western observers in film of Czechoslovakia's great jumping race, the Pardubice. It's a gimmick more recently followed by the Budweisser Clydesdales at Santa Anita, and one has to say that if Prague has the better coach, Santa Anita comes out some way ahead on the surroundings, California's backdrop of St George's Mountains being more pleasing than Prague's railway line and factories. But before anyone says 'typical Iron Curtain facelessness', just remember that the setting for Tokyo's 100,000-seater track is almost exactly the same.

Critics of the system could make much more of a meal of the four races that followed, because each was won by a horse carrying the all-red silks of Mother Russia. For however open-minded you tried to be, you would have to be an ostrich-style dolt not to notice how sparse was the applause as the Hammer and Sickle rose aloft for race after race, and to wonder how deep the wounds of 1968 run in Czechoslovakia, and how much the memory of the Soviet Union's 1956 invasion still lingers for the Hungarians. For a Britisher with most of our flag-waving a memory, there was, at the very least, a supreme irony in watching the nation which had made imperialism a dirty word, so trapped in such obvious problems of empire.

More than that, there did seem to be legitimate reason for query in the fourth Russian victory for any nation (and that includes Hungary) that had signed the 1979 Paris International Agreement on Artificial Insemination. For this race, the Cena Moskvy, was won by Gazolit, a handsome Russian three-year-old whose father died in 1975. Work that one out....Now some Einsteins among you may have cottoned on already, but back at the sunny bewilderment of the International Socialist Race Meeting it took that genial Hero of the Soviet Union, Nikolai Nasibov, to put me right.

In the Sixties, Nikolai used to ride the great Russian horse, Anilin, in such capitalist hotbeds as Cologne (Anilin won the Preis von Europa three times), Paris (fifth in the Prix de l'Arc de Triomphe) and Washington DC (second in the Laurel Park International). Nikolai trains Anilin's son, Gazolit, and he explained in glorious Pidgin: 'Veterinaire,

officials and the jockeys fully breeched and booted and wearing their country's own silk racing colours.

Apart from the sneakiest bit of absurdity in the sight of the little jockeys padding behind the white stallions, there were two slight snags to the United Nations idea. One was that there were only seven flags being marched along, the other that the Rumanian flag didn't have any jockeys with it. To their horsemen's great sadness, the Bucharest track has been closed down. There was also a good moment when some of the stallions seemed to be getting rather whinnyingly over-excited and threatened to reduce the whole thing to embarrassing farce.

But let's not carp at the parade. It was good, colourful theatre for the crowd, and was clearly explained (to all bar non-Czech speakers) over the PA system. So the stage was set. Perhaps we didn't have any of the big-deal Western nations, but there was a genuine international competition ahead designed to bring fun and enjoyment to all those gathered together.

The proceedings proper began with a 12-runner two-year-old race confined to local horses,

all of which carried unpronounceable names with the cryptic exceptions of Calvados and Boss. The turn-out didn't look too bad, although you had to be slightly pessimistic as to quality when you saw that one participant was by Royal David, an ex-English horse rated only 77 in Timeform's 1967 annual and sold for just 370 guineas.

That aperitif over, we came to the Cena Bucharest, the first of seven international events on this old and, one has to say, rather tatty racecourse at Velka Chuchle. The stands still had quite a bit of the old red-beamed Empire look, and hadn't seen the business end of a paint-brush for some time, which was perhaps excusable since the whole area had been under 6 feet of water a month before. But they were also built a disappointingly long way back from the action. The track, despite being very firm was, with its level mile-and-a-quarter circumference, a perfectly fair testing ground for the thoroughbred.

The Cena Bucharest had a total of 30,000 korunas in prize-money which stretched down to the fifth of the 10 finishers. It was won in brave style by the 20-1 Polish outsider Czempin from an East

laboratoire, frigidaire'. Anilin was kaput. Gazolit, the product of the freezer, was, to Western eyes, the first test-tube thoroughbred.

Now there are two ways to take Comrade Nasibov's news. The first is to laugh along with him, and to think that since Gazolit was clearly a racehorse (rather than, say, an antelope), and since he passed the dope test after winning his race, why shouldn't he get full credit for his exploits on the track. The second reaction is to throw up your hands in horror, and see AI as a fiendish Russian plot to end this sporting life as we know it.

The West tends to take the second view. A leading French official saw Gazolit win in Prague. Back in Paris he contacted other authorities, and it was confirmed that a horse sired by artificial insemination would not be allowed to race in Western Europe, and particularly not in Cologne, where Gazolit had been entered a month later.

In one sense, this ruling looks as rigid and archaic as the block on geldings such as the great American money-winner, John Henry, competing in top races like the Epsom Derby and the Arc de Triomphe. For both bans are put up 'in defence of

the breed', which is pretty ridiculous considering that John Henry can't breed, and that the only designs Gazolit is likely to have are behind the Iron Curtain, and then probably with a mare substitute in a Moscow laboratory.

But while the authorities look on shaky ground in not allowing the public to see the likes of John Henry, winner of the inaugural Arlington Million one week before Prague or watching Gazolit in action, and while also a long-term ban on thoroughbred AI looks difficult in view of its success with pigs, cattle and now top American trotting horses, the powers that be are sure as hell right to tread cautiously. If AI came in – and besides disease-prevention reasons for supporting it, there is in the United States an animal-protection lobby pushing it as an alternative to the 'organised rape' of the stallion barn – the whole infrastructure of the European and American breeding world would be changed at a stroke.

At present, a top stallion like Mill Reef serves about 45 mares a season in the 'natural' way at a sultan-like premium of £25,000 a time. With AI, the mares covered could in simple runaway theory

be increased to as many as a thousand, with a corresponding drop in cost but with a drastic undercutting effect on stallions in the cheaper range. And even if the numbers were limited, the prices that young unraced stock command would put horrific pressure on the honesty of the semen sample, particularly if, like Anilin, the stallion has gone to the great stud in the sky.

The Russian three-year-old, Gazolit, wins the day's most important prize in Prague, the 2,800-metres Cena Moscow (Above), and thrusts the question of artificial insemination of thoroughbreds before the public eye. It appears that Gazolit's dam, Gana, was fertilised with sperm which had been taken three years earlier from the great Anilin and kept in a freeze bank. Anilin, who died in 1975, was the best horse ever bred and raced in the Soviet Union. Ridden regularly by Gazolit's trainer Nikolai Nasibov (Left), Anilin won 21 of his 27 starts, was never beaten in the USSR, and carried the standard far and wide, winning the Preis von Europa in Cologne three years running, coming second in the Washington DC International and fifth in the Prix de l'Arc de Triomphe. But for all Gazolit's success no horse conceived by artificial insemination is allowed to run in the West and his own participation in Prague was the subject of some controversy.

Yet a lot of the European reaction is fear of the unknown, and so our leaders would do well to listen to the testimony of an American, Freddie Van Ledder, owner of the massive Castleton Farm, in Kentucky where he has 22 stallions and 250 mares, the best of the standard-bred (trotting) breed, and where all covering has been done by artificial insemination for the past five years. And don't let any thoroughbred breeders turn up a blue-blooded nose and say: 'It's all right for trotters'. Besides running a magnificent operation, Van Ledder has among his stallions the remarkable Niatross, whose 1980 winnings of one-and-a-half-million dollars topped even Spectacular Bid's record thoroughbred earnings.

It is Van Ledder's experience that with artificial insemination the incidence of disease is reduced: 'Our mares are a whole lot cleaner, and we have had no CEM [contagious equine metritis]'. But his organisation insists that all coverings are done on the farm where the semen is taken: 'We thought there was too much risk of mistakes or dishonesty if you start travelling the semen'.

Nonetheless, there are problems, as Van Ledder admits: 'Our stud practises a voluntary code limiting each stallion to 125 mares, but some people breed up to 300 to the one horse and this poses obvious threats of in-breeding. And we don't allow frozen semen. I know the Russians have done an exhaustive amount of work on this, but we weren't satisfied you could regulate it properly. As it is, we think we have the integrity thing pretty well under control. There is always a vet overseeing things, weanlings are freeze-marked, yearlings tattooed and if there are any arguments, a blood test usually resolves them'.

So food for thought for thoroughbred breeders, whose present planning already insists that any future 'AI operation' would only service the same number of mares as the present 'natural' system and would totally ban the fridge, but this still leaves Gazolit and the idea of other 'freezer' products out in the cold. 'I don't see how we can accept Gazolit's pedigree' says Charles Weatherby, British racing's head of administration. 'The Russians have given us no proof, and have sailed in the face of the main European agreement. And so, at the moment, no horse bred in this way will be accepted to race in our areas, nor would they or their progeny be allowed in our stud book'.

The problem may well get worse because one fanciful report has it that no fewer than 100 posthumous Anilin foals were born in 1981. Besides blocking much Russian participation in the international scene, this may well affect her satellite countries, who often use Russian stock but who, as in Hungary's case, are anxious to gain some foreign currency by selling abroad the produce of their flourishing breeding industry.

None of this should be taken as any reflection on Nikolai Nasibov and the rest of the Russian racing team. Nasibov made many friends when he rode in the Washington International eight times between 1958 and 1966, and with his big, pock-marked Mongolian face continually splitting into a grin, it was easy to see why, even if it was also difficult to imagine so big a man doing the weight for flat racing.

In fact, the four Russian victories that day in Prague must have represented a considerable achievement by Nasibov and his men, because Mr Zloti, their official delegate, told me that it had taken 12 days by road to reach the Czechoslovakian capital from their base in the Caucasus. They were, of course, too discreet to say so, but you would have thought the use of an empty Aeroflot to whizz them up in a few hours would not have been too much to ask.

Anyway, the Soviet monopoly was at last ended in Race 7 when two Hungarian two-year-olds battled out the finish. And then, to tremendous cheering, Race 8 brought the day's only Czechoslovak winner against foreign opposition as the local favourite Nicolas made a triumphant final racecourse appearance. This meant that only the East Germans and the Bulgarians failed to score. No great surprise to the Bulgarians who have still not built their long-promised racecourse in Sofia, but certainly a sadness to the East Germans, who have been a thoroughbred nation for over a century. And whose main track at Hoppelgarten is one of the showpieces of the Eastern Bloc.

The standard of riding could best be described as varied. Some of the jockeys, including a very dusky Bulgarian, looked fairly argricultural. But some, like Gazolit's rider, Victor Jacovlev, would not have looked out of place at Longchamp or Epsom. Victor also sported a crash helmet similar to the American Caliente type. No doubt Nasibov spotted the advantage of the Caliente during his trips abroad, and it was sad to see some of the other countries' riders wearing headgear which would hardly protect you from the wife's rolling pin, let alone a racing fall.

For instance, a Polish jockey had one of the terrible French hard-rubber *casquettes* with its elasticated chinstrap. The adjective 'terrible' is a personal choice because as vice-president of the Jockeys' Association in Britain during the Sixties, I sat on the British Standards Institution committee to develop effective head protection for British riders, and was appalled by the inadequacy of the French helmet. Its cover would not pass even the lowest of the impact standards we considered, and the elasticated chinstrap meant that the helmet could be removed by a kick from behind.

The grandstand at Prague racecourse, Velka Chuchle, is one of horse racing's great survivors. Not only has it withstood two world wars and a complete social upheaval but one month before the 1981 Socialist Countries International Meeting the whole racecourse and grounds were under five feet of flood water. Sunny weather brought dry ground and a 20,000 crowd, so that all reserved seats were taken.

Its only advantage was its lightness, something which, absurdly, was still important in France at the time because they insisted that a jockey's weight included his crash helmet. In Britain and other sane countries we had taken the view that the only important quality for a helmet should be its protective powers, and therefore a jockey should weigh without it. Even though visiting riders such as Lester Piggott insisted on using the Caliente helmet, the French continued on their stubborn way until one afternoon at Auteuil in 1976, when jockey Daniel Merle's helmet came off after a fall at the water jump, and a following horse kicked him on the skull – with fatal consequences.

You may detect a trace of bitterness about this report, but there are not many times in a life that you can be sure people are doing something as cross-eyed, and as dangerously wrong, as I was certain the French were doing about crash helmets. Six full years before Merle's death, I tried to warn the French authorities, but either I was too feeble, or they were too thick. There was no change then. There's no point in squabbling over the apportionment of blame, because nothing will alter the fact that Daniel Merle's two children were rendered fatherless on October 24, 1976, by an accident that should never have happened. So one can only hope

that the Eastern Bloc countries will now heed the Russian example, and realise that the minor economy of the cheaper, lighter helmet can be fatal as well as false.

Without carping too much about what was, in general, a thoroughly enjoyable afternoon, there were elements in the treatment of the horses – and of the racegoers – that also smacked of ignorance or false economy. For it only needs care to prevent horses getting a chafing scar all around the girth like one of the Russian winners, and if you are going to allow the racegoers to bet, and indeed to finance your operation from that function, it is surely only common sense to have some means of telling him how the betting is going.

The main argument in Prague against doing all this seemed to be lack of money, and when you looked at the drabness of the clothes, the smallness of the stands, the gimcrack state of the starting stalls and remembered how in 1977 the first Polish horses to run in England had made the long trek by road, just as the Russians had to this meeting, you realised how much we in the West take for granted. Racecourse bars and catering, closed-circuit TV, modern glass cantilevered stands, computerised betting, bookmakers' prices or Tote odds on display and jet-travel luxury for the top horses are

all considered commonplace in the West, but would be considered amazing, if not shockingly decadent, behind the Iron Curtain.

Since Western Europe has also found itself under severe economic pressure, you don't have to be a communist to wonder sometimes about the social wisdom of the ostentatious wealth that our racing often flaunts, particularly when the whole thing depends on the betting of the ordinary man in the street. The best answer is to visit somewhere like Hungary (as we did after Czecholovakia), and see what a burden the punter has to bear even in that reasonably successful economy. The 30 per cent betting deduction from the Tote doesn't just have to subsidise prize-money and racecourse improvements, it has to pay the keep of all the racehorses, studs, trainers, jockeys and lads.

Those of us who keep saying that Governments should keep their hands off racing, might like to note that in Hungary, as in many socialist countries, there is little direct Government interference. But how would we manage if our authorities had to shoulder such a massive responsibility? Maybe not as well as Hungary's Director-General, Dr Feheer, who in this odyssey round the racing globe must rank as one of the outstanding personalities in any country.

With his dark blue blazer, light grey slacks and urbane, arm-taking charm, Dr Feheer looked as likely an apparition in the peeling dullness of our Prague hotel as Lenin in the London Hilton. Not that there was anything pointed about the hospitality (even the Russian delegation was holed up in our hostelry), it's just that on a scale of one to 10 this dump scored about one-and-a-half. It didn't leak, there was food and drink and there weren't any bugs (not, anyway, of the creepy-crawly kind), but that was about where the good things ended. No lifts, no bath, one loo per landing and little choice of menu. Perhaps we were just capitalist softies, but I'll bet you the whole of Czechoslovakia to a Chinese takeaway that no Iron Curtain delegate would be seen dead in such a spot on our side of the River Elbe.

The trick, it seems, is not to notice it, but to try and play it rather differently when you get back home. That certainly appeared to be the Feheer method, although no one should underestimate what Hungary has had to go through in the 100 years or so which separate today from the golden times of the 1870s, when the Hungarian-born Kisber won the 1876 Epsom Derby, and their immortal mare, Kincsem, won all her 54 races. She triumphed in such distant spots as Hanover, Baden Baden, Deauville and Goodwood, where she took the Cup in 1878. As in the rest of Eastern Europe, this stock had been taken from British lines in the mid-19th century, but the cream was lost in the First World War, and 95 per cent of it in the Second.

There was also the revolution of 1956, and the social and economic rigidity which followed, none of which was likely to produce the bloodstock

investment that top flat racing needs, or even the affluent punters which are its bread and butter. Yet in Dr Feheer's 10 years, the betting turnover has doubled on what has become a 1,000 races-a-year operation, and you didn't have to travel far around the country to be reminded that the Magyars first ran an empire from Hungary over 1,000 years ago. And on these Eastern plains you only did that by having horsemanship high in the blood.

An hour-and-a-half's drive through the maize and sunflower fields west of Budapest, you reach the ancient city of Tatabanya, with its lake, its fine cathedral and its magnificent walled-and-moated 11th-century castle. It was here that the great family Esterhazy held sway before the lights started going out all over Europe, having such a leading thoroughbred stud and racing stable that they even brought men over from England to give them a touch of Newmarket.

Such patrician eccentricities are, of course, only history in this brave new socialist world, but if you travel a little way south of the city you reach the Diospusztai Menes, one of the five thoroughbred state farms, and since this is the home of champion sire Jolly Jet, who reached Tatabanya by way of top stables in America, Ireland and England, you wonder whether maybe the horses

are the aristocrats now. Certainly there seemed little extra that Jolly Jet could ask by way of treatment, and you could even argue that he had a better deal than his counterparts in the West. In order to combat disease, the Hungarians don't shunt the mares to and from the stallions' court, but put the stallion to all available mares on the stud, and then move him on after a couple of years. At least he gets a change of air, if not of occupation.

There were two other stallions to argue the toss over the 68 mares in the stud; the mating decisions for them, and for the other 500-odd brood mares in the country, being taken by a central committee of the racing authority. Before somebody produces the old joke that a horse made by committee was supposed to be The Definition of a Camel, we might as well face the fact that 400 matings is only a few more than those that have to be planned by the Sangster or Aga Khan empires and, in one sense at least, having all the stock of one stallion in one place does gives you an advantage. Instead of relying on wishful-thinking word of mouth as to how you think the progeny will shape up, you can see for yourself. There, at feeding time, were eight Jolly Jet colt foals haltered up in a line to take their evening feed from the manger before going out for the night. It was a good place to make a collective

judgment, and on that look Jolly Jet should be able to gain further honours on the sires' list, which he topped in 1980 with 16 winners of 32 races worth over a million forints.

But if the Hungarian system had its advantages in assessing young stock, it did seem to be taking the community spirit a bit far in the paddocks. In the first one we saw, there were no fewer than 28 yearlings. OK, so we know about the herd principle, but this was ridiculous. Still, take as you find, and the horses didn't look wormy or flea-bitten. And they seemed perfectly adapted to a single steel pipe, running three feet from the ground which fenced them in. 'Ah yes, they are the same thing as is mass-produced for water pipes', said Zoltan Prutkay, the young stud manager. 'The horses respect them, and the maintenance is far

The training centre at Alag, 30 kilometres from Budapest, was created in the early days of the century by Anglophile Hungarian aristocrats. Newmarket was their original inspiration but the leafy woodland rides and extensive sand gallops, where half of Hungary's 500 active racehorses are training, tend to be more reminiscent of Chantilly. Yet the traditions handed down are of British origin and the names in the local graveyard those like Wainwright, Reiff and Hesp. It was the former stable lad Robert Hesp who trained the immortal Kincsem to all her 54 successes.

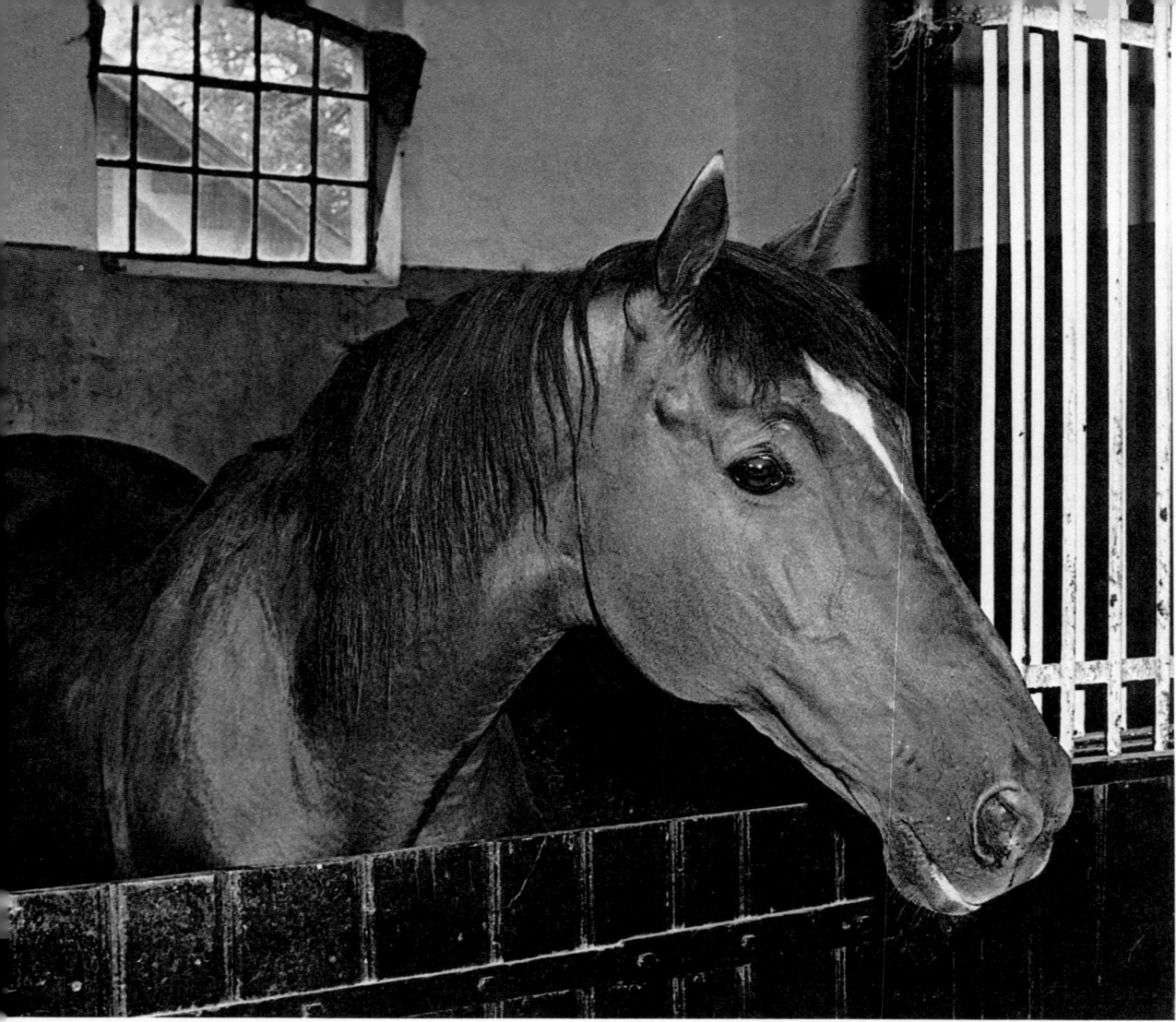

track, which is in Budapest and is called, as you might expect, Kincsem Park. It was during those self-confident days of the Austro-Hungarian Empire that Alag was conceived and finally built at the turn of the century. A reconnaissance was done at Newmarket, and many English jockeys and stable staff were recruited. Some of their descendants live on, and a sentimental journey out to the thorn trees and whispy grass of the Alag graveyard revealed names like Wainwright, Hesp and Reiff pushing up the Hungarian daisies. But many more must have been taken away on the two great war tides that have swept across Europe this century. Considering that, and the social revolution that followed the second war, the most remarkable thing about Alag is that it is there.

Having made that allowance, I have to report that Alag is no great advert for Communism as a racing man's perfect system. The initial planning was impressive. Ten separate trainers, each with his own barn laid out in a semi-circle round a trainer's bungalow like the one in which we had taken that so-necessary draught of schnapps in the early morning. There were plentiful sandtracks, Chantilly style, through the nearby woods, and out on the heathery grassland there was a mile-and-a-quarter turf gallop, as well as numerous jumps for steeplechasing, which is now almost defunct. But the whole place looked as if it hadn't had any money spent on it since the assassination at Sarajevo, and this observer was astounded to hear one of the gnarled old veterans with which the

better than wooden fencing'. Purists may choke, but seeing is believing.

For all his egalitarian friendliness, and simple three-room lifestyle, it was clear that Prutkay was as much a part of the pre-Communist legacy as the big, high-gabled barns that are so cool in summer, and so snug in winter. For Prutkay's grandfather had been married at Tatabanya Cathedral, his father was one of Hungary's leading riding masters, his brother was Dr Feheer's efficient assistant and Zoltan himself had represented Hungary in the European Junior Show Jumping Championships at Coventry in 1970. Through an interpreter, he spoke of the usual problems of fertility, of crop rotation (the same farm also has a big livestock side), and of the difficulty of getting staff who stay.

Prutkay also talked of the riding horses, which he manages to exercise in his few spare hours and which seem to be a major perk in any student or worker's day. For with no great export market, and very little jump racing, to absorb the unsuccessful flat-racer, there is clearly a reservoir of thoroughbreds to be retrained as riding horses if you have the stable room. A big stud built in the age of the horse will always have space, so, tucked away from the breeding stock in another barn, were up to 12 thoroughbreds and other riding horses which Zoltan and his men train in their nearby menage, and take round the local jumping shows

in the summer. Swallowing a glass of homemade schnapps in Prutkay's neat little sitting room, with its antique walnut dresser, elegant chairs and 1920s portrait of his father, you were struck by the old Magyar pride living through. There was no overt quarrel with the present system. In fact, there was clearly a desire to do his best for it and within it. But was there not a touch of wistful irony in the set of little 19th-century equestrian line drawings on the far wall? Their title was, 'La Vie d'un Gentleman de Tous Saisons'.

It was schnapps again with Zoltan's elder brother, Janos, as early as eight next morning. We were in the main reception lounge at the Alag training centre 30 kilometres from Budapest, a big, panelled hall still looking like the hunting lodge it was obviously modelled on at the turn of the century, antlers facing old hunting and racing prints on the walls. After the schnapps, the talk was of Kincsem and the great horses of the past, and with one of the diplomats who use Alag as a riding club coming in booted and spurred, the feeling that the equestrian torch has been passed intact down the years was irresistible.

Outside, where half Hungary's 500 active racehorses are trained, there was the same feeling, but you appreciated quite clearly the problems Alag must have had along the way. The other half of the racing stock is trained on Hungary's one race

place abounds say that he had visited Lambourn only the year before, and been most unimpressed. If you know the Berkshire training centre's sand, peat-moss, all-weather and marvellous natural downland gallops, and have also seen what Alag has to offer, you have to think that his eyes were not too open. Perhaps it was the schnapps.

But who are we to scoff? The Hungarians are hanging on to, and may soon considerably improve, a fine racing tradition under circumstances that our racing professionals could hardly contemplate. In 1980 Henbit took home £166,820 as the winner's purse from the Epsom Derby, while Arena, Hungary's top three-year-old, collected the equivalent of just over £6,000 for winning the Magyar Derby. As for personnel, remember that in Hungary trainer and jockey receive only five per cent of prize-money, half the traditional cut in Britain. So the disparity between the 1980 champion trainers is solar systems wide. Dick Hern's horses won 65 races and £831,964 to head the British list while Hazi Lazlo's team won 34 races and 1,093,200 forints, which represents only about £24,600, as champion Hungarian trainer.

Faced with such meagre rewards throughout the socialist countries, and with the need to re-invest in both bloodstock and buildings, most British trainers and officials would simply commit hara-kiri on a pitchfork. But that's not the way they look at it in Budapest. Wishful thinking, which we are so good at in Britain, finds no forints, and the achievements over the past few years should gain admiration in the lusher corners of the racing globe. Besides Jolly Jet, they have bought the brave front-running Tacitus, and the St Leger winner, Peleid, as sires from Britain. Off-course betting has been introduced–17 'shops' in Budapest alone–and there are plans to rebuild the stands at Kincsem Park.

The mastermind behind all this is, of course, the remarkable Dr Feheer, author, vet, and very high in the handicap when it comes to leaders of men. 'We already have the money,' he says of the Kincsem rebuilding project, 'but it will just take some time to get it through the official channels.' There's an opening of the palms, the hint of a shrug, but Dr Feheer doesn't win his battles by banging the table. Steeliness of purpose perhaps, but also real charm, deep affection for his racing family, and best of all, a belief that what he is doing for racing is to bring the greatest good for the greatest number. One immediate impression is that he is wasted in Hungary. But then you think of the great tradition he follows, of the size of his task, of his biography of Kincsem, and you know he is in the right place.

Already Hungary is showing that horse racing and the socialist system are not totally incompatible. It can make great progress if the country's economy continues to improve, but without heavy investment in the top Western bloodlines, it is hard to see how we can forget the heavy symbolism of the picture that hangs in pride of place on the weighing-room wall in Budapest. It is the family tree of Kincsem, the immortal mare who went through five countries and 54 races unbeaten. It shows her successful descendants across the continent. The last of them was back in the Sixties. It's going to be very difficult to see another Kincsem come.

Hungary's only racecourse, in Budapest, dates from the last century and is named, inevitably, after the great mare Kincsem (Bottom Left), one of the outstanding horses of all time. Foaled in Hungary in 1874, by the British-bred Cambuscan, Kincsem won all her 54 races over four seasons, travelling as far afield as Baden-Baden, Deauville, Goodwood and Hanover. Two world wars, however, have wrought havoc with Kincsem's descendants. Even if the old racecourse buildings are still intact, new blood is clearly needed. An example of that is the stallion Jolly Jet (Top Left), who now stands at the Diospusztai Menes, near Tatabanya, and who has a travelling record which Kincsem would appreciate. Born in America in 1963, Jolly Jet was one of the leaders of his generation before moving to Vincent O'Brien's stables in Ireland and then on to race and stand at stud in England. In 1975 he was exported to Hungary and topped the list in 1980. Now, because of Hungary's anti-infection principle of keeping mares in one place and moving the stallion only every three years, he can contemplate a whole barnful of his progeny (Above).

10
SOUTH AFRICA

'In a 52-year training career George Azzie won almost everything South Africa had to offer. He also left two other major marks on racing history by introducing Charles Engelhard to the sport and training that owner's legendary Hawaii; the horse later became Grass Horse of the Year in America and finished second in the 1969 Washington International'.

(Preceding Spread) Gold of many kinds is in evidence as runners race towards the finish at Gosforth Park, Germiston, 10 miles east of Johannesburg; the track is right beside the Simmer and Jack goldmine tower visible in the distance. Each year 30 meetings are held on the 10½-furlong circuit, where crowds can be anywhere between 15,000 and 22,000. Over R3¼ million are bet per day on the Totalisator, both on and off the course, as well as another R1¾ million with the on-course bookmakers.

(Top Left). In a 52-year training career the late George Azzie won almost everything South Africa had to offer. He also left two other major marks on racing history by introducing Charles Engelhard to the sport and training that owner's legendary Hawaii; the horse later became Grass Horse of the Year in America and finished second in the 1969 Washington International. Born in the coastal town of East London, George Azzie saddled his first-ever runner, Jack Sprat, to victory in 1922 and, before he retired in 1972, he had won over 3,000 more races, including the July Handicap, and South Africa's richest race, the Holiday Inns, on no fewer than six occasions. After his retirement, Azzie handed his famous establishment, some 15 miles from Johannesburg, to his son Herbie. Sadly, the young Azzie died in 1981, soon after his father's death. Now the Azzie banner is carried by George's grandson, Michael, who holds the licence.

(Middle Left). Before he sold out in 1981, Godfrey Gird had built up Maine Chance Farm into one of the biggest operations in South Africa with 100 mares and five stallions, including the list leader, Jungle Cove. Originally involved with American saddle horses he first started in the Wittehart Stud in the Beaufort West area of Cape Province and moved in 1969 to what was to become the Maine Chance Farm in the Robertson area. The farm's name was not adopted until the coal magnate, Graeme Beck, joined Gird in 1977. Beck continues Maine Chance's successful operation.

(Top Right). Turffontein racecourse is just three miles from the centre of Johannesburg, and only 100 yards from the now disused Robertson Deep goldmine. With a circumference of over 13 furlongs and a 45 foot climb into the straight, the runners know at the finish that they have been on the country's most demanding track. It is the home of South Africa's richest races, the 10-furlong, R250,000 Holiday Inns, and the 12-furlong, R100,000 South African Derby.

(Bottom Left). The son of a famous trainer, Herman Brown has risen to the heights of his profession himself. In 1979 he headed the South African list and his many successes encompass practically every big race, including numerous Queen's Plates.

(Bottom Row, Second Picture). Born in 1954, Michael Roberts was nicknamed 'Muis' (mouse) because of his diminutive size. But once embarked on his chosen career he soon built a giant-size reputation. In his 13 seasons up to 1982 he had been champion no less than 11 times. He seems set for many years to come.

(Bottom Row, Third Picture). Punters battle with the bookmakers' line at one of the 30 meetings held at Turffontein during the year. The course attracts up to 20,000 a day. Almost R4 million is bet each time with the bookies and the Tote, and off-course interest is even wider: up to R5 million can be placed with the Tote on a single meeting.

(Bottom Row, Fourth Picture). Jockeys leave the stalls at Newmarket, South Africa. Some 15 miles south of Johannesburg and 7,000 from its English racing namesake, Newmarket was started in 1938. It holds 32 meetings a year, contributing its part to what appears to be one of South Africa's most thriving industries.

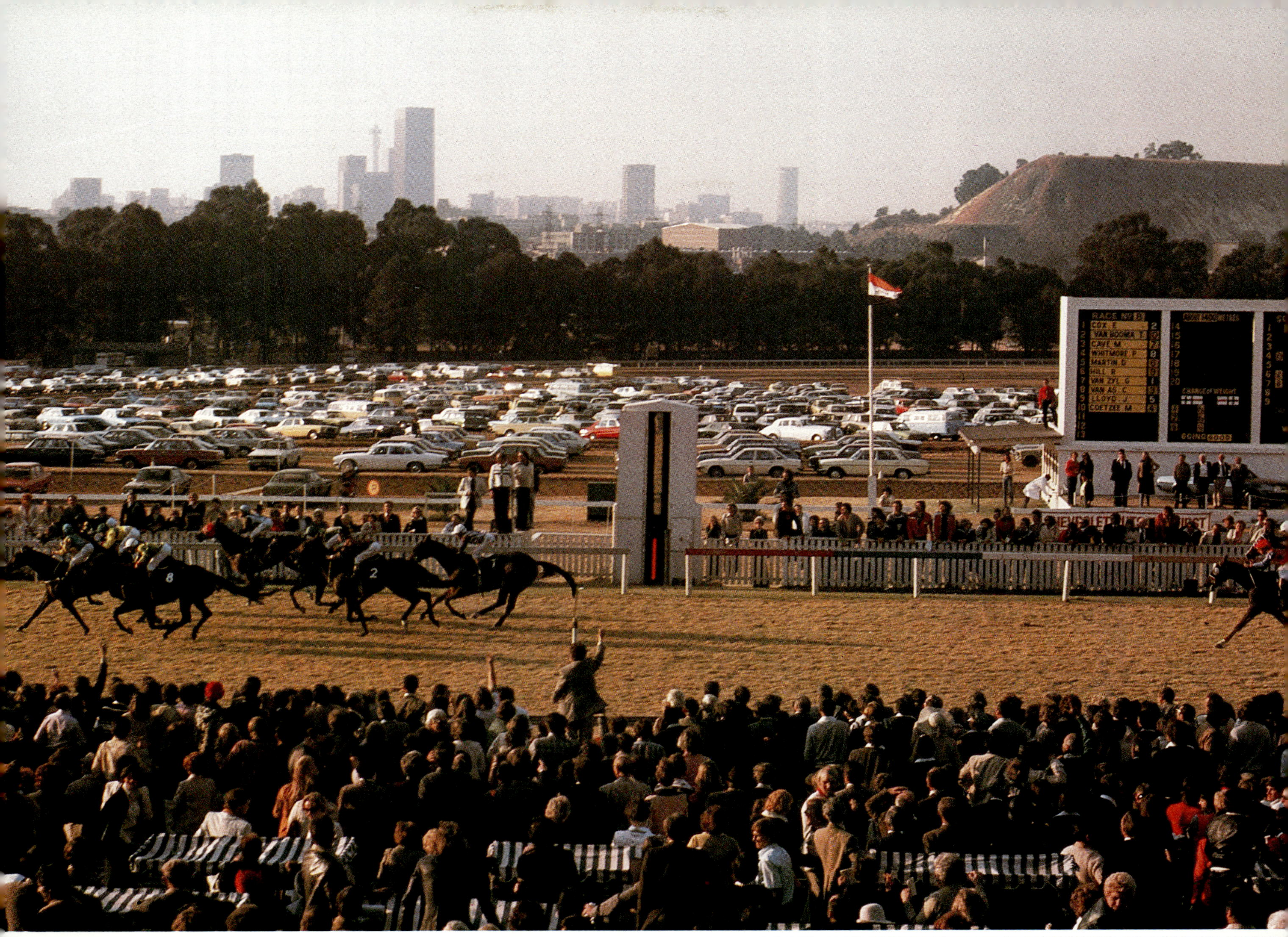
RACE No
COX E
VAN BOOMA T
CAVE M
WHITMORE P
MARTIN D
HILL R
VAN ZYL G
VAN AS C
LLOYD J
COETZEE M
CHANGE of WEIGHT
GOING

5
6
7
8
9
10
11
12
13
14

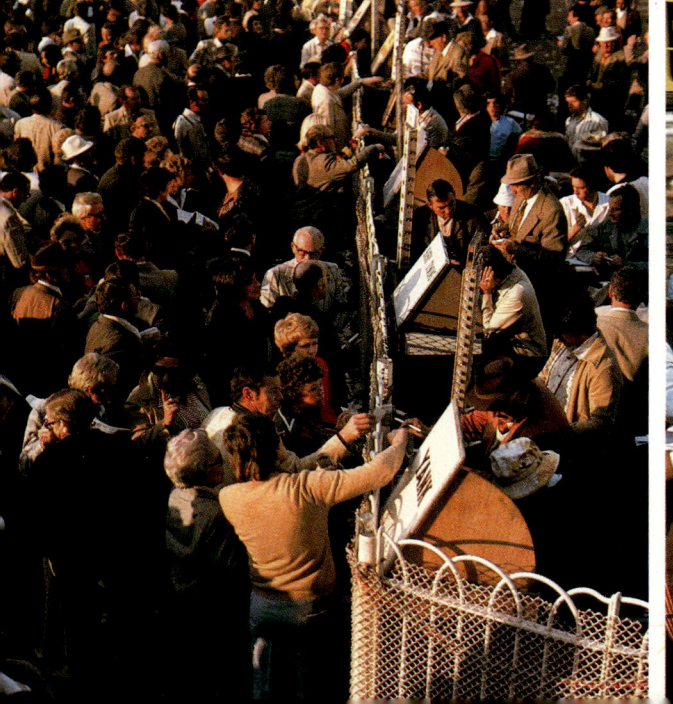

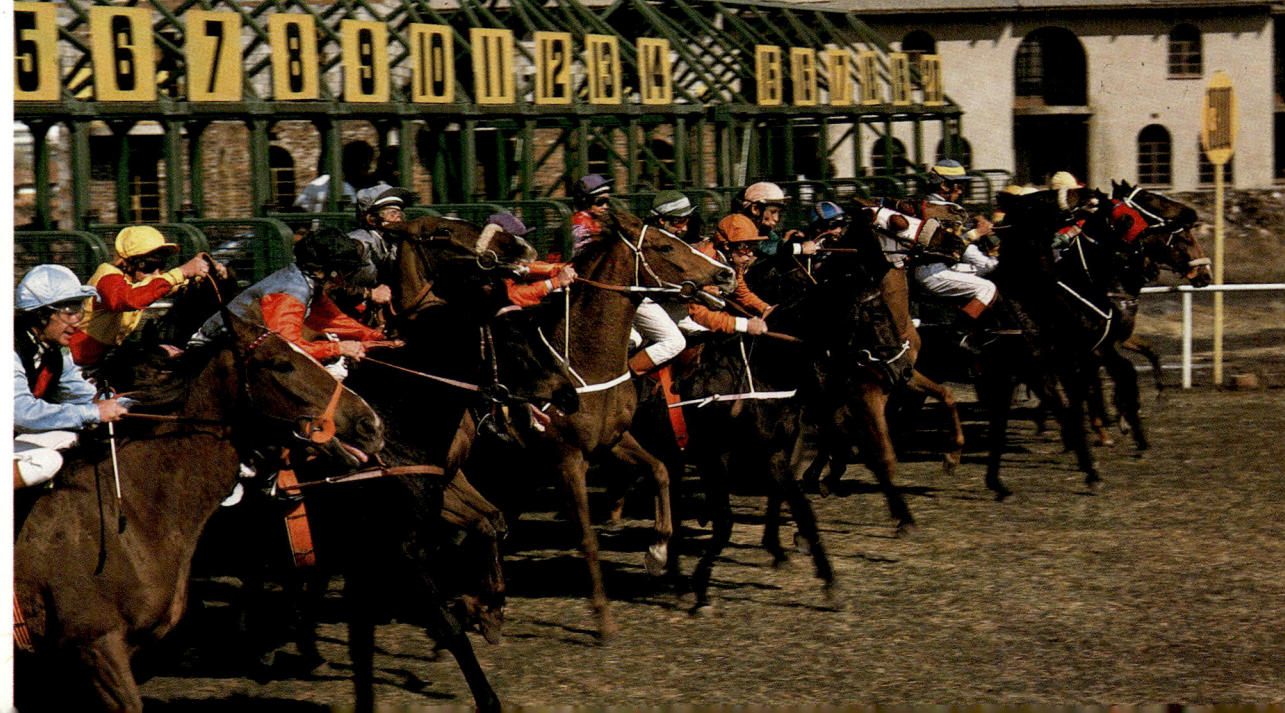

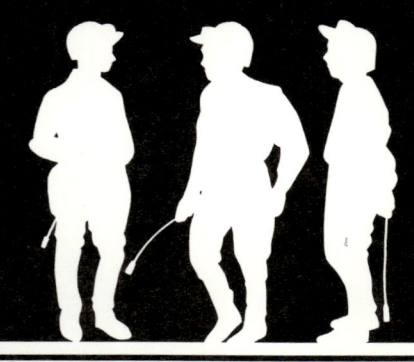

A WORLD OF
STRIVING

(Preceding Spread) To make them run. This stretch drive by Angel Cordero symbolises everything a jockey has been trying to do since the first starter called the roll; 112 lbs of man goading to maximum effort half a ton of the fastest weight-carrying creature the world has ever seen. But while the principle remains the same the world over, different racing territories develop varying racing techniques. Blinkers are much more common, as here, on the USA's dirt tracks than the grass tracks of Europe. Moreover, Cordero crouches very high up the neck, with the reins as short to the horse's mouth as possible, the whip in the vertical 'carry' and only the toe of his foot in the stirrup iron. In this fashion Cordero, born in Puerto Rico, has won over 4,000 races, including five in a single day in New York on eight separate occasions. He is now third only to Bill Shoemaker and Laffit Pincay in career earnings, which exceed $60 million. Cordero represents the American style to perfection and it should be compared with the European as represented by Piggott, Head and St. Martin.

The hand ride. Three champions, Lester Piggott (Top), eleven times top rider in Britain, and the French pair, Yves St. Martin (Middle) and Freddie Head (Bottom) depict the pros and cons of the latest refinements of the jockeys' craft in Europe. Although St. Martin approaches Cordero's streamlining (Opening Spread), the European style is usually more upright and can lead to moments (witness Freddie Head) of obvious excess. Europe's wide open grass tracks, plus the slower pace, demand however that a jockey is able to take a horse in hand early in a race. 'Drawing the bow' in this way requires all three riders to have their feet firmly 'home' in the stirrup irons. Piggott is a symbol of purposeful dominance, two athletes blended, the weight balanced over the mount's shoulder where a horse carries it easiest. But compare the shortness of the leathers of the three Europeans and Cordero with those of the leading Australians and you realise how far along the road from the old days of 'kicking them along' jockeys have come.

(**1**) *Willie Carson. Born Stirling, Scotland 1942. Four times English champion, winner of six Classics, including the Epsom Derby twice and the Oaks and the St. Leger in the Queen's colours (as in picture).*

(**2**) *Angel Cordero Junior. Born Santurce, Puerto Rico, 1942, son of Angel Cordero Snr. Won the 100th running of the Kentucky Derby on Cannonade. Lives Long Island.*

(**3**) *Yves St. Martin. Born Agen, France, 1941. Fourteen times French champion and winner of the Arc de Triomphe on Sassafras, Allez France and Akiyada, the latter in the colours of the Aga Khan, for whom he is now retained at Chantilly.*

(**4**) *Walter Swinburn. Born 1960, first winner 1978. Won Epsom Derby and King George VI and Queen Elizabeth Stakes on Shergar in 1981, during his first year out of apprenticeship.*

(**5**) *Steve Cauthen. Born Kentucky, 1960. Rode first winner in 1976 and 487 races and a record $6 million dollars in 1977. Won the American Triple Crown on Affirmed in 1978. Won the 2000 Guineas in 1979, within two months of moving to England where he rode over 100 winners in the 1982 season.*

(**6**) *Greville Starkey. Born 1939. First winner in 1955. Won four Classics and nine Group 1 races in 1978, including the English Derby and Irish Derby with Shirley Heights. Starkey also won the 1975 Arc de Triomphe on Star Appeal.*

(**7**) *Jorge Velasquez. Born Chepo, Panama, 1946. Six times champion of New York, leading US rider in 1967 with 438 winners. Has won the Man O'War five times, the United Nations four times, and the 1982 Kentucky Derby. Fourth rider in history to win more than $50 million. Lives in New York.*

(**8**) *Joe Mercer. Born Yorkshire, 1934. Won the 1953 Oaks on Ambiguity while still an apprentice. Has since won every other English Classic bar the Derby. Associated with all Brigadier Gerard's 17 successes and was champion jockey in 1979.*

(**9**) *Laffit Pincay. Born Panama City, 1946. Pincay has won over 5,000 races and more than $60 million, second only to Shoemaker in all-time prize money won. In 1979 he became the first man to ride winners to over $8 million in prize money in single season. Based in California.*

(**10**) *Phillippe Paquet. Born France, 1953. Apprenticed to Francois Boutin in Chantilly, he became French champion in 1979, although his trips to Britain for Boutin were dogged by ill luck. Won the 1976 Eclipse Stakes on Trepan (subsequently disqualified for failing dope test) and the 1980 2000 Guineas on Nureyev (subsequently disqualified for mid-race infringement). Moved to Hong Kong in 1981.*

(**11**) *Pat Eddery. Born 1952. Seen talking to Auriol Sinclair, one of the first successful women trainers after the Jockey Club finally allowed women to take out a training licence in 1966. Eddery has won the English Derby with Grundy and Golden Fleece, the Arc de Triomphe with Detroit, and been English champion four times.*

1	2	3	4	5
6		7	11	
8	9	10		

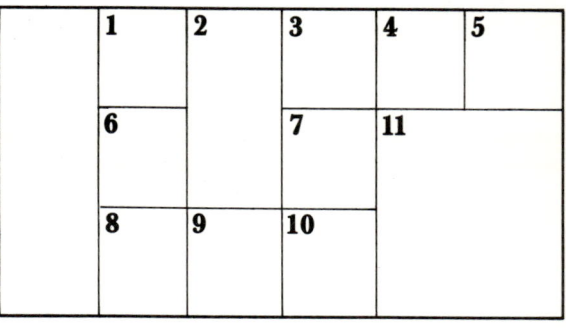

Two faces that have seen it all. Bill Shoemaker (Left) and Lester Piggott (Right), each a special genius on his side of the Atlantic. Different shapes, sizes, methods and background but both relying finally on a gift for making a racehorse race. Shoemaker, born in Fabens, Texas, in 1931, four years before Piggott's birth in Berkshire, England, didn't ride a horse till he was a teenager, nor a winner until he was 18. Piggott, from a long line of jockeys, rode his first winner when 12 years old. Shoemaker, only 4ft 11in. and 100 lbs, clamps very close to his horse. Piggott, 5ft 7in. and 117 lbs, is bent up, like a hair pin above the saddle. Shoemaker has won a record 8,000 races, including five Belmonts and seven Hollywood Gold Cups, and has been associated with such legends as Gallant Man, Damascus, Forego and Spectacular Bid. Piggott has won 4,000 races, 25 English Classics, including the Epsom Derby nine times. He has been aboard Crepello, Sir Ivor, Alleged and Nijinsky. Different wines perhaps and even better with age and at their best on the great occasions.

The most famous, and controversial, whipping action in the world is captured (Far Right) as Lester Piggott, on the left, just fails to drive Lady Pavlova past Trillionaire at the end of the 1978 Princess Royal Stakes at Ascot. Orthodox observation might conclude that Piggott rides too short to give his mounts any body assistance and that he appears to hit them too hard, thus affecting their balance. Yet he is supremely successful. As he brings his whip forward he also keeps a tight hold on the reins in order to keep Lady Pavlova away from Trillionaire. The hit he delivers will, moreover be backhanded, far back on the quarters, where the horse's impetus comes from, and his balance will be kept. Piggott in full blitz is no sight for the squeamish but in his later years he has rarely hit a horse unable to respond. In that sense he is the horse's and punter's best friend. He has helped them to run and to win.

However skilful the man employed, whatever the horse involved, everybody in racing knows that you cannot bank on a win until jockey and horse are past the post together. What happened to Geoff Baxter in 1982 at Epsom while riding I'll See You is an example. About to sprint away and win the Abbots Hill Handicap Stakes, run on Oaks Day, Baxter's saddle slipped. Instead of savouring victory he had to suffer a spectacular fall. A doughty jockey, born in 1946, Baxter survived well enough to walk in, be met by the horse's trainer Clive Brittain, and ride in the very next race. In that he finished 9th in a 10-horse field.

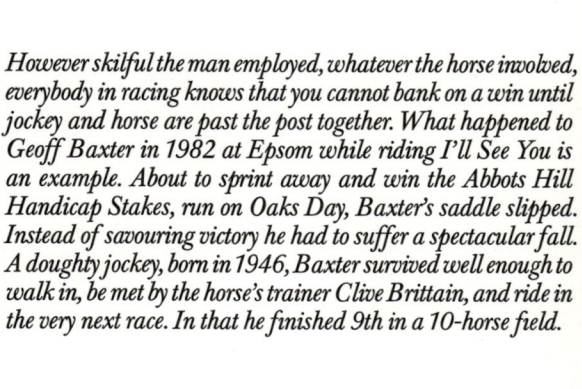

11
JAPAN

'We had been warned of the multi-billion-yen operation involved in Japanese betting, but after we had driven past the Emperor's Palace on a brilliantly crisp sunny morning, and seen the predictable string of Japanese joggers, we were still astonished by the huge yellow building with orange towers which looked for all the world like an indoor skating rink rather than the biggest single off-course betting operation any gambler has ever seen'.

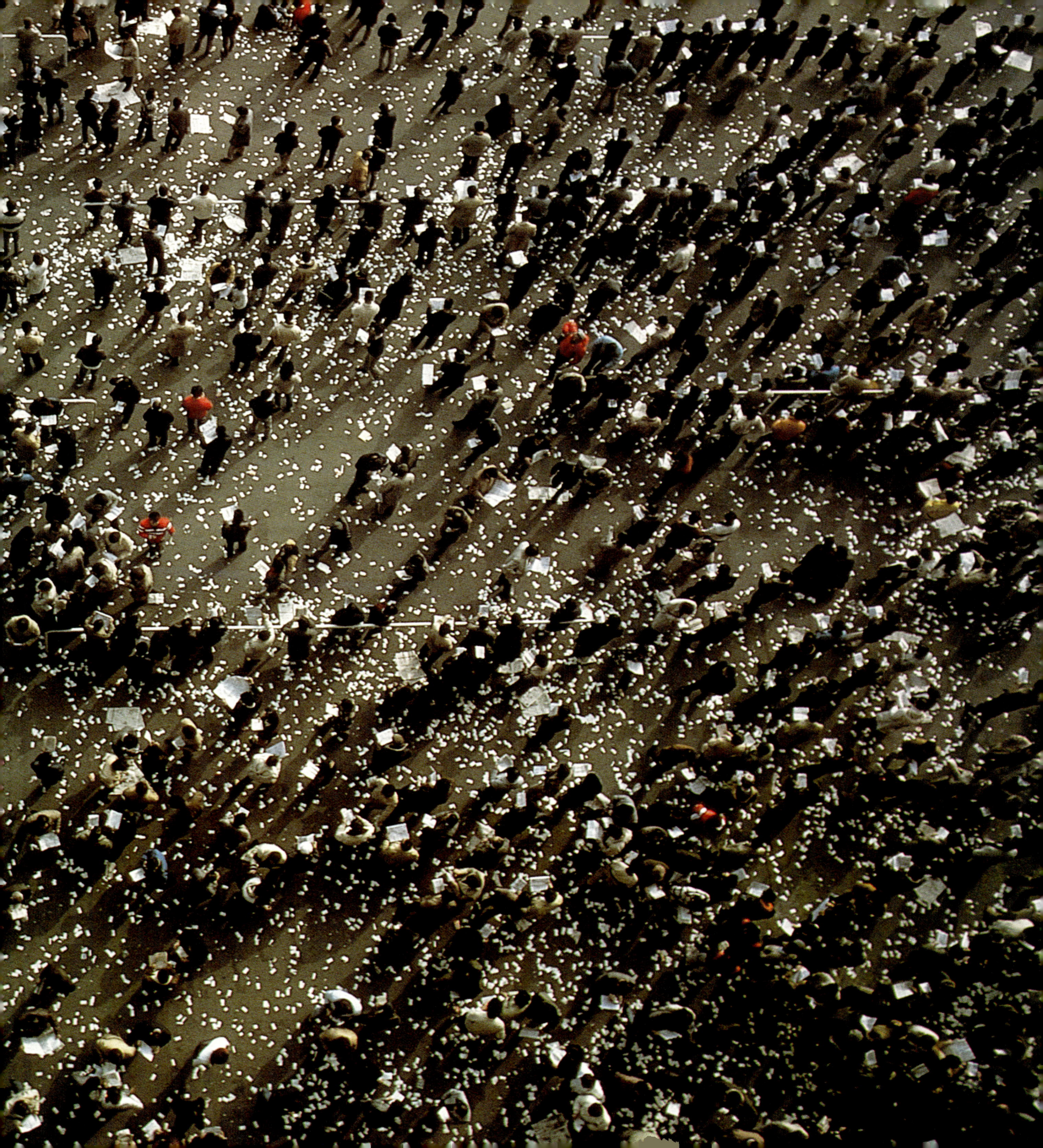

AS ONE or two people in the British automobile industry have discovered, when the Japanese apply their devastating logic to a problem it can be difficult to compete. Try a day at the races in Tokyo, as Gerry Cranham and I did in February 1980, and it's sayonara to any cosy assumptions about the sport of kings.

The first to go is the idea that you need to race six days a week to keep up public interest and betting turnover. In Japan, the government doesn't really approve of racing, permits it only on Saturday and Sunday, and forbids all other forms of gambling. Yet on the day we were there, 100,000 people at Tokyo racecourse bet 4,000 million yen (£8 million) which, with a further 6,000 million yen (£12 million), meant that in one day they had staked a 10th of Britain's annual total.

Granted only two opportunities a week, why, ask the Japanese, wait until the day is half over before beginning? On our Sunday, they started at 10am, held five races, took an hour's break for lunch, and then held six more. And given that punters then become so keen that there are capacity crowds at the main courses, why not open betting shops to allow participation from the outside? And why confine these outlets to dingy, dirty-windowed, smoke-filled parlours, British style? The Japanese Racing Association, which controls the sport under government mandate, has just 17 shops open at a weekend, but they are beyond a British bookie's dream.

We went to the biggest, Korakuen, on our first morning in Tokyo, and thank heaven for a good night's sleep, or the mind would have boggled itself to pieces. We had been warned of the multi-billion-yen operation involved in Japanese betting, but after we had driven past the Emperor's Palace on a brilliantly crisp sunny morning, and seen the predictable string of Japanese joggers, we were still astonished by the huge yellow building with orange towers which looked for all the world like an indoor skating rink rather than the biggest single off-course betting operation any gambler has ever seen.

The joke is that a skating rink is precisely what it is, but only on the top storey of the first of the three buildings used by the JRA, which has 13 separate betting floors, 19 escalators, more than

(Preceding Spread). A quiet day at the Tokyo racecourse. Every Sunday some 100,000 spectators turn up. Today there are a mere 50,000. Within an hour of the end of racing the torn-up tickets and discarded tipping sheets, littering the ground like confetti, will have been vacuum-cleaned away.

Time: 11.30am. It's Saturday in Tokyo. The world's biggest betting shop, with an exterior redolent of a cinema in Hollywood's halcyon days, is in full swing. It can accommodate 40,000 enthusiasts on five floors and cope with countless telephone bets from outside. Some are dealt with by operators like the young woman (Centre Far Right), a student doing a six-hour shift, others by an automatic betting system. 'Hai, thank you for your bet', the answer phone says when your transaction has been recorded and repeated back to you. Security is handled using remote-control cameras and on-the-spot betting transactions with sweet diplomacy by lines of ladies whom the microchip has not seduced: they use an abacus for their calculations. As a bettor you may, typically, guard against the Tokyo smog with a mask (Top Far Right) but one way or another, once you are hooked, there seems little defence against the lure of the easy yen.

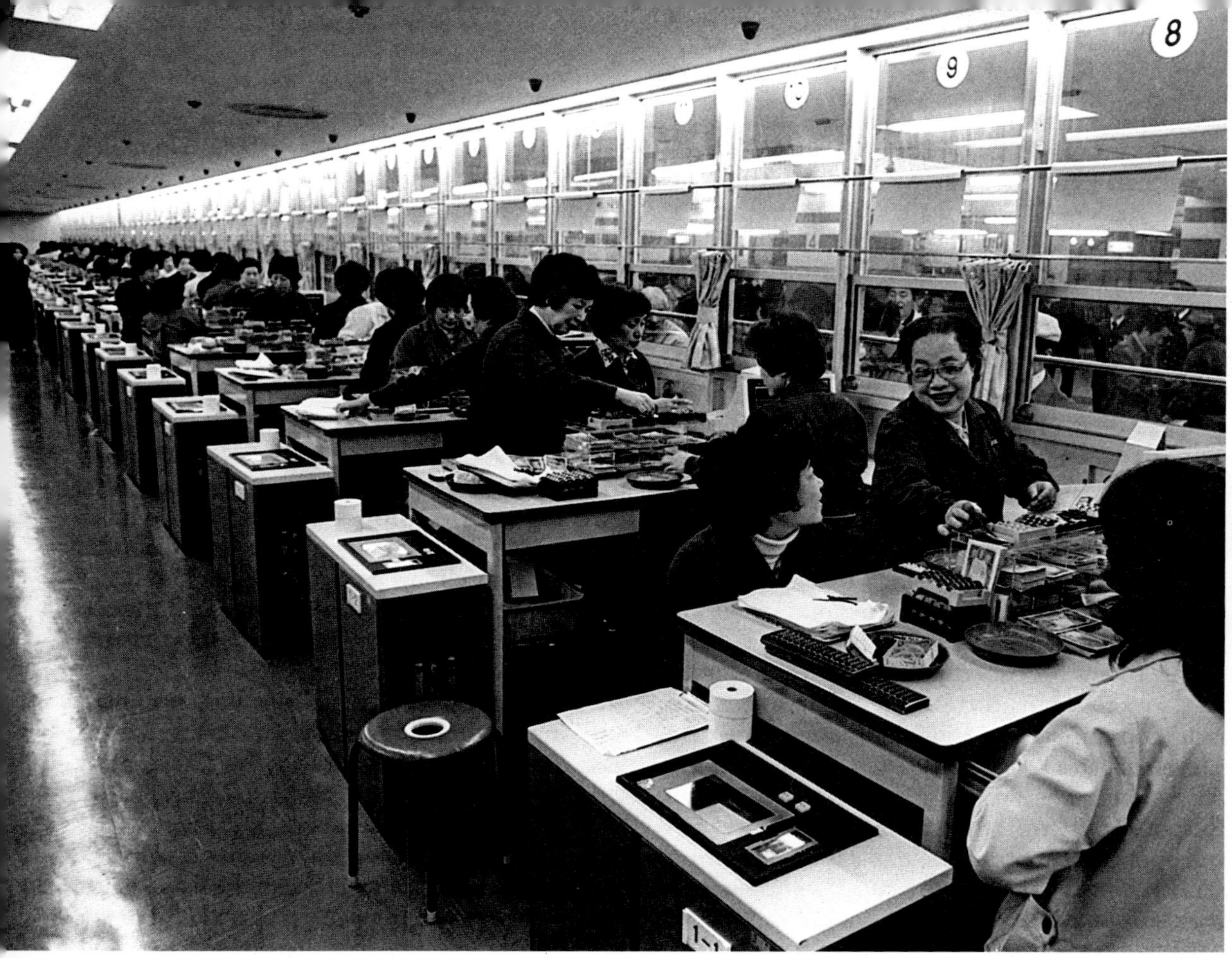
8
9

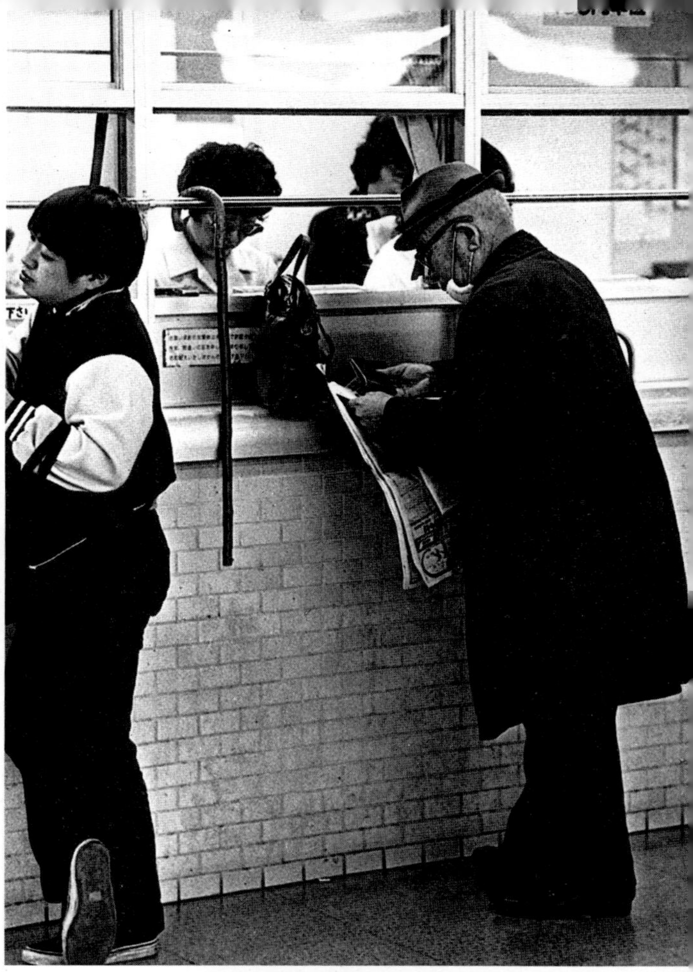

63
64
65
66
67
68
複合投票券
連勝式

B館
3F北
4F北
2F北

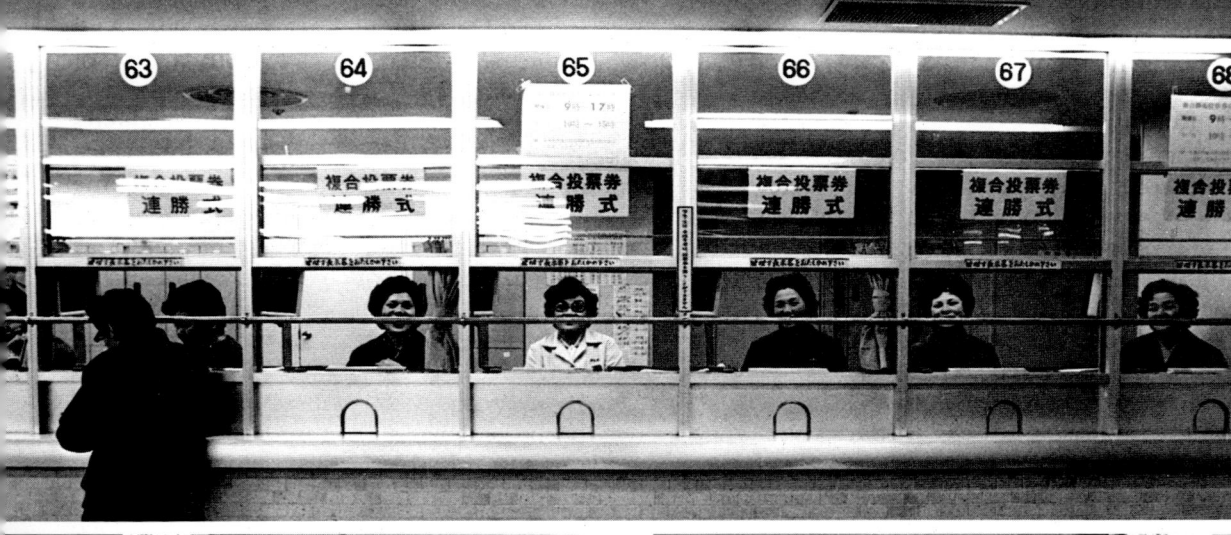

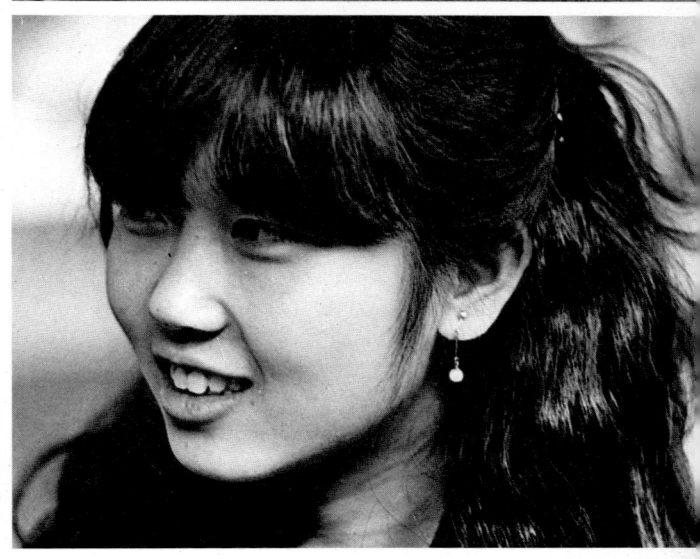

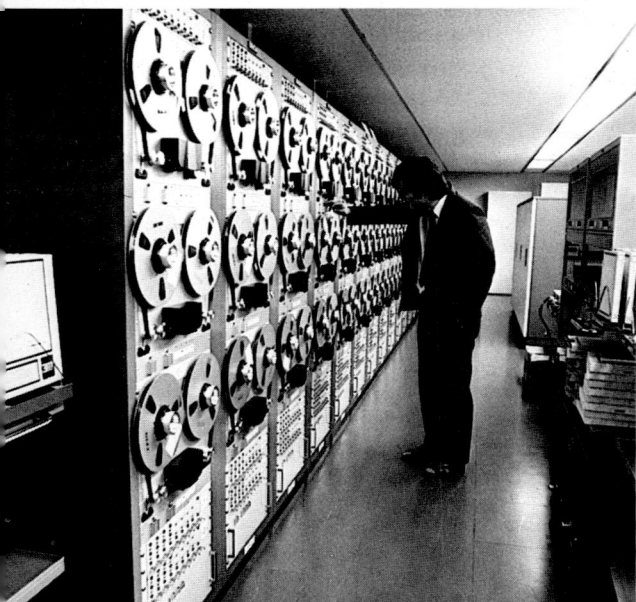

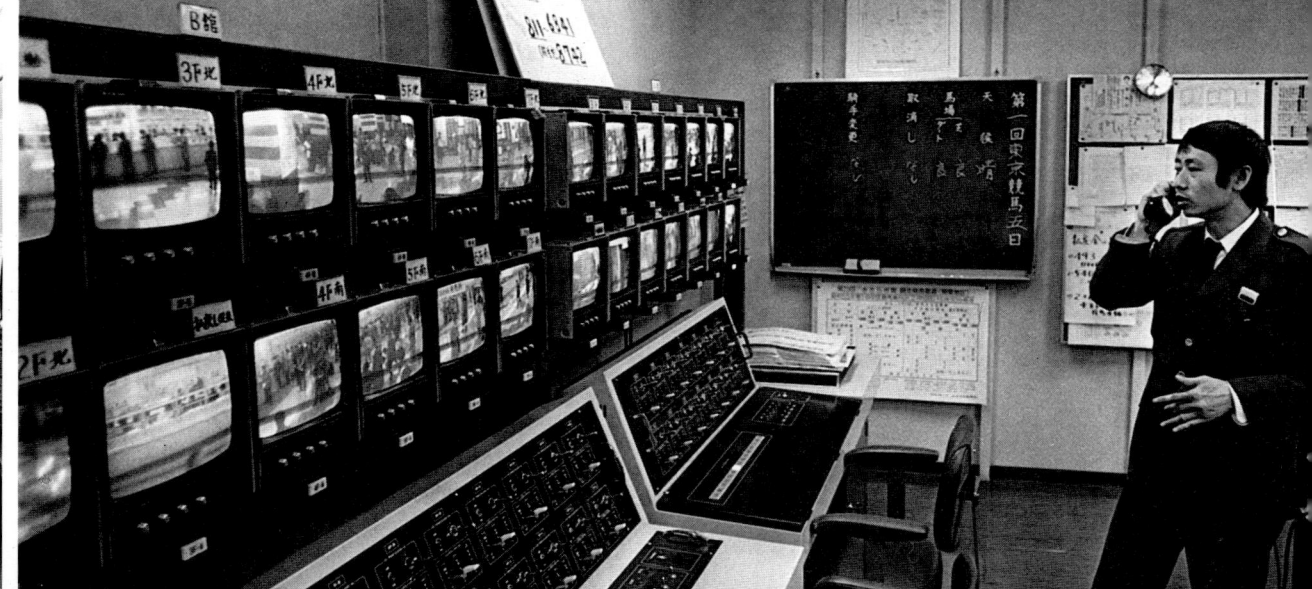

800 betting windows, 405 vending machines, a total floor area of 56,077.18 square metres; where more than 1,700 employees accommodate what can be a packed house of 40,000 punters betting 1,000 million yen (£12 million) in a single day.

The statistics are numbing, but they are not hard to believe after you have made the pilgrimage across the footbridge from Suidobashi Station. We arrived at 11am as they were broadcasting the third race and the place was less than a quarter full, yet in an hour's tour with the plant director, Mr Ida, I saw more betting machinery and more punters than you'd find in a week's tour of British betting shops.

What's more, much of the machinery would test a microchip's comprehension, pride of place going to the first and last rooms we visited. The first was the security room, which had lock-up TV surveillance, radio communication and fully-trained guards on a level that Fort Knox would envy. The last was the ARS floor. The initials stand for Automatic Response System, through which subscribers can call upon any of 256 lines and talk to an answering service which takes them in that entrancingly staccato Japanese rhythm through the whole betting process–number of race, type of bet, number of horse. So, at the end, the Tokyo punter has made an investment without ever getting near anything more human than the unwinking eye at the tape wheel.

But as always, the people are the most fascinating part of the whole operation. For if you have got the impression that the Japanese are orderly, you are not going to be contradicted by exposure to Korakuen. There is row upon row of bright, blue-bloused little Tokyo housewives perched patiently on the administration side of the betting windows, while out in the shimmering clean halls the serried ranks of Japanese punters endlessly ponder their selections. But, most memorable of all, is the white-desked, blue-carpeted telephone operators' room, containing more than 100 girls, each with her display screen, selection buttons and telephone dial, all continuously answering the phone so that the whole room is filled with that soft, sharp, breathless Japanese affirmative 'hai... hai... hai...', for all the world like a flock of birds calling at night.

It was all so much of a culture shock that it was good to try and talk to one of the telephone girls, and however inadequate our translated dialogue, I am happy to report that pretty Kayoko Yokobori seemed little different from any other 19-year-old student who opts for one of the slightly more conservative types of spare-time clerical work to help her savings. Yet Kayoko still bowed her head as she talked to me, just as the housewives had done by their windows downstairs, and even allowing for Japanese custom there is still an air of unquestioning acceptance which contrasts vividly

with the tumult and discussion which permeates the racing events that the whole Korakuen enterprise serves so remarkably.

The contrast is even more amazing on the other side of the grill. For these men are Japanese punters, so they tend to be that much more thorough. They have more tipping sheets, and often supplement their reading and public-address information by listening to the local radio reporting yet more news direct from the track. But they are punters nevertheless, so they should be subject to the same hopes and fears and frustrations as the rest of us, but after watching assorted groups listening to the finish of the 11 o'clock race, with the commentator working himself up into the usual orgasm of excitement, I began to see how 40,000 punters might be able to get into one betting shop and not blow the roof off.

Putting that number of, say Italian punters into one betting shop and then having the big-race favourite get beat, would be like putting a thousand tons of dynamite into Vesuvius. But here, while there was rapt chart-studying attention to the commentary, there were no oaths, no tearing of tickets, no clenching of the fists. I could finally believe Mr Ida's comment when I made several attempts via the interpreter to enquire what the punters did if there was some... er... excitement. The answer? 'They form queues'. And, when further pressed, perhaps with a hint of condescension: 'They always form queues'.

The 27-kilometre drive along the wretchedly narrow two-lane overhead freeway to Tokyo racecourse on the west side of the city gave us some chance to ponder the Japanese passion and attitude towards gambling. This is almost as contradictory as the way a country with such a mania for cleanliness that one man in 10 wears a surgical mask against flu germs, can also tolerate a large number of chain-smokers. You could write tomes on the possible pressures involved, but the best bet by far is that in a country–and particularly a 21-million conurbation like Tokyo–where the work ethic rules during the week, and where green recreation patches just don't seem to exist, the need for a release such as gambling becomes quite overwhelming.

Whatever the causes, you see another part of the astonishing effect once you get to Tokyo racecourse. For they have clearly got used to the odd punter coming down the road from the big city, and to the European racegoer it is as enor-

The ritual of the Tokyo betting shop is the same for all: never have one racing paper when three are available; pore over the facts, which go upwards rather than across and, if you are from the West, seemingly also from the wrong corner of the page; have infinite patience. Though the Japanese bettor has no great deal, in terms of the percentage he extracts from the Tote, for the factory workers who form the vast majority of racing followers, it is the only legalised gambling in the country, and a welcome break from the routine of normal life.

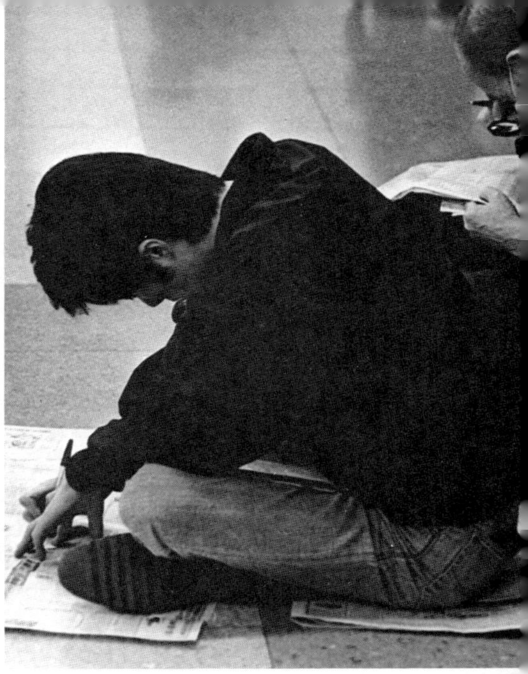

mous as suddenly being on board an ocean liner after being used to cross-Channel ferries. The great boat-like stand is two whole furlongs in length, and its five storeys include a gondola slung from the roof which, though it looks precarious from the ground, is still swanky enough to have spacious corridors and executive boxes with their own viewing balconies.

On the Sunday we were there the crowd topped 100,000, as it does every week (the record attendance is more than 130,000), and with only a mere 60,000 on the Saturday the place looked positively empty as we peered down at the punters' heads and the betting-slip confetti way below us, and wondered what terrible accident had occasioned the frequent stern notices to 'please ensure binocular strap is over neck'.

As you might expect from the land of the tea ceremony, Japanese racing is pretty big on parades, and with 12 races on the card there is more than a hint of the military about some of the manoeuvres. For instance, before every race the jockeys march into the paddock behind a martinet figure in full hunting kit, who halts at the head of the paddock and barks out orders for the mounting process.

Such parades appear to wait for no man, and certainly no jockey. Before the day's big race, two of the jockeys had been delayed by a presentation ceremony for the previous event, but the others got their mounting orders as usual, and at precisely 15 minutes to post time the procession filed its way through the non-slip underpass beneath the grandstand behind the now-mounted outrider, and the jockeys had to jump up on their horses as they were led past.

But clearly even the normal parades are not enough. On our Sunday, the lunch break was

There is nothing small about the racing scene in Tokyo. A field explodes from the start on the other side of the course away from the spacious stands, while in the sequence above another sets out right in front of those same stands. Japanese jockeys wear their owner's colours but the caps are coloured according to the draw, so that 1 and 2 have white caps, 3 and 4 have black caps and so on. The colours of the caps can be coupled in the forecast draws. It is not unusual in Japan for almost half a field of horses to have hoods on which cover their ears. This is done with the apparent intention of ensuring the mounts do not react badly to noise, but it is an equine reaction so rare in a trained animal as to make the Japanese practice seem bizarrely cautious.

A Japanese hero, jockey Hiro Yuki Gohara (on horse No. 7) rides with a considerable lack of concern. When he gets to the start he's likely to trot round with his feet out of his irons, for all the world behaving like a dressage rider. Concern for style, exquisite decoration and, above all, ceremony is a Japanese characteristic that bubbles continually to the surface in their racing. A former winner of the Japanese St Leger (Centre Right) is about to retire to stud. He canters round the track, parades before a bevy of girls while his connections, including owner, trainer and jockey, are garlanded with flowers, and he is himself given a wreath, not of laurels but carrots. An apt recompense for pounding out the furlongs at Tokyo, where the racecourse turns into the straight against the disordered design of the capital with hardly a trace of vegetation in sight.

enlivened by a glorious ceremony to mark the retirement of the previous year's St Leger winner. First the great horse was paraded in front of the stand with jockey and colours up, then he did a farewell canter round the track while the closed-circuit TV sets showed films of his greatest triumph. Finally he was brought back for a presentation of bouquets to all his connections, and he even received a huge red garland made almost entirely of carrots.

Once out on the track, events have a very Japanese flavour to them. After the horses have paraded past the stands, they don't just canter off to the start together in boring old orthodox European fashion, but scatter to the four corners of the track to re-group at the stalls before the off, some doing one long slow canter, some doing little sprints, some circling gently. It was as if you could hear a Japanese voice saying: 'Ah so, now the warm-up', and in that wonderfully logical way of theirs, had decided that some equine form of callisthenics was of more benefit than a mere canter to the start. Whatever the reasons, they result in the best-disciplined, quickest-loading horses in the world.

This lengthy pre-performance is also very much to give the public a view of their fancies and sharpen their betting appetite. Their interests are also catered for by jockeys carrying their start numbers on their arms as well as their shoulders, by cap colours always relating to the same numbers and by an information display board that even includes the horse's weight.

There is an admirable application about the Japanese punter. He looks at his racecard, glances at the indicator board, pores over his (to European eyes) totally indecipherable, not to mention absolutely upside-down, racecard, and listens to the local shortwave radio broadcast for even more news and tips. But there is more than a touch of unreality about the whole exercise because while the eager Japanese flock relentlessly towards any of the 2,000-odd Tote-only windows betting up to 17 thousand million yen (£34 million) a race, and 90 per cent of it on the Quinella Forecast, their chances of making it pay are drastically reduced by a take-out of no less than 25 per cent.

Yet unlike almost every other country in the world, racing's own interests get a bigger share of the slice than the government, whose take is 10 per cent to racing's 15 per cent. The Japan Racing

The jockey's quarters underground at the Tokyo racecourse are fringed with security and officials. The riders have to be resident there the day before the races start, submit themselves to being under lock and key, and not meeting anybody. Consolations are numerous, including food, on-the-spot medical care, television and magazines, and the benevolent eye of the man in charge, Takemi Kaga (Bottom Right), who was for seven times Japan's leading jockey and rode 1,100 winners himself. Exit and entrance to and from the course is by a tunnel under the stands, which has underhoof a rubberised surface to ensure the horses keep securely upright. Nothing appears to be left to chance; even the grooms wear protective crash helmets. The jockeys themselves maintain an immaculate appearance, even of their rubber riding boots, which get constantly washed. Saddling and unsaddling is done underground and the attention of jockeys to personal detail would not be so remarkable but for the fact that the programme waits for no one. The jockey who fails to be fast enough between races finds himself rushing out later to scramble into the saddle – after the parade.

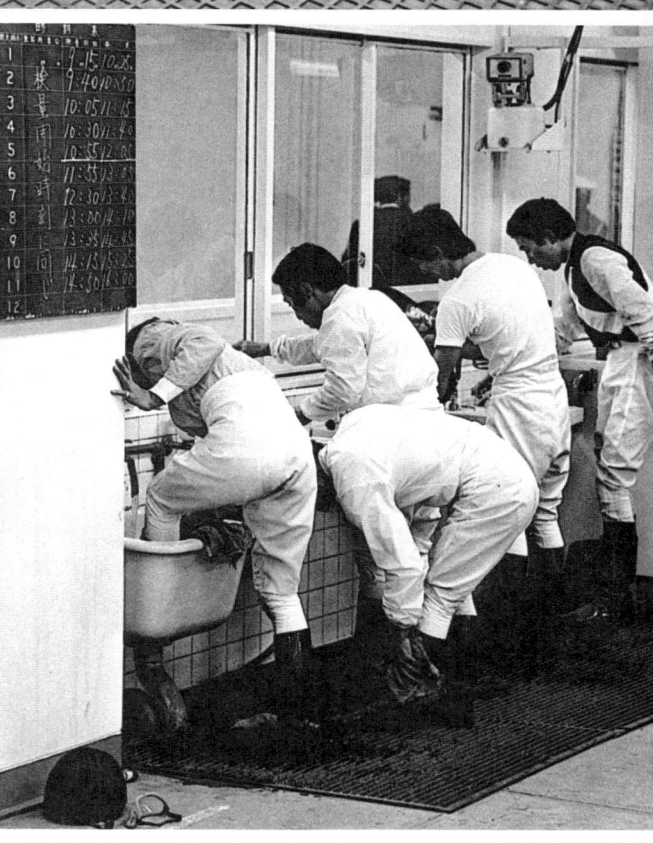
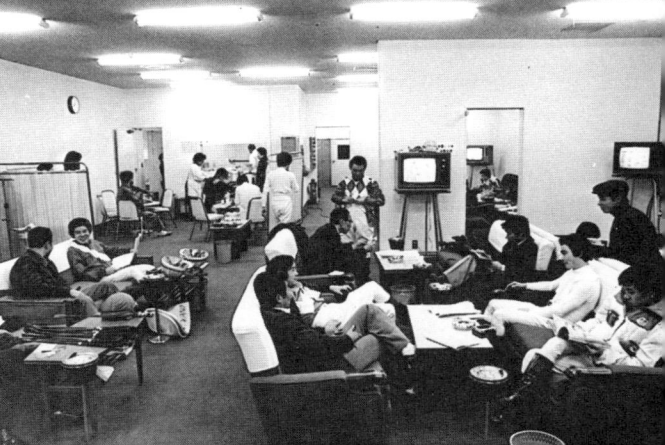

Association was set up under the wing of the Ministry of Agriculture, Forestry and Fisheries as recently as 1954. Official disapproval of all other forms of gambling still limits its operations to weekends only, yet in 1978, with only 10 JRA tracks and 288 racing days, their attendances amounted to more than 11 million, and their turnover was vast. So you can see that a 15 per cent share gives the racing authorities plenty of room for manoeuvre.

They certainly take their responsibilities seriously, for if the Japanese punter has a difficult percentage deal, he is at least served by probably the most supervised, and surely the straightest, racing in the world.

This supervision doesn't rest at endless video and film-camera scrutiny of races, or at the very latest forensic checks on the horses before and after they run. It's not even enough to have all the animals stabled at one or the other of the JRA's enormously well-equipped and closely-guarded training centres. No, in Japan they take the ultimate security step. They lock the jockeys up.

Of course, many countries shut the door on their riders once they arrive at the track, but in Japan it's taken a whole stage further. Following what were euphemistically described as 'some corruptions' 15 years ago, all jockeys are required to present themselves at the track an hour after declaration time, that is the day before. So even top multi-billion-yen jockeys, like Gohara, turn up like schoolboys early on Friday afternoon and clock-in to a pleasant but functional three-storey house on the edge of the fenced-off stable area. They have separate rooms, a communal lounge, a snooker table and a sauna big enough to bake a rugby team. But, and for jockeys on the eve of races it is a big but, they can receive no visitors or phone calls. If that happened in England, the Post Office would be bankrupt in a week.

Trying through an interpreter to explore what the jockeys felt, I didn't get much response, at least from the security angle. The usual reply was: 'The jockeys make good money, but they have responsibilities to the public'. But there was more reaction about being kept away from their families. 'Yes, they do miss their families', and, with a clear-eyed twinkle, 'some of them do worry about what their wives get up to'.

But the top boys in any country are very hard to beat and there was nothing to suggest that Japan was different. The style might lack a bit of sharpness, which is hardly surprising, since they only actually race-ride two days a week, but the riders as a group showed a competence and fitness you might expect of men who have to go through a rigid examination before they are finally allowed out on to the tracks as jockeys, and who have to pass physical tests, and even a 'medical brain-wave test' before they are allowed to start the apprentice course at Equestrian Park in the centre of Tokyo.

More of a question mark hangs over the ability

of the horses at the centre of this amazing circus. Naturally, it is a bit of a surprise to Europeans when they see racehorses not just with their manes and tails untrimmed, but in almost half the cases wearing a hood over their ears (no blinkers around), and all of them sporting a long, coloured plait stitched along the mane. Beyond that, several of them looked in poor condition even by February standards, and the animals competing in the 20-million-yen classic trial were the only ones a top European trainer would have been proud of.

That trial was the main race run on grass that Sunday – grass that in the bright, dry cold, which is normal February weather, was yellow and lifeless, with very firm ground underneath. The bulk of the card was run on the shorter (1,900 metres) interior dirt track, and it was on that surface that all the training was being done when we rubbed the sleep from our eyes at the Miho Training Centre on the Sunday morning.

I say 'was being done', because even at 5am when I first looked out of my bedroom in the luxuriously-appointed guest house where all owners and other guests are lodged, there were horses thundering round the floodlit training oval. Perhaps it was sleeping Japanese style – with a mattress set directly on the beautifully-woven rush-type floor – that was the problem, maybe it was indigestion from the delicious Japanese meal eaten while sitting cross-legged the night before, but we started off that morning by putting the worst pressure of the whole trip on Mr Inada, the long-suffering and ever-courteous JRA official who slogged round with us.

The crisis was over whether Gerry Cranham should be allowed to go into the centre of the training-track area to take a picture of the stand, (oh yes, a full-scale stand to watch the training) as it was silhouetted by the first fitful fingers of dawn. At one awful point, Cranham's powerful camera-swinging back could be seen storming off into the middle distance, while I tried to pacify the much-stressed Mr Inada, who kept repeating: 'Frankly speaking, Mistah Cranham, you are breaking the regulations'.

Peace was finally made as the light came up and we could see the full implications of Miho's training centre, which was opened in 1978, 180 kilometres from Tokyo racecourse, and which houses half of the 4,000-odd racehorses which are allowed to run at the 11 main tracks, and no fewer than 5,000 of assorted racing personnel. Quite a few of them seemed to be beetling around the endless walkways of the training camp, each category having to sport a different-coloured-and-

shaped cap, with only the jockeys, apprentices and specially-qualified 'training boys' actually allowed to go and gallop on the track.

Whatever you wore, you needed plenty of it, for the big electronic sign at the top of the water tower was showing minus nine degrees centigrade when we first arrived, and was still at minus four, when we left at 8am. Training was very much on traditional American dirt-track lines, with the careful clocking of gallops and then the slow walking of horses to cool them down. All that was of a perfectly normal standard, but unluckily or otherwise on such a fleeting visit, the impression of stable hygiene and discipline left more questions unanswered.

In the land where humans don one set of slippers to enter the house and another to go to the bathroom, it was disappointing to see only the droppings cleared away from the horse's box, the soiled rice straw being laid out in front of the stable block to dry in the sun and then put back again. If that is hygienic, then Dettol is an aperitif. More

---

(Left) At Japan's modern Miho training centre, where 5,000 people and half as many horses live and work, riders and mounts file past below early in the morning. The temperature on this occasion was still below freezing.

(Centre) A smog-masked lad follows his horse out on to the track at Tokyo racecourse for a full-scale trial in the shivering cold. The number 88 is the horse's training number and L indicates the barn he's in.

(Top) Trotting out for a day in the snow-covered fields: a herd of yearlings at the stud farm of Mr Yoshida. It is here that the stallion My Swallow stands and many of the yearlings bear proof of their ancestry in their father's striking markings, a white face and a chestnut coat.

seriously still, when I asked one of the grooms to move a horse across his box for a photograph, there was no easy clicking or shooing his charge across. He just reached across the yard, grabbed a long pole and prodded the animal around the space for all the world as if it was a man-eating tiger.

The first thoroughbreds didn't arrive in Japan until 1895, and the sport did not take much of a grip until the ravages of war destroyed it, as it did much of the country, in the 1940s. Therefore, it was not surprising to hear one of Japan's most enterprising young stud owners declare: 'Our problem is that we have no tradition or experience of caring for the thoroughbred horse'. Teruya ('Terry') Yoshida's family run the leading Shadai farm in snow-clad Hokkaido (North Island) and

has made educational forays to Europe and America. We were watching one of the first foals of the year staggering around the paddock in living proof of why the Japanese like to delay their breeding season until the snows have gone.

The snow, in fact, is not a real problem, as the success of E. P. Taylor's Canadian studs has proved. Far worse is the limited basic horse knowledge, and the deficiencies of calcium and other minerals in the grass. 'We have very advanced scientists working on it', said Terry, 'so soon we should be able to feed them right. But to get good blood and to look after them well... that is also the problem'.

At the Shadai Farms, the building and the condition of most of the horses was a tribute to progress. But it didn't always seem the same in other fields we looked at, and stud pundits in some parts of the world would have been horrified to see 20 yearlings out in the snow browsing on a huge old dunghill.

For some 30 years the Japanese have been importing stallions and broodmares of high standard from Europe and the United States (including seven Derby winners), but the results have been frankly disappointing. Several Japanese horses have run in top races in America and England without making any impression. Of course, you can argue that playing away from home is an almost hopeless disadvantage, and November 1981 saw the first running of a major international race in Tokyo. Such events may show the Japanese horse in a reasonable light, and having foreign competition, both equine and human, will hold a beneficial mirror up to the Japanese scene.

Some of the practices the mirror revealed would make most Western people raise their eyebrows and their stallions wince. For any English horse which expected to settle into some equine geisha house would have forgotten about the Japanese work ethic. In Europe we consider 40 mares enough for one stallion to cover during the five-month breeding season. In Japan, your would-be sultan is faced with the daunting task of managing 60 to 70 mares in a season shortened by the winter snow.

Admittedly, with the exception of poor old High Hat who, at 25, was looking his age, all the stallions we saw looked fit and ready for the long months of philandering, but it is still legitimate to wonder what state the likes of such recent imports as Huntercombe and My Swallow would be in by the close of their season. So the reports from British Bloodstock agency men that these Romeos still looked in the pink by the end of May is no small compliment to Japanese stud management.

If the management of stallions in Japan is a bit out of step with Western thinking, so too is the handling of the young stock. For while we are all used to getting young horses ready for the sales by their second autumn, and then having them at a trainer's stables to learn to race, and often to run, early the next year, Japan has a much slower progression. Over there, the young stock are kept at the stud until the middle of their two-year-old season before being sent to the training centres, and once installed there is no close season at the turn of the year, as in Europe. We watched the first big classic trial for three-year-olds while we were there, and that was in early February.

This system may give animals more time to mature and it certainly leads to extremely well-broken racehorses. Nowhere in the world did we see horses behave better on the track and at the starting stalls. But discipline can be imposed quickly whilst true racing ability can take generations to develop, and it's that which remains unproven.

It's not that some pretty good blood isn't bashing around. Seven Derby winners have been imported in the last 25 years. The great success of Tesco Boy and Tribal Chief has made the brilliantly fast Princely Gift line the most sought after strain in Japan. Moreover, while it may be true Japan has, at times, been something of a dumping ground for unsuccessful European stallions, such criticism cannot be levelled at fine performers like Pitcairn, Sun Prince, and Yellow God. Their departure East was later seen to be a major loss by local breeders. But racing empires are not built in a day and, at the moment, the Japanese racehorse still seems to lack international class.

Of course, trying to compare horses running

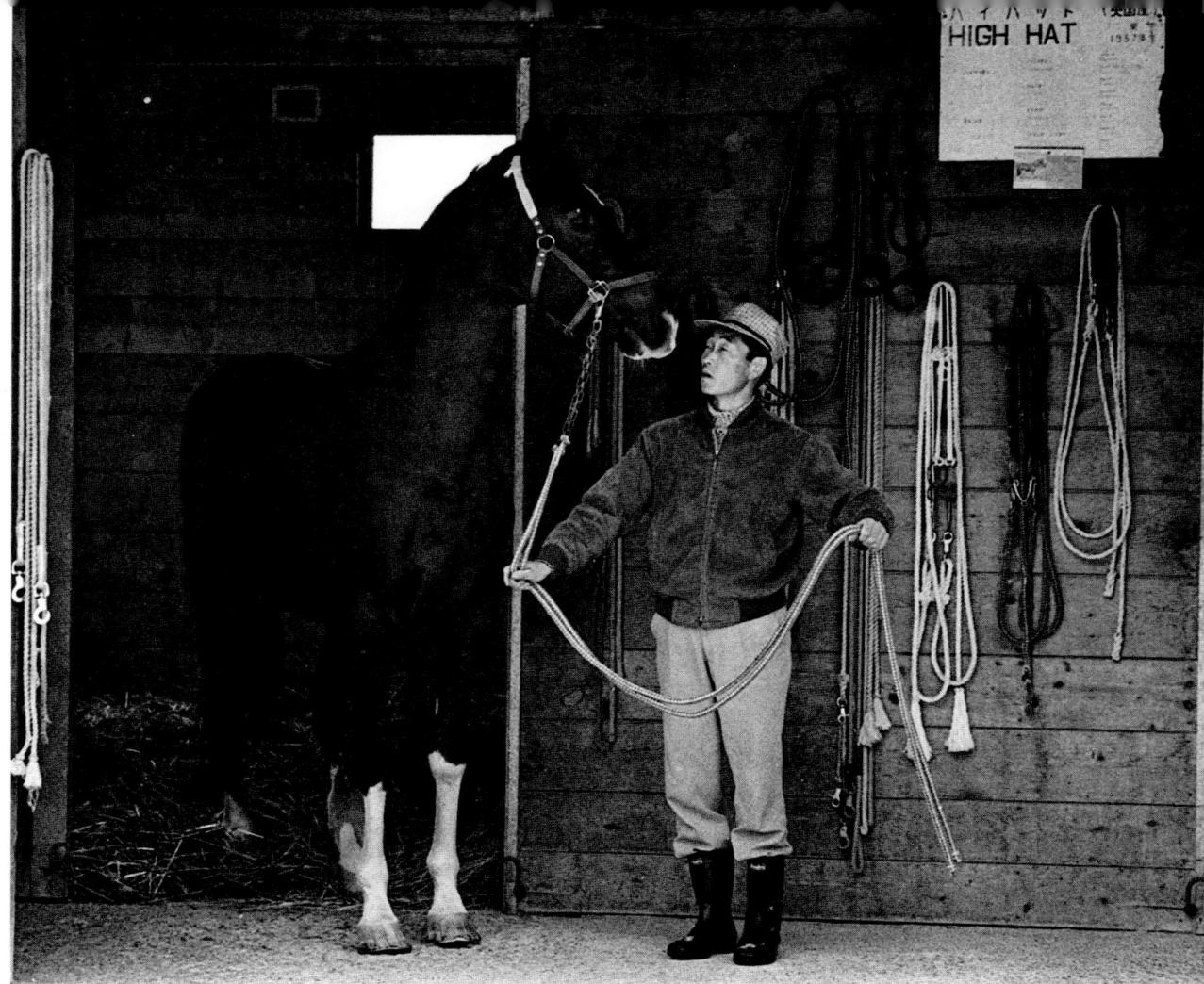

in one corner of the globe with those in another, is almost as unrewarding an exercise as arguing over the respective merits of Muhammad Ali and Gentleman Jim Corbett. But it is on record that the few Japanese horses that have tried their luck overseas have cut no ice at all, the best effort being by Speed Symboli, who in 1967 finished 5th in the Washington International at Laurel Park.

Tokyo's new international race, albeit without European participation in the first year, was a great local attraction and will be a major breakthrough. Yet the suspicion lingers that if the top horses from Europe, America or Australia faced a Japanese starter, they would at this moment prove much the stronger and, indeed, no local horse finished nearer than fifth in 1981. The Japanese are, after all, still labouring under the disadvantage of starting their breeding operations almost from scratch 30 years ago. They don't have the big American and European market to test their stock in, and their standard and practices of horse care and training have not the pressure of foreign competition. But anyone who has seen what they've achieved in so short a time would be crazy to discount them.

One final memory reminds me that their potential is far from being confined to the tremendous financial clout of a gamble-hungry citizenry. Amid the paddocks and barns that make up one Mr Shigoe Yoshida's highly successful stud in Hokkaido, there is an elaborate marble tomb. It is built to the memory of his horse Tenpointo, the first animal to top seven billion yen in Japan. Before his accidental death, Tenpointo was scheduled to campaign in Europe to prove his country's worth. It was a brilliantly clear February morning, with the snowclad fields set in perspective by the volcanic peaks of Sapporo in the background. Mr Yoshida explained with gravity that ever since Tenpointo's death, race fans have beaten a constant path to the farm to pay tribute at the tomb. Then, quickly and silently, he took a candle himself, lit it and placed it beside the plaque commemorating his horse's deeds.

Japan may be short of some things yet. But it certainly doesn't lack drive or a sense of history.

(Far Left) Teruya 'Terry' Yoshida, who gesticulates with his hands to emphasise a point, is the man in charge of the most successful stud farm in Japan. He is the new, computerised world of Japanese racing, while behind him is Shigoe Yoshida, who represents a slightly older, equally celebrated era, but one rooted in a somewhat less-bustling farm.

(Centre) At Shigoe Yoshida's farm the past is revered. Beneath an elaborate gravestone lies the magnificent Tenpointo, once the hero of all Japan, who broke a leg and, unlike the famous Mill Reef, did not recover. Now thousands of fans beat a path to his grave to pay their respects, leave flowers and light candles, just as Mr Yoshida does, in memory of the great horse.

(Above) The end of a glorious road: when High Hat was in England he carried Sir Winston Churchill's colours with distinction. He finally wound up, happily, as a stallion in Japan. But now he is on his last legs, literally, and shortly will die.

12

HONG KONG

'The biggest double take in the whole racing scene is to drive through the heavily built-up surroundings of the Happy Valley track and see a string of racehorses walking up the one-in-three slope, and then disappearing into a high-rise apartment block halfway up the hill. No, your eyes have not deceived you! They are going back to their stables in the Shan Kwong Road. Anywhere else in the world, you would think it all quite ridiculous, but in Hong Kong, with its premium on space and its genius for improvisation, it quickly seems obvious'.

THE ROYAL CAR swept up the floodlit Happy Valley racecourse and, with the flash-bulbs popping as Her Majesty the Queen stepped graciously on to the track, a great buzz went up from the 30,000 capacity crowd. But no, this was not a big patriotic cheer from an otherwise appreciative audience–it was the fevered reaction of the Hong Kong punters as the Quinella Dividend shone out on the electronic results board.

That moment on May 5, 1975, came in the middle of the most remarkable decade in the history of Hong Kong racing, or indeed of any single racing centre in the world. For it was only in 1971 that racing turned professional at Happy Valley, yet by 1980 it was collecting over 12 million Hong Kong dollars (about £1 million) a race, and had channelled it all efficiently enough to have built at Sha Tin, in the New Territories, the most modern racecourse on Earth.

The whole thing would be quite ludicrous by anything other than the standards of this tiny capitalist colony which somehow flourishes right on the toe-nails of Communist China. After all, on the original little (29 square miles) Hong Kong

Island, there is hardly room to swing a cat, let alone gallop a racehorse. Yet right in the middle of the whole seething four million-man ant-heap, there is Happy Valley, just off the Wongneichung Road, not only surrounded by tower blocks but using a couple of them as stable blocks, and their roofs as exercise yards.

But Happy Valley is quite a normal idea compared with Sha Tin, set at the end of Tolo Bay across the harbour from Hong Kong Island and northwards through Kowloon and the Lion's Rock Tunnel. Faced with the wish and the money to build a new racecourse, but having nothing but rocky, sea-girt mountains to build it on, what did they do? They moved one of the mountains into the sea! The raised sea-bed gave them the racecourse, and the eaten-out slabs of mountain gave them priceless new building land. The genius of simplicity.

It's true. The exact statistics (everyone in Hong Kong can give you statistics) are that 250 acres were reclaimed from Sha Tin Bay, giving a million square feet for the racetrack, and the shifting of 13,995,071 cubic yards from hillside to recla-

mation site at one lorry-load every eight-and-a-half seconds finally left 161 acres of new building land whose market value would far exceed the £60 million cost of the whole project. And if you don't believe me, read the enthusiastic jottings

(Preceding Spread) When you haven't got space, use the roof. The hubble-bubble of life on Hong Kong island, make a racehorse's life seemingly impossible. But that's no problem for local genius and these horses from the city's Happy Valley racetrack take their exercise on the roofs of their stables.

The mountains of Mourne may have swept down to the sea, but at Hong Kong's Sha Tin Bay they filled it up to create the world's most remarkable racecourse (Above). Over 5 years, 13,995,071 cubic yards of mountain were moved at 7½ lorry loads a minute to fill in 250 acres of Sha Tin Bay. The racecourse has every modern facility, including a giant video matrix board screening the race and replays. Hong Kong's money and massive labour market mean that there is no shortage of manpower at the starting stalls, even if the fairer sex claim their share of the tasks available. But this is the tip of China and few opportunities are missed for celebrating local style and it is racing's blessing that gambling is also endemic in Chinese life as the punters (Bottom Far Right) show, studying the form at one of the colonies 114 betting shops away from the racecourse.

of the British media persons who were given a typically generous facility visit to this new jewel of the East in 1979.

As family matters (the birth of a son) kept me from that not-quite-teetotal voyage, I travelled in some cynicism to this outpost of the galloping game which, just as we in Britain were claiming that the whole deal was financially impossible, had apparently discovered all over again that El Dorado starts at the betting window. But to paraphrase Robert Louis Stevenson, to travel cynically is a lot easier than to arrive if you are dealing with Hong Kong, and you don't really need Her Majesty's visit to make the point. Just look east up the city any Thursday night during the October-to-May season, and you will see the big red bulb proclaiming its 'House Full' warning from the top of the Happy Valley grandstand.

Happy Valley was the original seam of interest, when it wasn't being hit by the plague or the terrible fire of 1917, and to judge from the statistics (oh yes, plenty more of them) and our own observations, there is an awful lot of precious metal still to come. But the big surprise is that the accent behind this slickest of racing operations is just that British military crispness that gets so derided in Britain itself for lack of professionalism. The difference is, of course, that in Hong Kong, those concerned get paid handsomely for their labours, and those in charge have thoroughly cordial relations with the government. Who wouldn't, with a taxation pay-out in 1980-81 season of £55 million, and a further £11.2 million going to charity?

In many ways it is the last, and by no means the least successful, flowering of the old military colonial system. Slacks and open-neck shirts may be all right for morning work-outs, but at the races themselves tailored grey or fawn suits are uniform for the impressive array of handicappers, starters, stipendiaries and other officials. The lack of the brown trilby hat thought so essential by British racing officialdom is the only concession to the heat. Hong Kong is a small racing circus of just the two tracks, 700 resident horses and 63 race-days, but it didn't get its reputation for runaway intrigue for nothing, and no army of officials, however crisply dressed and starchly loyal, would have had a hope without strong and intelligent leadership from the top; and in this the role of Major-General Bernard Penfold, as the Hong Kong Jockey Club's general manager in the Seventies, is all-important.

Tall, courteous, and with that diffident sense of command that being effectively in charge of Hong Kong racing in the crucial years from 1972 to 1979 has brought, Bernard Penfold can look back with quiet pride on the job he took when he retired as GOC of the British Army's South East District.

The £60 million spent on making Sha Tin the most modern racecourse in the world included a whole battery of floodlights. They enable early birds to start work by 5.00 a.m.

Diplomacy would not let him be drawn into making too invidious a comparison between Britain's confusingly structured racing government (his present part-time post is chairman of the Horse Racing Advisory Council), but it was with some wistfulness that he said: 'The great thing out in Hong Kong is that I was allowed to get on with things'.

Penfold was not originally very keen about going. 'I fitted in a visit between shooting dates', he said. 'But once I got there I was hooked. It was so buzzing, so throbbing with activity. I am a doer, and it suited me'.

It might be added that few places can have had a new appointment that suited them better, for Penfold complemented his expected military efficiency ('I tried to travel to the main places in the world to find the best ideas available') with political finesse and social conscience. He helped outmanoeuvre ethical opposition to increased betting by arguing that if people were going to bet anyway, they might as well do it within the law, and when he utters the old politician's line: 'I felt I represented the silent masses', his record makes you think he meant it, for he encouraged his stewards (six Europeans, four Chinese) 'to spend, spend, spend for the integrity of racing'. His own keenness extended to the development of the middle of Sha Tin racetrack as a landscaped, flower-filled area for the general public's use throughout the year.

Penfold's term of office had twin achievements–the building of the new racecourse at Sha Tin, and the opening of the off-course betting shops. The one was very much dependent on the other, and both were possible only because of the seemingly insatiable appetite of the Chinese (90 per cent of the colony's population) for gambling. In fact, the story of the last 20 years can be seen not so much as the stimulating of the gambling instinct as of the controlling of it.

In the 1961-62 season, the turnover was 170 million Hong Kong dollars. By 1971-72 it had risen to 570 million, but by 1979-80 it had gone right through the roof to 6,480 million. To generate this, the annual number of meetings had risen from 31 to 63, and the off-course handle from nine per cent of the total money wagered in 1973-74, when the first off-course betting shops opened, to 58 per cent

Former British trainer Eric Collingwood (Top Right) oversees jockeys weighing out including Lester Piggott, in checkered silks, and French star Philippe Paquet, who is married to the daughter of Australian legend George Moore, seen bottom far right with his jockey son Gary. Both George and Gary won France's Prix de l'Arc de Triomphe, an honour shared by cue-holding Pat Eddery (Third Right). With Eddery is Hong Kong regular Bill Hartack, winner of five Kentucky Derbys in his native America. The trainers include Britain's popular Frank Carr (Right) and former Epsom Derby winner Gordon Smyth (Second Right). The British flavour is not unfitting, since the great surge of the Seventies was masterminded by Major General Bernard Penfold (Top Far Right).

in 1979-80, when 114 shops were in operation.

Psychologists, anthropologists, psephologists and whoever, can ponder the reasons, but these figures state clearly that for the Chinese temperament in general, and for the Hong Kong Chinese in particular, horse-racing and the gambling offers a much-needed release to the lifestyle. Of course, the trick, or maybe the joke, of it all is that this sort of gambling is an inexact science. Hong Kong, after all, is one place in the world where you should be able to get on top of the game. Every horse, every jockey, is known, and with not more than two meetings a week there is ample time to study every considerable nuance of the race ahead. The newspapers give really serious study, not just to races but to the morning work-outs. Television replays of previous races can be endlessly watched, and when your average Chinese punter gets ready to do battle at Happy Valley, he is usually equipped with a short-wave radio and an earpiece to give him last-minute guidance. And yet for all this welter of information, the outsiders still come up, and the favourites get beaten just like anywhere else in the world.

If you listen to the crowd in Hong Kong, you have the ultimate proof that punters don't want to believe that racing is straight. For with the massive concentration of interest, there is more speculation, if not downright allegation, about surprise results than anywhere else in the world. Yet they keep coming back, and trainers will tell you that owners there are pretty good losers, even if the regular news of horses moving from one stable to another suggests ownership is a volatile condition.

The one unforgivable sin is to come up on an unfancied horse, and just before we arrived young Jimmy Bleasdale had lost his contract and received a far-from-happy welcome after landing a winner on a horse called Joyful at 40-1. As the leading British rider out there at the time, he was understandably unrepentant. 'The horse had disappointed last time, and we agreed to ride him from way off the pace', he said. 'I didn't think he had much chance, but the others went very fast and fell in a heap. I wasn't going to risk my career by trying to get him beat, so I gave him a couple of cracks, and we got up on the line. You should have seen the reception party! No one said a word'.

Not for the first time, all the most professional of assessments, even the most helpful of omens (like most racehorses in Hong Kong, Joyful had had his name changed–from the staid-sounding Whatcombe of his English racing days) had been made fools of by a horse. But let no one think that those involved with the animals, or even the horses themselves, are joke figures any more. That may have been so in the good old days at Happy Valley, when bewhiskered cavalry officers galloped round on tiny little China ponies which were handi-capped according to their size. But it certainly doesn't apply now, when the fortunes to be won and lost have ensured the keenest degree of professionalism, not just among the resident participants but those from outside, be they trainers or jockeys, who want to get in on the act.

After all, George Moore, who has frequently headed the Hong Kong trainers' list, with his son Gary leading the jockeys' table, has the most com-prehensive of backgrounds. He long ago establish-ed himself as one of the outstanding jockeys of the

century, not just in his native Australia, but in France, where he won the 1959 Arc de Triomphe on Saint Crespin, and in Britain where he took the 1967 Derby on Royal Palace during one meteoric season. Yet nobody can point a finger at George and say that he simply has the best horses, as might be said of some trainers in other places. For in Hong Kong, with most of the races handicaps, only horses of limited price and ability are allowed in, until recently all of them bought by the Jockey Club and shared out among would-be members on a ballot basis. Therefore, to win the most races you have to understand your animal and his capacities better than the next man.

'Of course, it's a different game out here', said Gary Moore as he towelled himself down in the Hilton Hotel sauna one afternoon. 'Just two tracks, and always the same horses, so it means that everyone knows every move, and that doesn't make things any easier'. Apart from his pedigree, Gary has a riding reputation big enough to get himself flown across the world to take the winning ride on Gold River in the 1981 Arc de Triomphe within 24 hours of winning the last race at Happy Valley on the Saturday. 'With my father and my brother John we have got quite a family set up here', he said. 'It's not Chantilly or Newmarket, but it's special in its own way.'

It's hard to nod your head if you are being pummelled on the massage table, but it looked as if some sign of agreement came from the French jockey, Philippe Paquet, who was also preparing himself for the night's racing at Happy Valley as part of the annual busman's holiday which had originally led him into marrying George Moore's

daughter, Michelle. 'Hong Kong ees deeferent all right', he said in that Sacha Distel way of his. 'Happy Valley is very tight, only fifteen-hundred metres round, and the sand track inside, that's even tighter, while Sha Tin is a lot bigger – two-thousand metres round and a one-thousand-metre straight. You can ride another sort of race there'.

Quite a few of racing's riding family tend to gravitate to Hong Kong these winters. Lester Piggott, in his most relaxed casual-shirted mode, had been the first person we met in the Hilton foyer. 'I can't just freeze to death in England', he said over lunch. And that evening Paquet and Bleasdale were among the winners at Happy Valley. The smallness of the track area (the whole thing is only 45 acres) may be good for spectators and TV monitors, but it puts pressure on the trainers, who used to have only this place to operate from, and jockeys. Brian Taylor had a horrible fall when his horse failed to turn, and hit the outer wall.

The biggest double take in the whole racing scene is to drive through the heavily built-up surroundings of the Happy Valley track and see a string of racehorses walking up the one-in-three slope, and then disappearing into a high-rise apartment block halfway up the hill. No, your eyes have not deceived you! They are going back to their stables in the Shan Kwong Road. Anywhere else in the world, you would think it all quite ridiculous, but in Hong Kong, with its premium on space and its genius for improvisation, it quickly seems obvious. There are 63 stalls in the latest 1971 building, and don't think the horses always have to potter (with muffled hooves to avoid disturbing the neighbours) down the hill to the track for exercise. If it's just walking or lunging they need, their route is in the opposite direction. They go storey by storey up the walking ramps, and, yes, out on to the roof.

Such training arrangements may have been typical Hong Kong solutions to supposedly insoluble problems, but obviously they were far from ideal, and so, when Sha Tin opened in 1978, it was welcomed by professionals as much for its training facilities as for its space-age racecourse. Sha Tin has 10 two-storey blocks, each with 50 horses in 12ft square loose boxes, it has both sand and an all-weather track within the 1,900-metre turf course, non-slip-surfaced underground tunnels to reach them, a swimming pool for aches and pains and the best veterinary back-up in the East. In short, as good training facilities as any on-the-plant racehorse could expect anywhere.

When you think of some of the cobwebby little yards back home in Britain, of the chickens and beetle juice behind Kuala Lumpur's sweltering stable line, of some of the muddier corners of the great American backstretch, going round the Sha Tin horses with Noel McAfferty, the ubiquitous stable manager, seemed like viewing some modern boys' boarding school. The trainers were the housemasters, and the mafoos (chinese lads) the teachers and cleaners.

On the same line of thought, contrast the twin tower blocks housing 300 mafoos and their families at the far end of the track, with some of the broken-sofa rat-holes that have done service as lads' quarters in Britain over the years. Or, even more poignantly, with the swarming, floating slum over the hill from Happy Valley that is Aberdeen – at an estimated 10,000 people, the largest water-borne gathering in the world.

'It's not quite like Malton', says Frank Carr whose Whitewall stables at that Yorkshire training centre were for long a mecca for anybody who liked the heady scent of a good racing scheme. Frank, along with Eric Collingwood and Gordon Smyth, is a contracted English trainer at Sha Tin, and listening to him talk over breakfast in his fifth floor luxury flat overlooking the racecourse, it was clear he had settled well in the new life.

'Out here everything is done for you', he said. 'Food, transport, lads' pay, insurance, every-thing...all you have got to do is to train the horse, and have him right on the day'. Frank hasn't got much hair left on top these days, but he didn't work his way up from being a half-a-crown-a-week Irish stable lad without having plenty between the ears, and there was a lovable craftiness about the way he talked which emphasised the importance of getting the calculations right, and reminded you that relationships with heavy-punting owners are matters of some finesse.

On that side, you would expect the locals to have the edge, and certainly in the short time that Hong Kong has been professional, such men as Allan Chan and ex-jockey T. C. 'Top Cat' Cheng have developed into top-class trainers, as well as highly-tuned diplomats. With fanatical interest,

If you are a Hong Kong racehorse you soon learn that you are special. Early morning exercise (Above) is under floodlights while the big city sleeps all round. But the meandering journey back to the numbered stalls is sometimes a battle against cars if not placards!

an efficient press but only two meetings a week, every conceivable facet of every race can be discussed. 'After we have finished work in the mornings, we usually go to meet some owners', said the former Irish champion jockey Johnny Roe as we sipped coffee at Frank Carr's table. 'And those owners want to know everything'.

Although leading Australian, as well as English and Irish, jockeys have visited, and are resident in, Hong Kong, big efforts have been made to recruit and train local boys. Recruiting is no problem since a jockey's life holds promise of gold-mines, and there must be half a million Chinese boys small enough to apply. But training is quite a task, since none of the boys are likely to have any riding knowledge.

So jump into a train and rattle round the coast past the Sha Tin New Town, past the futuristic University, and, always the contrast, past also the huts and lean-tos that spring up all around like insects under the glittering new-laid stones. Eventually you go past rice-fields and trees until you reach Fanling, still only 25 miles from Kowloon, where a car will whisk you up through the market and the military post to reach Beas River Country Club, which is not only a country club, but also the home of the Jockey Club Apprentice Training Scheme.

This school has the typical hallmarks of the Hong Kong success operation. It is really 'moneyed military' with a social conscience. You can almost hear the original orders being barked out. ['Got to teach these local Chinese chappies what racing is all about. Right, collect information from all available sources. Arrange extensive curriculum stressing basic equitation and education, with quite a few runs and cold showers included for character building. Get knowledgeable racing-officer figure to run the course with local sergeant-major type to put 'em all through their paces. Now pick the most likely sorts from your candidates' list, and within a year you will have a fine-looking home-grown apprentice'.]

Now we can all make jokes about the military, just as they can laugh at some of us thirsty members of the press, but you cannot laugh at success, and having made the pilgrimage up to watch Ian Tedford and his team at Beas River, I am sure success is the word. Old-fashioned some of his approach may be, but no more out of date than insisting on an equine equivalent of the three Rs. Every apprentice has got to be able to walk, trot, canter and jump without stirrups and, however small, to be able to vault into the saddle unaided. One of the lasting memories of this trip was of the class of 12 tiny would-be jockeys lined up in front of us, and, to staccato Chinese commands from the instructor, each swung his right leg forward and then catapulted it and themselves back in an arc to land in the saddle. It was so similar to the martial arts set-up that you feared that one false command might leave you with 12 headless horses.

After six months, the apprentices start to ride gallops in the morning, and then those who develop go on to be jockeys. Already a local product such as Tony Cruz has shown that good instruction married to energy, enthusiasm and talent can make up for what amounts to a standing start at the riding game. Naturally, there is quite a weeding-out process as the course begins, but the real problems and the failures start once it is over. For having slaved away for every waking hour while he is at the school, the young and impressionable apprentice will find that once he has finished his early-morning riding stint (and with a 4.30am start, it is some stint), he has plenty of time on his hands, and no lack of racing followers with suggestions as to how to spend it.

Indeed, there you have the fundamental dilemma of Hong Kong racing. It has such a following, and is so well run, that it can provide practically anything that money can buy within its strict geographical and climatic confines. But, among the millions in so small a place, can it prevent the corruptions that have been so

temptingly available in the game ever since Adam bit the apple and decided to gamble on whether one horse could gallop faster than another?

On the plus side, the Hong Kong Jockey Club has more to be proud of in its achievements during the Seventies than any other racing authority in the world. Look at this list: Professional racing, off-course betting and new pick-six and other exotic bets introduced, which in turn have funded a gleaming new clubhouse and floodlights for night racing at Happy Valley, and a whole new racing Camelot at Sha Tin, with its computer Tote, its immaculate dining facilities, its huge 32,000-bulb Video Matrix board, and its 30,000 capacity grandstand, at 16½-acre floor-space the largest single building in Hong Kong. And if, because of the lack of space and suitable minerals, no local horses will be produced, the standard of newcomers has improved out of all recognition from the bad old days when Hong Kong was the rubbish heap of British and Australasian horseflesh. Private purchases are allowed in, as well as the old block-buying-then-ballot-out scheme, and the best

recent horse, Silver Lining, would probably not be far behind the top handicappers in Britain.

Better still, the Hong Kong Jockey Club, for all its built-in establishment bias (every big wheel from Jardine Matheson downwards seems to be on the board), has never wavered from its commitment to the community. 'When I took over', said Bernard Penfold, 'there was, of course, the commitment to Sha Tin, but there was also a similar one to Ocean Park [an oceanarium] which was going to cost a hundred and sixty million dollars and be one of the largest and most modern of its kind in the world'. Penfold's efforts on these projects caused the recreational park within the Sha Tin track to be named after him, and the tradition continues apace, the Jockey Club contributing no less than 140 million Hong Kong dollars to charity in the year ending June, 1981, and that in addition to the 662.7 million dollars that would have already gone in betting tax.

Nevertheless, the dilemma that every extra dollar wagered increases the pressure for possible corruption, remains. Back in 1971, a really bad

doping case revealed two rival gangs at work and ended in jail sentences for several leading figures. Extensive testing facilities have ensured that nothing as simply crooked as that has happened since, just as the huge off-course Tote operation has taken much of the sting away from illegal book-makers. But while the retiring Senior Stipendiary, Kenneth Stewart, could say: 'I think we have it as well under control as casino racing can be', it's hard to forget the words of one senior rider: 'Of course you have to be careful. Yet though they have the best race patrol cameras and early-morning-gallop watchers in the world, you can still hide a horse pretty easily'.

It's a pressure cooker all right, and a long way from those old English aristocrats racing their home-bred colts and fillies.

Hong Kong prides itself on producing its own, so why not jockeys? Up at the Beas River Club, within shooting distance of the Red China border, a selected input of Hong Kong would-be horsemen are drilled in a manner deriving more directly from a British cavalry school than Kowloon.

13
MALAYSIA

'It was 100 degrees even in the shade. Out by the rails, people were using racecards and newspapers to keep the sun off their heads and I would never have survived to pen these words if my new friend, Mr. Yeap, had not let me shelter under his umbrella and then got his mate, Mr. Tai Ching Kid, to bring me a carton of cold chrysanthemum tea. It's probably dreadful stuff in a temperate climate, but there it tasted like champagne.'

KUALA LUMPUR has many things–a beautiful mosque, the ultimate in colonial railway stations, street restaurants after dark, a Chinese temple, taxi drivers with a life expectancy of about three days…and the hottest jockeys in the world.

Before Messrs Ooi Choon Hock, Lam Mun Chiew and the bearded Subian Bin Dalwee start sending writs, let's stress that we are not doubting their honesty, even if we are querying the KL punters' scepticism. Apparently they won't risk their dollars until they see their fancy ready and mounted on the track in front of them. And so it's the jockeys who go out in the midday sun, a quarter of an hour before each race.

Talk about mounted sauna baths! It was 100 degrees even in the shade. Out by the rails, people were using racecards and newspapers to keep the sun off their heads, and I would never have survived to pen these words if my new friend, Mr Yeap, had not let me shelter under his umbrella and then got his mate, Mr Tai Ching Kid, to bring me a carton of cold chrysanthemum tea. It's probably dreadful stuff in a temperate climate, but there it tasted like champagne.

Mr Yeap is an electrician with a novel line in infallible systems. The KL racecard (the most complete we saw anywhere in the world) carries photographs of various stages of previous races. Mr Yeap studies the furlong-from-home picture, and he assures me that by concentrating on the stride pattern of the horses he is making a handsome profit. Cynics might think it more logical to study the tension on some of the beaten horses' mouths, but let's not crib, for Mr Yeap gave me a winner, and, what's more, one ridden by a ghost. Not a very substantial ghost–about five feet five, with thinning hair and just a hint of the thickening waistline you would allow in a man who was to be 53 next birthday. It was Ron Hutchinson, for so long Britain's favourite Aussie with his bobbing style like a dinghy behind a speedboat, but who, we thought, had departed the jockey's life when he retired in England two years earlier.

Although he finally quit under unhappier circumstances six months later, the 'Bobber' wasn't dead then, not by a jugful. Race Three (no fancy

(Preceding Spread) No longer do just mad dogs and English-men go out in the midday sun in Kuala Lumpur. While the temperature in the shade is a sweltering 100 degrees or so, the horses and riders are led out. KL punters are so sceptical they won't put their money down until the parade is under way.

The study of form and the moment of decision brings about the same serious intentness beneath the shade of the umbrellas in Kuala Lumpur as anywhere else in the world. According to Mr Yeap (Left) the best system involves studying the stride pattern of the horses in the racecard photographs. Such scrutiny puts pressure on jockeys and officials alike. Ron Hutchinson (Far Right) ended a distinguished international career at Kuala Lumpur and like him the starter Y.M. Tunku Khalid bin Tunku Yahya (Top Right) tries to keep his cool.

titles here) was over six furlongs, with 12 runners and a 180-degree turn at halfway hectic enough to worry a Cresta rider. But our Ron was out of the gate and up the inside with all the dash of a 20-year-old, and he and his mount held on in a driving finish to yelps of delight from Mr Yeap and his team.

There were nine races that Sunday, and plenty of colourful reminders that we were almost slap on the Equator. After each event, the paddock area was swept by three dumpy, pink sari-clad Indian ladies, and every parade was led out by a doddery-looking white horse ridden by an amazingly ancient scarlet-coated Indian called Bekbang. Considering the heat, the sharpness of the track, the 30,000 capacity crowd and the fact that most professionals insisted that Kuala Lumpur was far worse appointed than Ipoh or Penang, the other two tracks in Malaysia proper, the racing was excellently organised.

But it was a pity that no means had been found to water the turf to something slightly the bouncier side of concrete, and that there were only two handlers to help load the starting stalls. That process therefore had to depend to a quite unreal extent on the outsize personality of the starter, Y.M. Tunku Khalid bin Tunku Yahya.

'All jockeys are my children', Mr Yahya (or should it be Mr Tunku?) said expansively as the 10 runners arrived for the seventh race. 'I am an old man now, but I have been a rider. I know their problems. The horses at home and on the race-course are two different animals, but some committee they think they should be the same, that the horse walk into the stalls by themselves, and so I do my best with two handlers and three shutters'. It wasn't a bad best, either, despite the eventual winner's breaking out early, and the 18-year-old stalls showing clear signs of mortality. Perhaps a set of 'Waikato' specials from New Zealand would be the answer.

Kuala Lumpur is a Tote-only show, but the activities of the illegal bookmakers are such that the Tote offers a 15 per cent reduction in the last five minutes before the off. With a 42 per cent Chinese population, there is plenty of the gambling fever that has made such an Eldorado of Hong Kong racing but, as ever, a great number of punters like to believe that it is only total wickedness that prevents their selections winning. 'This is the dirtiest game in the world', said Mr Yeap impressively, as his fancy trailed in fifth, and back beneath his multi-coloured umbrella I wasn't going to suggest that maybe for once the what-the-photos-say system had failed him.

Whatever their rating on the international disgruntled-punter list, Mr Yeap and his team are unique in one respect. For more than half the times they go racing in Kuala Lumpur – photo-tips, chrysanthemum tea, booed jockeys and all – they do so without a horse in sight.

Unlikely though they sound, these 'ghost races' are a great success at each of the Malaysia Racing Association's four tracks, Ipoh, Penang and KL, plus Singapore. For while they haven't got enough horses to keep all four going at once, there is no shortage of punters. So as the Saturday-Sunday card moves on from one track to another every month or so, the other race clubs remain open as the only places where you can legally get your money on.

But these other courses become much more than giant betting shops. Nearly 50 per cent of the normal capacity crowd shows up, and then goes through the motions of raceday. The loudspeaker checks off runners and riders, rattles off the latest betting news, announces the horses are on the parade and going to the start, and then delivers graphic commentary. The people flock from paddock to grandstand just as usual, and as their massed vocal tones changes from chattering starlings to roaring tigers, some of them even have binoculars raised to the points on the track where the commentary says the action is happening.

But that betting fever can go too far. Leading

An imperially positioned race track (Above) still needs the native touch (Right). Out on the palm-fringed track (Top Far Right) the competition can be as hot as the temperature and draws riders from as far as Britain. English Derby winner Ernie Johnson is pictured in full action (Bottom Far Right).

trainer Ivan Allan said: 'If a horse throws its jockey, some of them will laugh and think it part of the spectacle, nobody shows any concern. Of course, they only come to gamble. This is not racing, really, just an organised casino'.

Allan has, at 37, the sort of cool eye but warm touch which would make him a top trainer in any country. Listening to him both then, and in a previous visit to his home base at Singapore, it's clear that while the Malaysian climate and system may be totally different from Europe or America, considerable skills and understanding are needed to come out on top.

Most of the 800-odd horses on the circuit have no pretensions to being more than mediocre. Hutchinson's winner, Pathfinder, had been rated only 65 by Timeform back in England, where a top-class horse would be 130. So, having found the right level for him to win a race, the trainer's job is usually to 'finesse' him into being suitably handicapped for a second success, and so on. While

Mr Yeap's more cynical friends may think that this is simply obtained by a major application of brakes by the jockey in previous races, they need reminding that camera patrols and stipendiary stewards keep a pretty intensive surveillance.

Kuala Lumpur itself may have some way to go, but at Singapore's beautiful Bukit Timah track, the system looked as strong as anywhere in the world, and, following the Australian pattern the morning newspaper carried a full stipendiary's report on each of the previous day's races. Lester Piggott, Taffy Thomas or any other visiting knight of the pigskin will tell you that benefits of the doubt are not lightly given, and even such things as an intended change of tactics have to be explained to the authorities beforehand.

That other disgruntled punter's cry, that every winner (or loser) is doped, is hard to stand up against the intense scrutiny now available. While controlled medication is permitted, it has to be administered with veterinary supervision, and horses are put through not only a post-race analysis, but pre-race testing in which Singapore has led the world.

So to stay on top, a trainer has to understand his horses, and under equatorial Malaysian conditions there are some pretty major problems. For instance, quite apart from the rock-hard nature of the track, a place like Kuala Lumpur isn't exactly Warren Place (Newmarket's most famous stable) when it comes to stable arrangements.

Below the tall palm trees in the early morning, we picked our way past scratching, curly-tailed dogs, scurrying chickens and yawning, towel-skirted Indians, to the 40-horse yard of Alan Heddle. With his crisp moustache and the Scottish inflections unremoved by all these expatriate

years, there's more than a bit of Somerset Maugham about 'The Major'. But he has run a successful ship for years now, and seeing him wander about it you realised that there was more to keeping it afloat than asking the lads how they were.

For a start, it cannot be that easy to know how many lads you employ at any one time. If skilled labour, good work riders, experienced and responsible head lads, are hard to find, unskilled labour is not. In the parade ring at the races there had been two attendants at every horse's head. In the stables there is one groom to every horse, and all he ever does is clean out the shavings bed (not much straw used), and wash and groom his charge after exercise. Well, not quite all. 'To some of these chaps, the horse becomes almost a second wife', says Alan Heddle. 'They sit all day talking to the dumb fellow, and some of them are convinced that the horse is speaking to them'.

Most of these grooms are Boanese, from northern Sumatra, that nearby but mysterious Indonesian island. No Chinese, and only a few Indians, will take the job, and although the grooms have developed an affinity with horses, there is little instruction to take the process further. It's perhaps a surprise, then, that some of the horses *have* gone farther, most noticeably Jumbo Jet, who ran in the Washington International for Ivan Allan.

Another Allan graduate was successful with the American trainer, Charlie Whittingham, in 1980, and Ivan explains: 'While most of the horses are only platers by British standards, the top horses are not bad, as unlike Hong Kong we are allowed to import our own buys. With prizes like the 200,000 dollar Queen's Cup you can spend a bit'.

Butterfly Boy, the latest Allan champion, was trotting round the dusty excercising ring with the gleaming coat which betokens the ultimate in racing luxuries, the air-conditioned box. One happy day, all boxes will be so equipped, but until then most horses will be shielded from the sun, but not the heat, and sooner or later will be afflicted by the dreaded dry coat.

This ailment (real name anhydrosis) is what it says it is, for after some time in the tropics the sweat glands just cease functioning. In Singapore, the redoubtable Dick Tibbatts, starter, apprentice-school trainer and retired admiral, got me to ride in one of his licensing trials over hurdles. It was, so he said, to test the competence of would-be jump riders and, as a cracked-up ex-jock, I was loaded on to a dry-coated ex-crock of a nag. It was about four o'clock in the afternoon, and when I pulled up after working a mile at a reasonable gallop, my shirt was already soaked through. But when I reached forward and patted the horse on the neck, there was only one damp patch up towards the poll. All the rest was as hot and dry as dust in the Sahara.

Obviously there are grave risks in racing in such temperatures when the body does not lose heat and there was a dreadful occasion a few years back when three horses keeled over just after the finishing line. Nowadays, the absolutely dry-coated horse is not allowed to race, but as most

Trainers like Singapore's Ivan Allan (Right) have to adapt to the limitations of Kuala Lumpur's chicken-pecked training facilities (Top Right). Exercise has to be taken very early (Top Left) to avoid the heat and with only a few loose boxes with air conditioning most horses have to be protected from the heat by canvas awnings. As a consequence most of them eventually succumb to the dreaded 'dry coat' (inability to sweat) but local aid (Far Left) remains unknotted. Trainer Alan ('The Major') Heddle (Left) has come far from his native Scotland.

horses go that way eventually, one of the trainer's most important tasks is to spot the signs early enough. 'There are no hard and fast rules', says Ivan Allan, 'but you tend to find that a very free-sweating type will go dry quicker, and often horses by the same sire will turn. For instance, I have had three horses by Manacle (sire of the 1980 European champion, Moorestyle), and they all went dry.'

When dry coat sets in, a trainer can either get the horse into an air-conditioned box and cool him out or, more likely, pack him off to the 'spelling' station up in the hills. The word 'spelling' comes from the Australians, whose year-round racing, and intensely demanding big-city carnivals (three

races in a week are commonplace) make a break (a 'spell') away from the track a necessity. But the principle of cooling off in the hills comes from the Indian cavalry regiments and the best colonial merchant families in the days of the Empire, and it was with thoughts of them, and of Malaysia's more turbulent recent past, that we set off on a most spectacular journey, from Kuala Lumpur to the 'spelling' station in the Cameron Highlands.

A few words of advice. If you are thinking of making the trip, make sure you get an air-conditioned car and your own driver. Then you might avoid either dry coat or sweaty coffin. I can't remember how we found Anwar, only that he

suddenly appeared, that he charged very reasonably, was enviably clean and could negotiate the mechanised whirlpool that is Kuala Lumpur without a tremor. All those qualities were conspicuous by their absence in the taxi driver who collected us from the airport. It was a bit unnerving when the lid of the boot came off in his hand when he loaded the luggage, and downright terrifying when at the first traffic lights we realised that he had no brakes, but just slowed down by gear-changes. How we made the hotel that night is to be found in the memory file alongside riding a novice hurdler at Newton Abbot and discovering just before the start that the horse was blind.

The Cameron Highlands are only 80 miles north of Kuala Lumpur, but it's a four-hour drive. The first part, up the Ipoh road as far as Tapah, undulates gently through sweeping rubber plantations and great rows of oil palms like giant pineapples, and wouldn't take very long if the narrowness of the road and the litter of smashed-up lorries in the ditches didn't discourage overtaking the Buicks and bullock carts. But branching right after Tapah, you have every excuse for going slow. Firstly because you are winding your way up 5,000 feet in 10 miles, and secondly because it is one of the most spectacular jungle drives in the world. Thick, green-creepered trees tower above, and the bends in the road tease you with sudden distant glimpses of tea plantations across the valley.

For the horses, sore or dry-coated after bashing round in the heat down below, the 'spelling' station must seem like paradise. Even early in the afternoon there was a sweet touch of coolness in the air for the horses lazing out in the little fenced paddocks or the shady green-roofed stables. Up to 45 animals can be boarded, and the change in climate is such that besides the purple beauty of the bougainvillea and the startling orange of the central flame tree, there is the practical luxury of rows of tomatoes and green vegetables.

Set on the edge of the plateau to which

William Cameron gave his name in 1885, but which was only opened up properly in the late 1920s, this racehorse haven was started in 1929 by Paddy Boyle, an army major based in Singapore. It has survived not only changes of management, but the onslaught of the Japanese occupation in 1941 and the nervous years of The Emergency after 1948. But horses and horse people don't usually get hung up on history, and so the jungle keeps its secrets as Dr Dick Coughlan and his team continue to run this equine convalescent home.

For all Anwar's efforts at translation, our talk with the head man, Ascalana, was strictly pidgin-English stuff. But apparently the normal thing is for horses to stay for at least two months, and apart from benefiting from Dr Coughlan's veterinary skills and the milder climate, they ease aching joints by standing in a pool of the river below. There's a staff of 17, not including a grizzle-headed old boy who claimed to stand 78 years old in his crumpled linen skirt. Ascalana assured us that the horses loved it up there, and as a grey, New Zealand-bred six-year-old called Valentino II was led by, I could swear I saw him wink. The men didn't look too bothered, either, and were clearly at ease with the horses. Some of them cannot do too much for their charges. Scientists in Singapore analysing the pre-race dope tests were once baffled by a new drug. It turned out to be nicotine. Nicotine? Yes, one heavy-smoking groom couldn't wait any longer for his horse to give his sample. So he gave one of his own. Greater love hath no man.

The Cameron Highlands, a 'spelling station' high in the Malaysian heartland, gives racehorses a chance to recover from the rigours of the track and particularly to recondition after the problems of 'dry coat'. The cooling air of the Highlands allows the glands to function again and therefore gives the racehorse a new lease of life. All the same they are unlikely to match the longevity of some of the locals (Above).

A WORLD OF
TRADING

(Preceding Spread). At the sales an owner is not just getting a horse, he is buying a dream. For here he sees no silks, no jockeys wielding whips, no straining beasts. The animal is just led round and round the sawdust circle while the auctioneer recites a litany of possible achievements and potential buyers try to catch the rostrum's eye while looking disinterested at the same time. It's as good an example as you can get of the absurdity and yet rationale of the whole business: just a horse walking round. All it might ever do is run fast or produce something that might run fast. Yet the thoroughbred is now an international commodity and Newmarket's Tattersalls Sales, pictured here, did more than 20 million guineas of business at their two major yearling sales in 1982.

Sales, as here at Newmarket, involve contemplation, calculations and the unfathomable matter of what goes on in a horse's head (**5**). It has been so since Richard Tattersall founded the firm in 1766 that has become famous all over the world for the sale of bloodstock. The famous Rotunda (**10**) dates from his day, with its statue of a fox and surmounted by a bust of George IV, who counted Richard Tattersall among his friends. Originally sited at Hyde Park Corner in London, moved in 1865 to Knightsbridge Green, it was not until after World War II that the Rotunda moved from Britain's capital to its present site. There it resides today, like a small temple, in the midst of an escalation in prices that Richard Tattersall could not have contemplated even in his wildest dreams, and a cast of international characters that he could never have envisaged.

Like Welsh-born trainer Ron Boss (**4**) with his then patron, on the right, Prince Torki M. Saud, who could not have been the first to realise that silver tongues as well as rugby players are reared in the valleys of Wales. Or three Irish stalwarts (**3**) who are, left to right, Mick O'Toole, Jack Doyle and Adrian Maxwell, caught in a rare moment of silence. And complexities of the modern catalogue? At least Dr. Edouard Pouret (**7,8,9**), centre in his French grouping, with trainer John Cunnington on his left, is not a man to be daunted. Neither is Bruce Hobbs (**1**), who has been engaging in such study for a lifetime. Hobbs sticks to traditional English checks for the occasion, while Henry Cecil (**13**), with his wife Julie, reflects a new zip-up sartorial age, as does English bloodstock agent George Blackwell (**6**).

But whatever the cloth, the mode at Newmarket has usually been to dress up for the races and down for the sales. Witness Dick Hern (**14**), catalogue under arm, talking to his old mentor, the late Jack Colling; Robert Sangster (**12**); and Ryan Price (**11**). French trainer Francois Boutin (**2**) would however look elegant, come what may, even in an abattoir. And that, whisper it softly, is where some of the horses will be heading if all the talk and dreams come to naught.

1	2	3	4	
	5	6		
7	10	11		
8		12		13
9				14

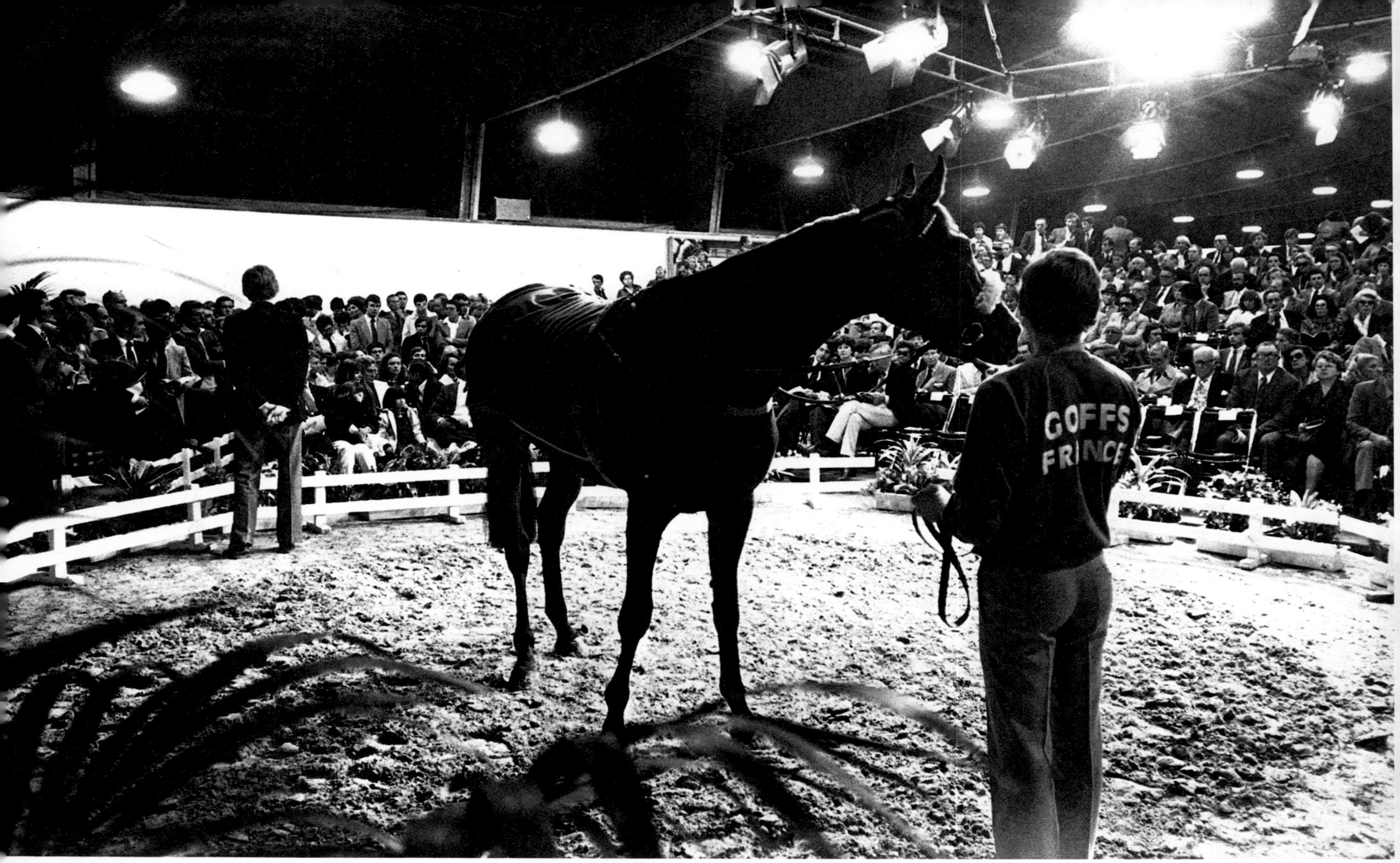
GOFFS
FRANCE

1980 SARATOGA YEARLING SALE
146
140000
NOW BID

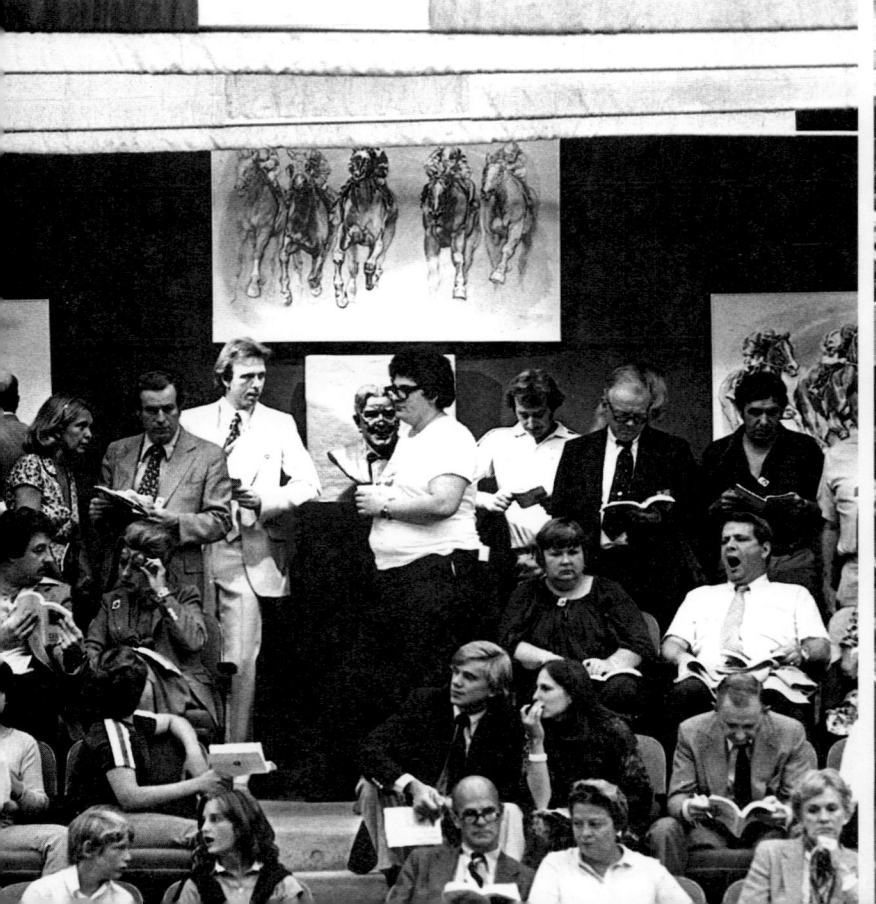

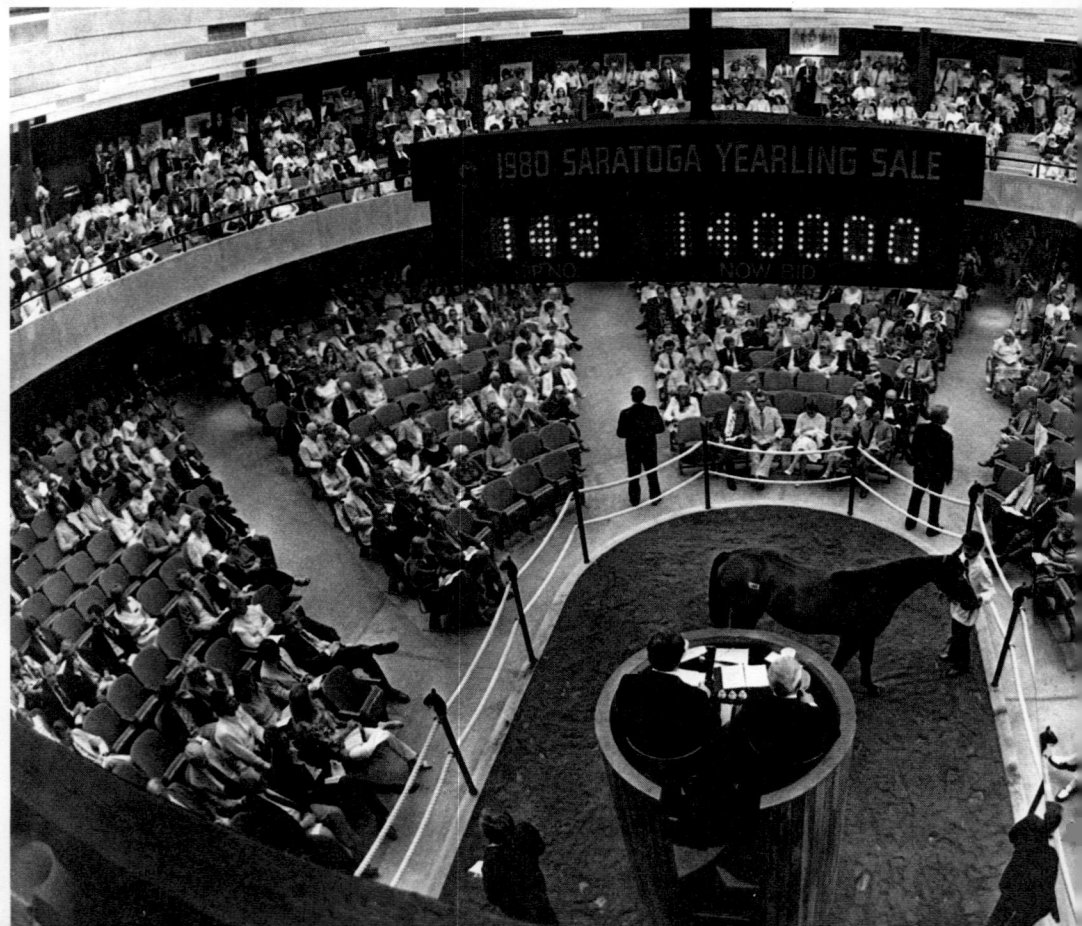

In a perfect world, sales and racing are made to mix and that certainly happens at Longchamp and Saratoga. Both of them use the trick of selling under lights when the day's racing is over and in Longchamp's case the Goff's France sales (1) at the Polo Ground, adjacent to the course, is on the very eve of the Arc de Tromphe in October. There, instead of the deliberate cap-and-anorak scruffiness of the English sales, the business suit is de rigueur, as witness (2) Alec Head and his father Willie, who begat a truly remarkable racing dynasty. Both men have trained Arc de Triomphe winners ridden by Freddie Head, the son of Alec and Ghislaine (on Alec's right), who also rode the 1979 winner Three Troikas, trained by his sister Criquette. At Saratoga in August (3,4), the immediate priorities are somewhat different: it is so hot outside that the air-conditioned cool of the sales ring is blessed and welcome relief. Once there, however, whatever the lateness of the hour, it is still serious work for the likes of E. P. Taylor (5, with pipe) and Leslie Combs III (seated alongside him), whose Windfields and Spendthrift Farms are as famous as any in the business.

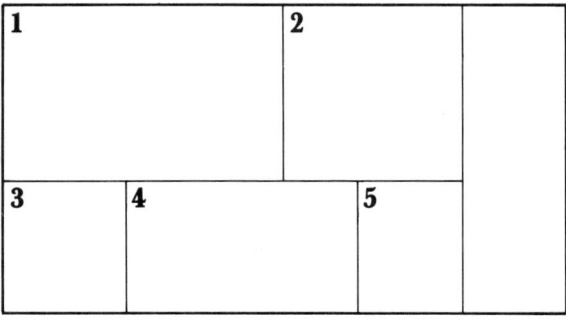

Going, going, gone.... The auctioneer's gavel bangs down, another lot is led away, and owner Phillip Solomon (**1**) makes a note in his catalogue. But the build-up to that climax is, to the connoisseur, one of the varied delights of being at the sales.

There is to be observed, for instance, the fine, old English way as personified by Captain Kenneth Watt (**2**) long-time senior partner of Newmarket's Tattersalls Sales, the leading sales in Europe. With trilby hat and slightly crumpled tweed suit, Watt approaches the hassle with all the good-mannered charm of a country squire asking the villagers to contribute to the Harvest Festival. 'Are you still with me sir?...Ah yes, a really lovely filly this, a hundred thousand and she is still cheap, gentlemen....'

There is the passionate Celtic approach, depicted in the bespectacled, hectoring style of Tattersalls' Irish representative, Sir Peter Nugent (**3, 4**). 'Now come on...it's against you in the gate...a really magnificent colt this...you are going to lose him...for the last time then...the bid's on my right....'

And there is the double-barrelled American approach as illustrated by John Finney and his senior auctioneer Ralph Retler (**5, 6, 7, 8, 9, 10**) at Saratoga's Fasig-Tipton Sales.

Atop their rostrum the selling pair attack with great American bustle and the bids are acknowledged in an undulating tobacco auction chant. 'Fifty thousand fifty thousand, who'll give me sixty....' It certainly gets through the lots quicker, even if there are times when you think the price of rose manure must be going through the roof.

	1	2	3	4
		5		
		6	7	10
		8	9	

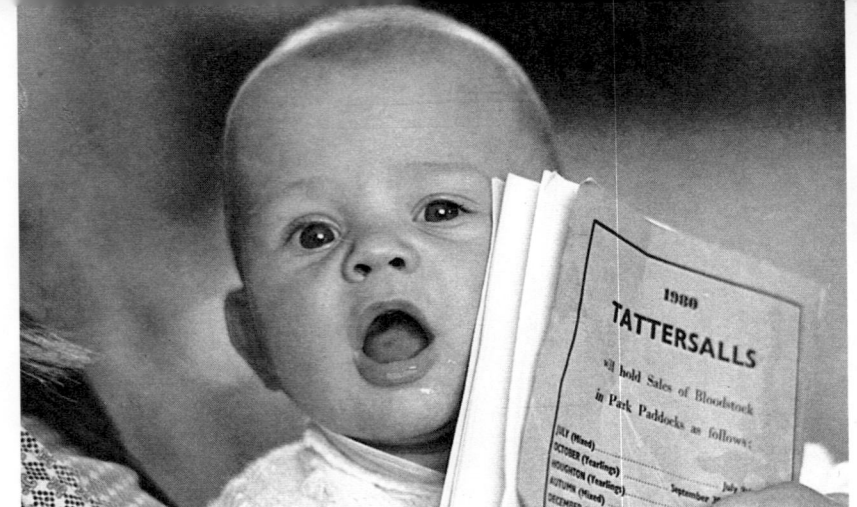

Whether they are babies, bearded or bald, racing folk tend to be steeped in the whole background of their sport, including breeding. Young Master James 'Fozzie' Stack (1), for example, does not just hide behind a sales catalogue. Shown an oft-repeated video of his famous father Tommy and Red Rum in their historic 1977 Grand National victory he can pick them out. By contrast Humphrey Cottrill (2) is a man with a 70-year advantage over Master James. After spending most of his life training horses, Cottrill went into retirement by undertaking the management of the burgeoning empire of Prince Khaled Abdulla.

The racing empire of Paul Mellon (right in picture 16) has been thriving for some 30 years on both sides of the Atlantic. But for all the success he has had in his native America, the pinnacle moments remain the European triumphs of Mill Reef in the Epsom Derby and the Arc de Triomphe in 1971. Mill Reef's trainer, Ian Balding, on Mellon's right, will be able to smile about those victories forever.

If Balding and Mellon knew what it was like to be associated with a champion so did Laz Barrera and Louis Wolfson (respectively left and right in 13), who will always be linked in the memory as the trainer and owner of the immortal Affirmed, American Horse of the Year in 1978 and 1979. Barrera, a native of Cuba, and Wolfson, who is from St. Louis, illustrate the international appeal of the racing game.

So to does Sheikh Mohammed Bin Rashid al Maktoum, presenting the Dubai Champion Stakes Trophy at Newmarket to Mrs Elizabeth Roberts (15), part-owner of the 1982 winner Time Charter. Sheikh Mohammed, a son of the ruler of Dubai, is defence minister of the tiny but influential Gulf State, and its sponsorship of the historic Champion Stakes was further evidence of British racing's good fortune in attracting Arab interest in the Seventies.

Agent Billy McDonald (3), the man who bought the dual Arc de Triomphe winner Alleged, hails from a spot more conventionally associated with the world of flat racing, Northern Ireland, but Sourien Vanian (6) comes from Armenia. And the assortment of trainers depicted here is equally, if not more wide ranging. Gordon Campbell (10), the trainer of the crack Flying Paster, hails from California, as does the incomparable Charlie 'Bald Eagle' Whittingham (8). Buddy Delp (4) hails from Maryland and, in the unlikely event of his never training another winner, will always be remembered for Spectacular Bid. Angel Penna (11) has made his mark in Argentina, Venezuela, France and the USA.

Penna has successfully raided Newmarket, as does Bill Watts (14) from his Yorkshire base; the Jordanian Michael Albina (5) from his new stables in the town; the Barbadian Michael Stoute (9), trainer of Shergar, the 1981 English Derby winner; and the Norman Francois Boutin (12), who brought Zino from Chantilly to win the 1982 2,000 Guineas.

They are all part of 'the great triviality,' a phrase beloved by Phil Bull (7), the bewhiskered guru from Halifax whose Timeform books and individual horse assessments have been the greatest advance yet in making a logical analysis of the sport.

1		2	3	4		5
6	7		8			9
10			11			12
13		14	15		16	

(1). *Racing can be a serious business and Lady Beaverbrook and her trainer, Dick Hern, ponder some weighty matter. Along the way, nonetheless, they have had plenty to smile about, most notably with Bustino, who won the 1974 St. Leger in the Beaverbrook maple leaf colours.*

(2). *Trainer Jeremy Tree's credits stretch across races at (unusually) all distances in all the major countries of Europe.*

(3). *Unlike many people in the game Barry Hills is just about as shrewd as he looks. During a long spell as a lad at Newmarket judicious betting accumulated for Hills sufficient capital to launch himself on his career as a trainer in 1969.*

(4). *An impressive trio at Epsom on Derby Day. On the left is Sir Noel Murless who, from 1935 until his retirement in 1977, became the most distinguished member of his profession. He won 19 English Classics, including the 1967 Derby with Royal Palace, owned by Mr. Jim Joel, on the right. Old enough to have fought in World War I and generous enough to have made his black-and-scarlet colours a byword for fair play over 40 years, Jim Joel had many fine winners but sadly only three other Classic winners besides Royal Palace. With them is France's Alec Head, a man with an equally distinguished career.*

(5). *Sheikh Hamdan al Maktoum (centre right, with black top hat) after the success of his brother Sheikh Maktoum's filly, Widaad, in the Queen Mary Stakes at Royal Ascot in 1982. Together with their other brothers Sheikh Mohammed and Sheikh Ahmed, these sons of the ruler of Dubai have made a stunning investment in British racing.*

(6). *Just in case anyone thought it was an insular game the good Lord invented Maurice Zilber, one-time Egyptian gambler turned trainer.*

(7). *Dr. Carlo Vittadini had a long association with racing in his native Italy before he became involved in ownership in Britain in the late Fifties, his crowning moments coming with the victories of Grundy in 1975.*

(8). *Guy Harwood has become the technocrat among British trainers. It has brought him to the head of his profession and dragged many rivals into the 20th century.*

(9). *Harry Wragg was born in 1902 and between 1919 and 1946 had a brilliant career as a jockey before becoming one of the very few riders to be equally successful as a trainer.*

(10). *Since childhood Daniel Wildenstein has followed racing but it was when he teamed up with trainer Angel Penna at Chantilly in the Seventies that he really set the turf alight.*

(11). *The moment of triumph they all seek. Shergar stands, ears pricked and resplendent, in the Sandown unsaddling enclosure in April 1981. The Aga Khan and Dickie McCabe share, as owner and lad, the hope of even bigger things.*

(12). *Stavros Niarchos, the great shipping tycoon, first came into racing in the late Fifties. His Pipe of Peace was third to Crepello and Ballymoss in the 1957 Epsom Derby. He then went out of racing for some 20 years before returning.*

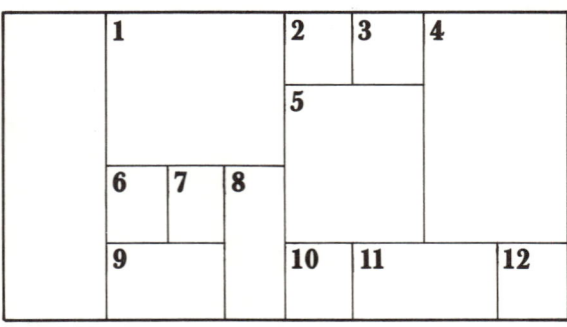

ACTING
STEWARDS

EARL OF HALIFAX

EARL OF DERBY

DUKE OF DEVONSHIRE

LT. COL. SIR JOHN HORNUNG

T. F. BLACKWELL ESQ. M.B.

CAPT. J. MACDONALD BUCHANAN M.

14
AUSTRALIA

'More than half the men at the hotel cocktail party seemed to be in full grey tailcoat Ascot kit, and at least one of the women had enough foliage on her head to make our irrepressible Mrs Shilling look to her ribbons. Once we finally made it back to the Flemington car park, the air of deja vu was even stronger. So much so that it became impossible to get the photograph to symbolise the great Australian picnic. The grey suits, the summer dresses, the champagne bottles, the white table cloths and the alcohol-flushed faces looked just like Royal Ascot on a sunny day'.

BY 9AM on Melbourne Cup day, thousands of festively-clad people, and whole regiments of champagne bottles, had already hit Flemington racecourse. Having been there since dawn, we beat a retreat to the Old Melbourne Motor Inn. It was sanctuary sought but hardly found, for by the time we finished breakfast the courtyard of this period piece among Melbourne hotels was filled by two white horses, by their riders in full scarlet-coated hunting kit, by a shivering school-uniformed girls' band and, as if you had to ask, by waiters bearing trays of champagne, enough to fill the fountain....

It's part of the vitality, and just occasionally the tedium, of Australian life that all sorts of major and minor events are seen as a challenge to prove that Oz is best. The Melbourne Cup is no exception, and ever since the first race in 1861, the Australians have set out to show that not only is this two-mile handicap the greatest single sporting event in the land, but that it assumes more respective importance than any other horse race in the world. From what we saw of the 1980 running, the challenge is still being met, but from our position wedged into the Flemington stands (and at the critical moment actually being perched on the roof), we were unable to check on the familiar claim that all Australia stops for the Melbourne

Cup. But it seemed that anyone not aware of the race by the traditional 2.30pm starting time on the first Tuesday in November was either living out beyond the aborigines or had a baby in the pouch.

The full media hype, built direct from one year to the next, first hit us in Honolulu which, even if it is still the wrong side of the Equator, is a hell of a sight better place to get stranded in than Vladivostok. For besides being one of the original surfer's paradises, it boasts an Australian consulate bursting with antipodean information, which was just as well, because by pre-Melbourne Cup Saturday we were meant to be reporting direct from Flemington on the Victoria Derby.

Our supposed round-the-world-in-80-racecourses tickets had turned out to be distinctly hobbled gift horses, carrying the dreaded affix SA (Space Available). With an empty plane you got the full first-class caviare treatment, but with overbooking you were turned out into the Los Angeles night or, in this instance, the Hawaii dawn, and with no guarantee of space for days ahead the only way we made Melbourne was to buy tickets on Canadian Pacific, which I had always thought was a railway line.

Happily, a fellow Space Available deportee turned out to be the world's greatest authority both on Honolulu hotels and on Australian racing,

with a direct line to the biggest betting chain in Sydney. After he had fixed us up with a luxury hotel room on Waikiki Beach, with a telephone link to the commentary on the Victoria Derby, any plea for sympathy, written glass in hand beneath the massive Baobab tree under which R.L. Stevenson penned some of his masterpieces, could only be a candidate for Whine of the Century.

The luck held in a big way when we finally staggered red-eyed into Melbourne on Sunday afternoon, and within three hours were sipping the golden bubbles in Robert Sangster's regal first-floor suite looking out over the Hilton swimming pool. If there was ever a better guide to the Melbourne Cup than this friendly visiting millionaire from our own country, he can only have graced the pages of social-climbing fiction. For not only was the former pools tycoon the single most influential entry into Australian racing circles in recent years, but his vivacious wife, Susan, had been the uncrowned queen of the place during her earlier marriage to Andrew Peacock, the most glamorous politician in either main party. And even more important than all that, Sangster's horse, Beldale Ball, was going to win the Cup....

Even struggling along in the Sangster's wake was the most extraordinary advantage to an

arriving Pom, not least in avoiding the two gaffes ('It's an eight-day cocktail party' and 'A very ordinary handicap') which Sangster himself dropped about the Melbourne Cup on his first visit. Cocktails there were in plenty, and bevvies of owners, trainers and jockeys kept coming out of the woodwork, but of all the Sangster introductions none compared with that to Colin Hayes, who on Melbourne Cup Tuesday must have completed as extraordinary a day as any trainer in history.

When we first saw him at 5.30 that morning, it seemed that the jinx that had haunted his Melbourne Cup attempts for 25 years, and which in 1979 culminated in the fatal accident to his top-rated Dulcify, had hit Hayes again. For, as he came out to the little blue hired Toyota on the top of the parking block, with his hat and tie and warming anorak, more like a caring professor than a racehorse trainer, Hayes told us that his elder brother, Arthur, had died the day before. 'He was my biggest supporter', said Colin, as he drove us the five kilometres to Flemington. 'Our father died when I was only nine, and being 12 years older than me, Arthur was the one to lean on'. Then, softly but with a deal of emphasis he added: 'I hope that doesn't mean the Melbourne Cup luck is going against us again'.

The record books will tell how the worm finally

turned to the tune not only of that elusive Melbourne Cup victory, but with six winners overall (three in Adelaide), and the Trifecta (first three placings) in the last race at Flemington. What no set of statistics can describe was the extraordinary aura of quietly beaming serenity with which Colin Hayes sailed through the day. Thirty-three years and twenty-one days since this former Electricity Trust clerk trained (and at that stage also rode) the first of more than 3,000 winners, it was almost as if Hayes had a line open to the Almighty, that all those years of struggling, the risks, the bereavements, the strain that caused major open-heart surgery, would be repaid in one great surge of the tide.

Of course, such thoughts were a long way from the sharp sunlight of Flemington on big-race early morning, with the track stretching itself awake without the packed car parks, crowded stands and booming public address that are its much-pictured clothing in the afternoon. Jockeys and trainers were sweatered against the chill, the horses looking workaday, not yet the gleaming hopefuls of the paddock parade. And after them came all the

(Preceding Spread) 'Normally I never touch it, but on Cup day anything goes…'. In fact, the day of Australia's Melbourne Cup is in some senses, as here, indistinguishable from Royal Ascot. But if the big hats, the dressing-up and the champagne are familiar, nothing in the world could match the local assertion that on this day of the year, if on no other, the whole world revolves round Australia's premier racing event.

Each year, the money bet on the Melbourne Cup makes it the country's biggest betting race, a fact in part reflected in the starting price, 11-1, of the eventual winner in 1980, Beldale Ball. Such is the hold the event has on all and sundry, including matronly ladies, that the nation addresses itself to the problem of picking a horse from the early hours. Come the dawn everybody who's anybody is interviewed for his views on TV and radio, until finally a stake has to be placed, perhaps with bookies where, at the end of the day, the only consolation is the shade.

microphones and notebooks when he first went to Australia, until the great Bart Cummings (a record seven Melbourne Cups to his name) took him aside and told him: 'You've just got to realise that it is all part of the game over here. It's the shop window and we are selling the merchandise'. Sangster's a changed man now, but even his new-found fluency was tested by the first question in an interview at the 1980 Melbourne Cup: 'Did you sack Piggott?' referring to Lester Piggott's replacement as Sangster's first jockey in the Vincent O'Brien stable. 'Or did Piggott sack you?'

To say that Cummings's red owl-face looks lived in is like suggesting that Tokyo is a bit short on garden space. But true to his word, he was available to all and sundry on Cup morning, so that by 7am he had done three radio and four TV interviews, as well as overseeing the final preparations of his three runners for the big race.

camp followers, fans, touts, media hacks and pundits of all ages, watching, pointing and endlessly building the buzz of the special day.

Aintree at dawn has its gladiatorial pre-Grand National drama. Churchill Downs has the Kentucky Derby's all-American dream up ahead, and when you look out at Tattenham Corner and Epsom's horseshoe gradients you have got two fabulous centuries of racing history to fall back on. Flemington may not beat those famous tracks on those points, but it has them all licked when it comes to public involvement. Whereas in England and France it can often be difficult to get connections to talk about their horses, and in America there is not always that wide interest if they do, in Australia you have the double-up of total interest and ultimate access. The Melbourne Cup is Australia's biggest single sporting event; it has been resident on the front pages for at least a week before Cup Tuesday, and so those involved with the runners might as well be ready to talk when they hit the racetrack.

Robert Sangster, 43 years old and reticent by nature, was horrified by the onslaught of cameras,

Colin Hayes between six o'clock and eight, probably talked as much to the public as to his staff, and quite often to both at the same time. The questions are much the same at one end of the world as at the other. How is he feeling? How will he like the track, distance, going, or jockey? What are the dangers? Australia was different in the amount of work the trainers were doing with their horses on big-race morning, when many had a 'breeze' (a sprint) and Hayes's four runners had 20 minutes' very sharp trotting, and in how early all the verbiage (even I was dragged in to give a visiting Pom's impressions) hit the air. We had been back at the hotel only 10 minutes, and ducked into our bedroom to avoid the white horses and the school band, when the television began to thump out a massive preview.

The almost casual openness towards the press was matched by a distinct lack of protocol

hang-ups in trainers' attitudes to their horses. Accustomed to the don't-go-near awe with which racehorses are treated in England, it was a refreshing surprise to see the Australian horses treated much more like pleasure animals than prima donnas, and my first memory of the race-track is of one rider leading a horse on either side of him as if he was taking two hunters down the road. So with all this digested, it was amusing to note the contradictory air of tradition that still comes like cream to the surface.

More than half the men at the hotel cocktail party seemed to be in full grey tailcoat Ascot kit, and at least one of the women had enough foliage on her head to make our irrepressible Mrs Shilling look to her ribbons. Once we finally made it back to the Flemington car park, the air of *deja vu* was even stronger. So much so that it became impossible to get the photograph to symbolise

the great Australian picnic. The grey suits, the summer dresses, the champagne bottles, the white table cloths and the alcohol-flushed faces looked just like Royal Ascot on a sunny day.

The mini-skirt caused a glorious rumpus when exhibited atop Jean Shrimpton's legs in 1965, but in 1980 some serious woman-watching soon discovered at least two totally see-through dresses, one lady with 21 porcupine quills quivering from her headdress and another very fit-looking 'Sheila'

They come to the Melbourne Cup alive and dead. The 100,000-plus crowd is ant-heap thick in the public enclosure (Below) and if the smarter car parks (Left) may have more space neither area lacks for lubrication. But some spectators are stuffed before proceedings commence. The legendary Phar Lap won The Cup in 1930 but now trundles out from Australia's National Museum to oversee the action on the first Tuesday in November.

inadequately covered in a cave-girl tigerskin. The attitude, therefore, has much of the carnival of Epsom Downs about it, and without the advantage of the infield on which to loose the freest spirits the two elements have to co-exist.

There was Prime Minister Malcolm Fraser getting a splendid cheer as he walked past the members' stand, and being roundly booed at the cheaper ring. There was the bucket-headed reincarnation of outlaw Ned Kelly swaying gently in drink just outside the unsaddling enclosure. There was the stuffed body of the legendary 1930 winner, Phar Lap, and the comic torso of a pantomime horse whose two constituents made a tipsy attempt to lead the runners into the paddock, thereby breaking Mrs Patrick Campbell's most famous rule: 'I don't care what you do as long as you don't do it in the street and frighten the horses'.

In fact, there was a nasty moment when the favourite, Hyperno, the 1979 winner, reared at the sight of his disconnected imitators. But all was well, and the truth is that good horse though the seven-year-old Hyperno is (he had won $A529,295 at post time), he and his 21 fellow contenders were a long way from being the fragile three-year-old classic hopefuls that skittle on to the course at Epsom. The Melbourne Cup is not a Derby or an Arc de Triomphe; it is an exact Southern Hemisphere equivalent of the Grand National at Aintree without the jumps.

At 3,200 metres, the Melbourne Cup is, like the Grand National, the longest race in its discipline. Being a handicap, it is open to almost anyone and, with $A310,000 overall prize money, always attracts a huge field. The magic element of luck can never be dismissed, which means that everyone can have their opinion, and bet their dollars as they like.

Such is the Melbourne Cup's hold on Australia that to suggest that it is more event than championship can be sacrilege, witness one infuriated letter from Earls Court when I mentioned same in my Sunday Times column. But the Grand National comparison is not only accurate, but respectful. For, by and large, the runners are older horses with more stories to them, more medals won, than any fly-by-night three-year-old, and so the race hardly ever lacks the drama of the greatest occasion. All it misses are those little Croesus paragraphs which appear after the Derby or the Arc de Triomphe telling you how many millions of pounds the winner was worth in stud value as he went past the post – rather hard to relate to Melbourne Cup winners, since most of them, including Phar Lap and Tulloch, the two greatest, have been geldings. Although the 1980 champion, Beldale Ball, was, so to speak, fully equipped, not even his greatest admirer could claim that this victory with only 49.5 kilos (7st 8lbs) on his back put him into the multi-million-pound-sire bracket.

So it is as a sporting event that the Melbourne Cup asks to be judged. Its impact was recognised by Robert Sangster at the victory ceremony. The man who over the years had been through similar triumphs after the English and Irish Derbys, and who only a month before had been in the winner's circle for the Arc de Triomphe, now stood before 100,000 people at the track, and the rest of Australia by telecast, and said with moving sincerity: 'This is the greatest day of my life'.

In fact, it was the most successful ceremony of its kind I have ever seen. It was so positioned (at the rails end of the parade ring) that the maximum number of people could see it. And it was uncluttered. Only Beldale Ball, his 'strapper' (groom) Akke van Dolan, trainer Colin Hayes, jockey John Letts and Mr and Mrs Sangster remained in that far end of the parade ring. Gathering hordes of photographers and pen-pushers were kept 20 metres back. Above all, it had a bit of style.

This style was in no small way due to the Governor-General, Sir Zelman Cowen, who conducted the presentations with a fine blend of pomp and humanity. For instance, he preceded the actual presentation and the speeches from Sangster, Hayes and the bespurred Letts by calling for individual rounds of applause not only for those

principals, but for Akke van Dolan. And he had done his homework, so that he was able to name her, and mention her Dutch origins and Indonesian upbringing. That surely is a touch other racing countries could imitate.

As always after a big race, inquests raged. Had the other jockeys erred in letting Letts lead from start to finish on Beldale Ball? How had Hyperno got shut in so that he never had a chance of getting nearer than seventh? Why had the New Zealand mare, Blue Denim, got so blocked before finishing like a rocket? And could the massive haemorrhage which killed Big Print at halfway have been foreseen?

Fearing a fall in attendance, the Victorian Racing Club had held television at bay until four years before, but now willingly submitted to its clutches. An impressively unencumbered space was made available immediately outside the weighing room, and every conceivable participant was dragged there to be interviewed, not necessarily by the genial host figure but, so it seemed, by the individual journalist who had sought out the participants. Clearly on Melbourne Cup Day a notebook is not enough; every ambitious hack must also have a microphone with which to take his chance of addressing the nation.

The day's statistics don't need to be pushed very hard to tell their story. The gate was 101,300 compared with 40,000 at Longchamp on Arc day, and 26,000 paying (300,000 on the Downs) at Epsom. The on-course Tote 'handle', which would be doubled by the 200 registered bookmakers, was $A1,695,136, and the off-course Tote Monopoly state total was $A9,240,330.50 on

Packed crowd, crammed car park, clustered sky line and multi-runnered race track for the 1980 Melbourne Cup (Top Left). The sweetness of triumph as Adelaide jockey John Letts is led in by Susan Sangster on the US-bred, former English racer – Beldale Ball (Centre). Then the formalities (Above) presided over by the Governor-General Sir Zelmen Cowen (at microphone), and applause for all the principals, including Beldale Ball's lad Akke van Dolan.

each race. That is all heady stuff, as was so much of the impressively organised afternoon, though I'm bound to say that the men-only stand above the weighing room was an absurd anachronism. But it was still the biggest day of all, and if a nation can't make that work, it might as well give up and turn to bingo.

So we packed these memories, and the picture of Mrs Sangster, flanked in happy reunion by Andrew Peacock as well as by Robert Sangster, standing barefoot on the table at Maxims belting out Waltzing Matilda before passing round the country's most coveted trophy as the loving cup, and moved on the following day to Sydney....

Apart from beating an impending airline strike, the idea was to get out into the country and take the temperature of the sport at the less glamorous end. Well, it was hot enough to keep the bush fires burning up in the Blue Mountains, and the dust flying at Hawkesbury, but the world's healthiest racing harvest was still coming in.

Hawkesbury's race track is set in racing country 40 miles west of Sydney, and some 10 miles short of that mountain range which the pioneers didn't cross until 1813. Hawkesbury is in theory one of the second-division 'provincial' tracks among the 128 racecourses in New South Wales, some cut above the true 'bush' meetings. But at first sight it looks like a baked-out gum-tree version of Huntingdon without the jumps. Some of the outbuildings appear to have been there since the first meeting in 1871, and to the visiting eye one or two of the horses swatting flies in the saddling stalls didn't seem much younger.

First impressions lie, for modest little Hawkesbury, where a notice warns that 'shirts, shorts, socks and shoes must be worn in the Members' is just one example of the great Australian racing boom showing what can happen

if government and racing authorities have a reasonable understanding about the state of the industry. With more than 20 meetings in its last financial year, this little patch of dust, this Aussie 'gaff', this other Hexham, grossed receipts of over a million dollars.

When you are told that Hawkesbury's average gate, including 700 professionals, is no more than 2,200, you will appreciate that all that money did not come from ever-clicking turnstiles, and in fact the authorities in several states are clucking about falling attendances, and we were among only 1,500 people on our race day. But while Hawkesbury's average off-course turnover (Tote only) and approximately 6½ per cent to Government and 3½ per cent to racing in general, is $A860,000, its most interesting figure is the average on-course Tote handle of $A220,000, of which the course is entitled to six per cent.

That massive on-course statistic from so small a crowd suggests a truth evident throughout this enormous, empty, seven-state, four hundred-race-course, 14 million-population continent, that what the Australian punter lacks in numbers he makes up for in keenness, matching all bar the obsessive Hong Kong Chinese and the gamble-starved Japanese in eagerness, and leading the world in informed aggression.

Before anyone starts crowing about Tote monopolies, let's add that on-course bookmakers play a major role. At Hawkesbury, there were no fewer than 34 operating on the local meeting, and another nine on racing in Melbourne and Brisbane, and the battles that ensued were almost as lively as the equine athletics out on the track, one man turning over as much as $A100,000 in the day.

That 'book' belonged to slim, smart-suited Robbie Waterhouse, heir apparent of the third-generation bookmaking genius of his family whose eight members presently operating are dominated by his father, Bill, who as a sort of satchel-carrying Kerry Packer remains the only

Melbourne Cup triumph in different forms. For Colin Hayes (Far Left) it is the most bitter-sweet day imaginable. He has finally won the race which has always escaped him and even killed his best ever horse, Dulcify, in 1979. He has also won five other races on the same day, but everything is overshadowed by the death of his older brother Arthur on the eve of The Cup. For Robert Sangster (Above Right) the strain, this once, is beginning to show. Beldale Ball's victory is not only the most international of justifications for his far-flung, 250-horse, six-country racing empire, it is the final tying of the friendship knot with Melbourne. He shook the Australian capital in previous years by referring to The Cup as 'just an ordinary handicap' and by eloping with their most glamorous politician's wife, Mrs. Susan Peacock. Now Mrs Sangster, she has become the vivacious queen of the Sangster operation (Above Left) and all parties, including her former husband Andrew Peacock (Left), forgot their cares to accompany her in a performance of 'Waltzing Matilda' on a table at Maxim's on Cup night.

man to have laid a single million-dollar bet and come out the other side (although not without some twitching of the taxman's nostrils). A study of Robbie's figures ($A80 racecourse fee and 1¾ per cent tax, made up of ½ per cent to racing and 1¼ per cent to government–and he lost $A8,000) showed the true incentive to the Australian horse player–if he works at it, he can win money.

To the visitor from Britain, where the true professional punter is about as common as the platypus in Perth, this sounds suspiciously like sales talk. But Waterhouse, with his tie swinging in the merciful breeze, was insistent. 'Do you realise', he said, pointing to the wary-eyed throng out front, 'that there are at least fifty, if not a hundred, out there who make a good living out of beating the book. So they have to graft. A man like Don Scott [a millionaire from punting] will do 30 hours' study before a Saturday's racing. But they have no deduction on winnings (in Britain 4 per cent), and the only way we can beat them is to be as informed ourselves, and offer true value in the market'.

Still better from the racecourse point of view, the same successful punters keep a weather eye on the Tote, and if the prices ever seem out of line they have a quick lunge at the machine with its resultant six per cent bonus for the track. In a financial sense (minimum first prize $A1,500) it was all too good to be true, and in watching the actual racing there wasn't even the cold comfort of finding that it was some competition for broken-down donkeys.

True, the first glimpse of the saddling area, with its rows of covered concrete stalls, smacked of some Indian market, and the 10-strong squad of blacksmiths hammering away to get the racing plates on beforehand, and off while the wretched animal was still blowing afterwards, seemed a bit makeshift. But on closer inspection many aspects of the afternoon stood up to any comparison.

That old caravan at the back of the stalls turns out to be a fully-equipped laboratory for pre-race blood tests, which are not yet used in Britain. That old stable in a corner collects post-race samples for as strict a no-medication analysis

Top Australian jockeys: Adelaide-based John Letts (Top Near Right) who rode the 1980 Melbourne Cup winner Beldale Ball; Malcolm Johnston (Top Far Right) the young Sydney star who rode the remarkable Kingston Town; Harry White, (Bottom Near Right) the crack Melbourne jockey who rode the 1979 Cup winner Hyperno; and Brett Thompson, (Bottom Far Right) the young man from Wangunui, New Zealand, who has become the first jockey to the Colin Hayes stable. They are obviously fine riders but is the Australian style, which favours much longer leathers (Left) than currently used in Europe or America, too loose and old-fashioned or are they the only place in the world to have it right? Class jockeys will always show through but looking at a typical Australian finish makes you wonder whether too many riders are trying too hard in a whirl of whips and spurs.

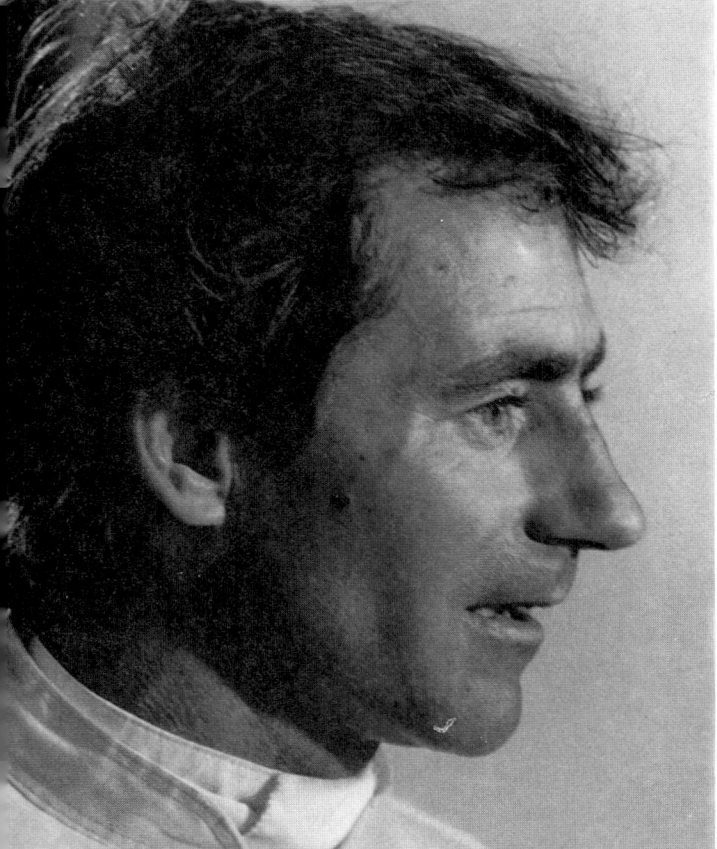

as our own. Those two amateur-looking video cameras actually give a clear and quickly-replayed picture of every race. Those plans on the club-room wall would make the British Levy Board wince. Those four be-blazered men are, in fact, stipendiary stewards with an impressive knowledge of tactical possibilities, and those deep-stirruped jockeys may look a bit like Banjo Paterson in full flight, but you have to wonder whether their British counterparts would sprint unraced two-year-olds round a right-angled bend as effectively.

Returning from this six-race, 75-runner meeting, it was really only in the area of riding and horse-care that doubts arose. In his native country, the Australian jockey is considered the best in the world, and of the few who have come to Britain in recent years at least three, Breasley, Williamson and, for one meteoric year, George Moore, were a match for anyone. But at a considerable risk of sounding like a prejudiced Little Englander, I have to report that the riding of the very best jockeys (at Flemington) and of the good journeymen (at Hawkesbury), was something of a disappointment.

Fundamentally, the Australian jockey rides like the English and French jockey of 15 years ago, and the American of 25 years ago. That is, he rides with deep enough stirrup leathers to be able to pivot the leg off the knee and basically propel the horse along by kicking him with the (often spurred) heels. It is undeniable that this method gives better lateral control than the much-shorter-leather technique first adopted by the Americans and then pioneered in Europe by the two super champions, Lester Piggott and Yves St. Martin. And it is also a fact that riding with ultra-short leathers can be a positive disadvantage on a tired horse that has almost ceased to generate much momentum. St. Martin once told me: 'When the very heavy going comes, I have difficulties'. And when Australian Bill Pyers was riding in France, he was always doubly effective in soft ground with tired horses.

But in Australia, with its commendably tough supervision of jockey's efforts and no animal-welfare lobby restricting the use of the whip ('Hit right out' is a frequent and all-too-apt commentator's description), many jockeys using their (to us) old-fashioned method seem to be in danger

Hawkesbury Race Club, 35 miles west of Sydney is a long way from the real bush tracks but the dust still flies and the battle lines of 43 bookmakers, including nine offering odds on 'out of state' races, perfectly illustrates the strength of the Australian betting market. During the day Robbie Waterhouse will turn over more than 100,000 Australian dollars and still come out losing, which the racecourse certainly will not. Besides collecting an 80 dollar fee from each bookmaker (who also give ½ percent of turnover to racing), Hawkesbury is entitled to take 6 percent of the Tote handle, which averages over 200,000 dollars a day.

W. WATERHOUSE

RESULTS
PRICE FLUCTUATIONS
MELBOURNE
BRISBANE
RESULTS
TRACK
WEATHER
TRACK

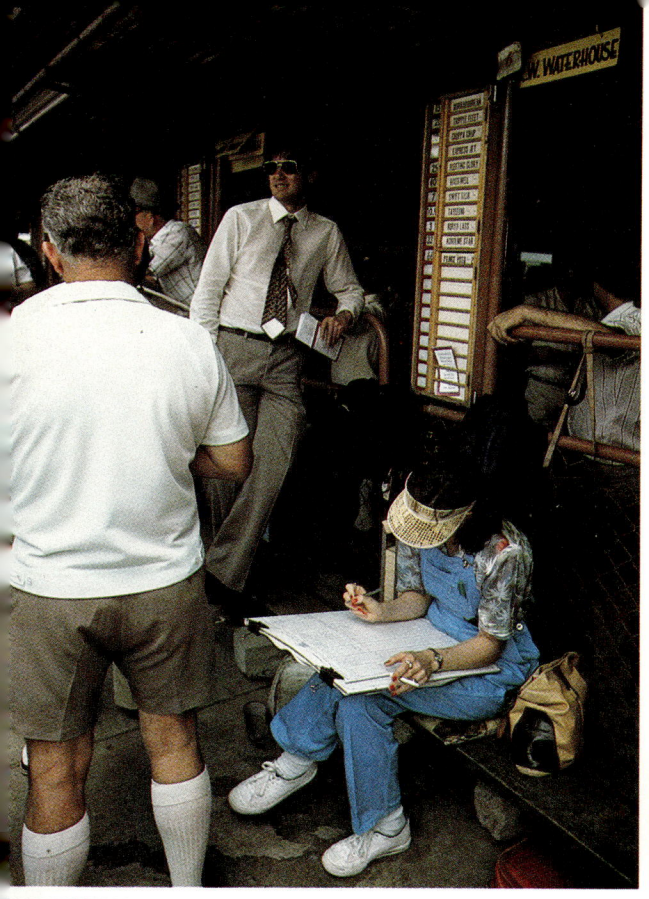

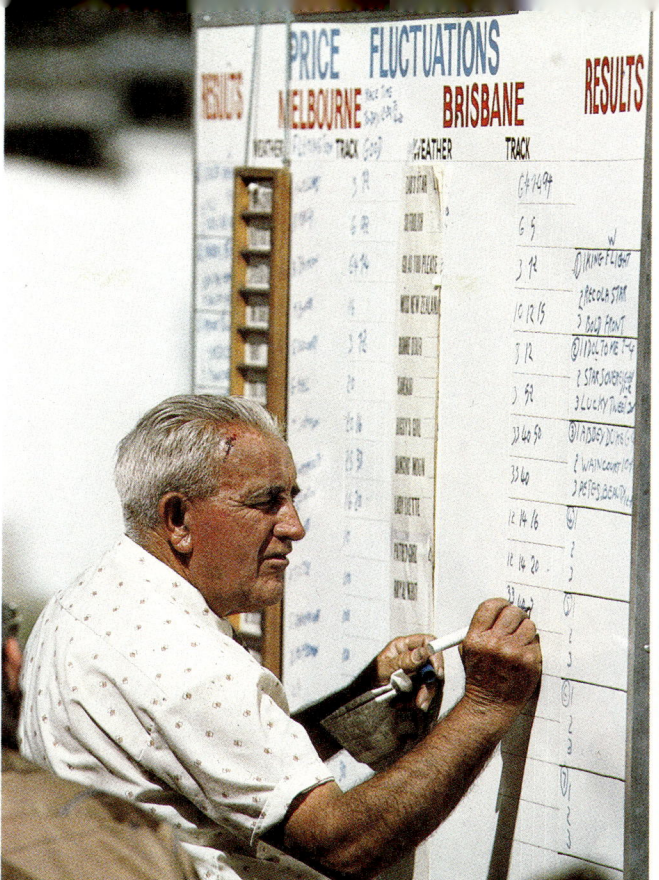

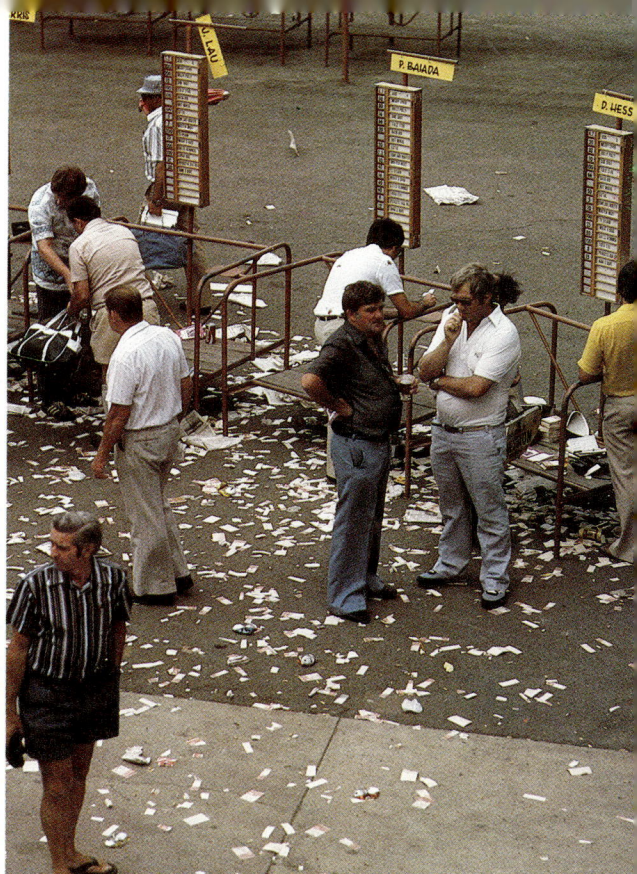

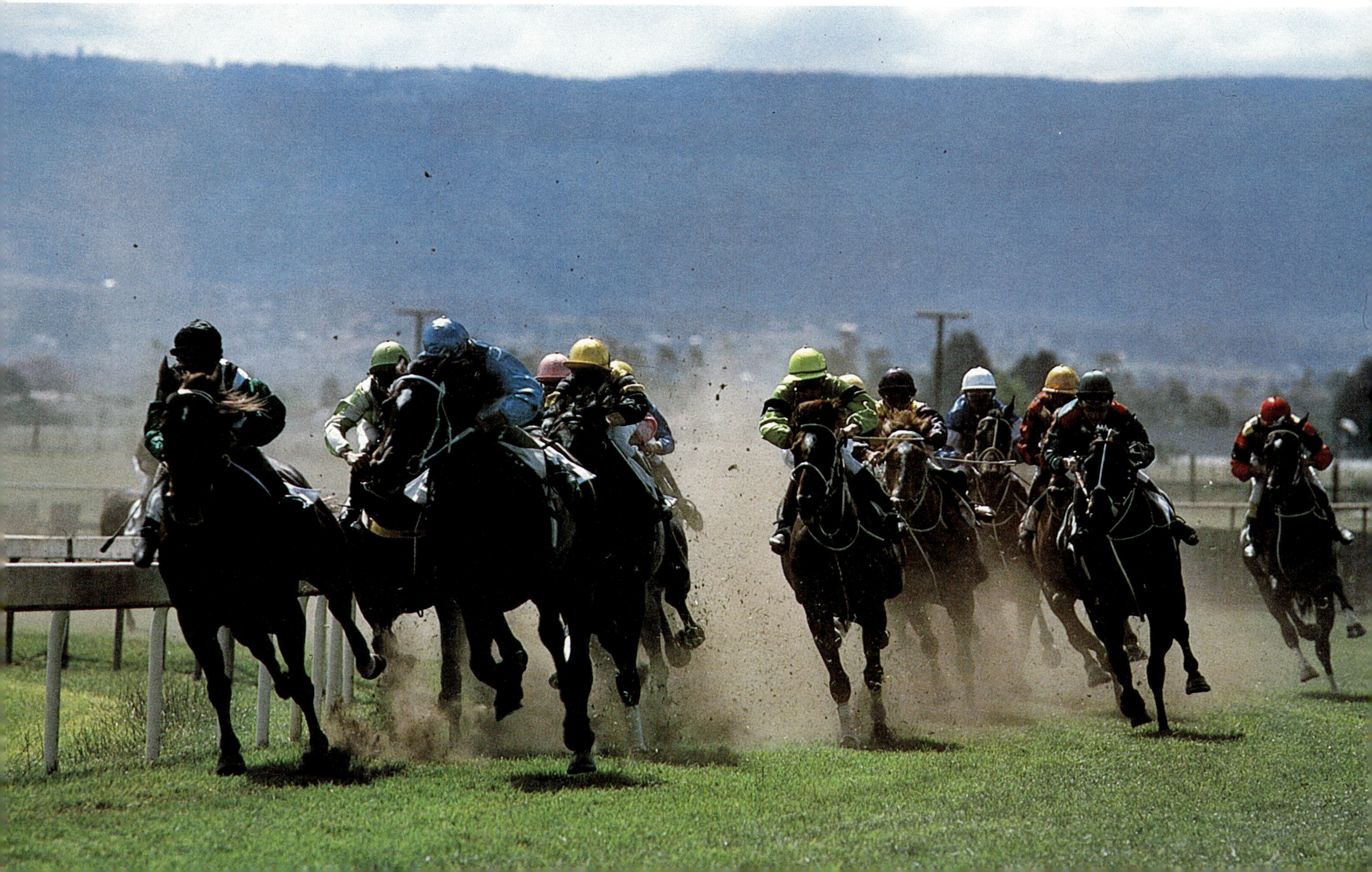

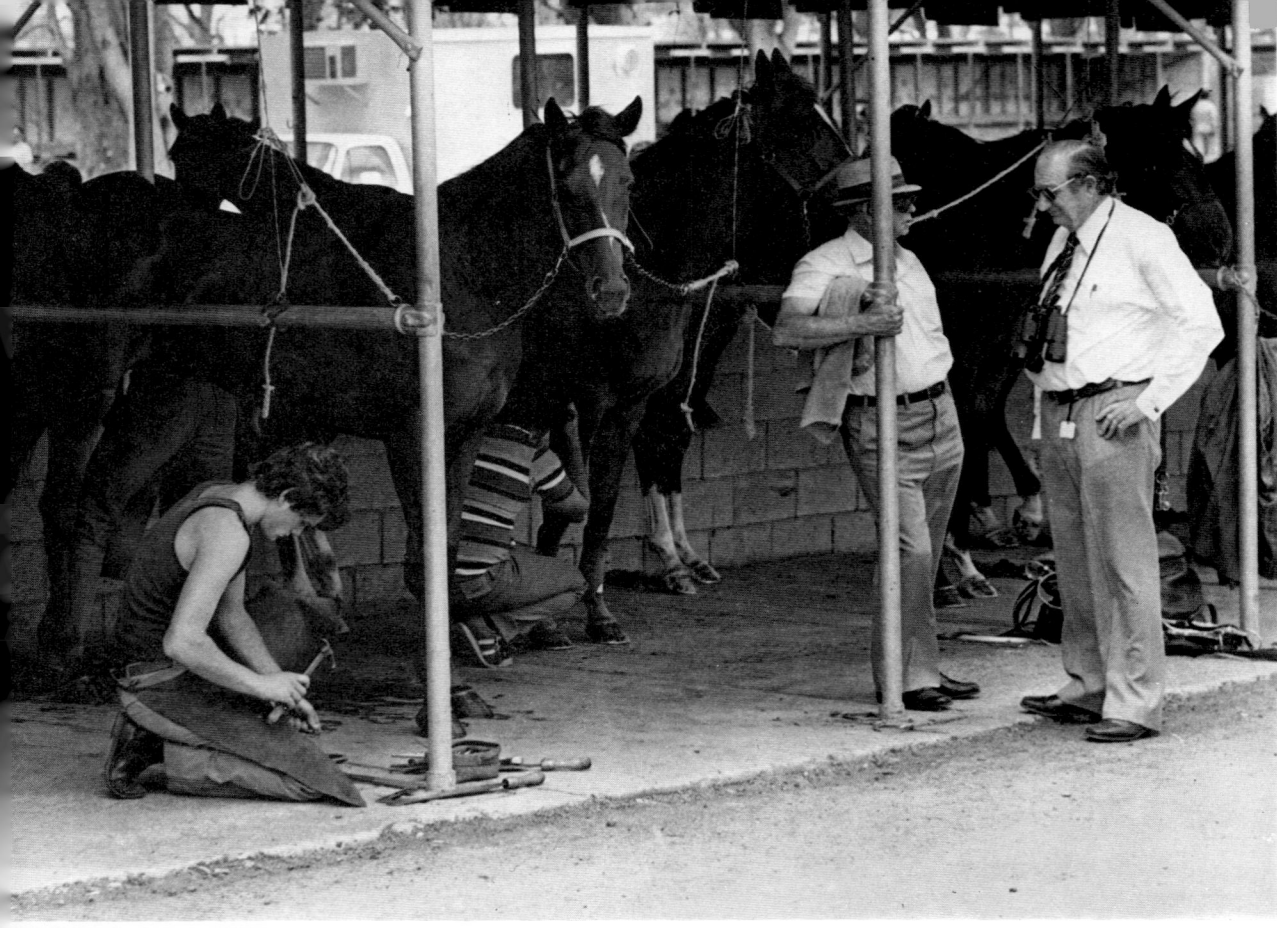

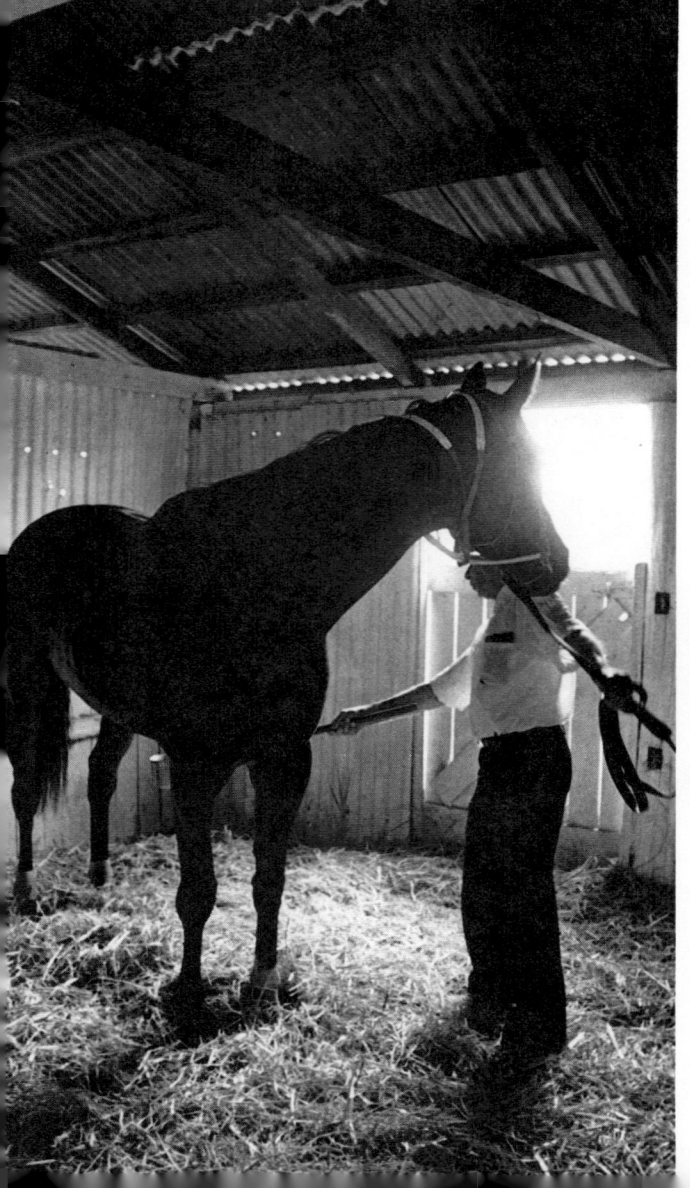

of going faster than the horse. However much energy a rider may expend, the only way a horse can be made to go faster is to put more power into the thrust of the hindleg stride which propels him forward. He may be induced to greater thrust by hitting, whipping, shouting or just competitive instinct, but none of those in themselves actually provides the thrust. The only way a rider can assist directly is by pressing down in the stirrup irons and adding his weight to that of the horse's at the moment of propulsion.

That is not opinion, it is a matter of fact, of basic animal dynamics. But with the memory of too many jockeys flapping and whirling away like overwound clockwork dolls, comes the opinion that a shorter-stirruped, closer-to-the-horse method, would give the horse more leverage and freedom, and that a more selective use of the whip, hitting on the horse's quarters would be more effective. In the closing stages of one Flemington race, a leading Australian rider hit a filly in the stomach. She promptly cow-kicked, losing both her momentum and a race she would have won.

The short-leathered riding method can have major drawbacks as best chronicled in John Hislop's definitive race-riding manual, 'From Start To Finish'. But while recognising that the only chance I would have had against the top flat-race jockeys in my riding days would have been to put up some steeplechase fences, I believe that a modification of the European method will soon arrive in Australia. Malcolm Johnston, 24-year-old Sydney star, is doing it already, and if everyone isn't following suit within 10 years I shall put a crate of

the best stuff in the Flemington weighing room.

Yet such observations should never dilute one of the abiding truths about race riding – that how a jockey uses his head and hands is far more important than how he sits. Correctly reading your own horse's mood, and the play of the race around you, wins far more races than all the walloping and kicking ever can.

Back at Flemington on the Saturday, four days after the Cup, there were two perfect examples. Roy 'The Professor' Higgins kept coaxing a little extra all the way to the line, and 'Handbrake Harry' White got that crafty old veteran, Hyperno, up to win the big race with just one brief flourish to galvanise the horse, and then grabbed his head again before Hyperno could resent it.

Just as this intangible touch brings the great riders to the top of the heap, so too with trainers. If they consistently head their profession, you can be sure that there is something more than efficiency in their operation, that special gypsy intuition which recalls Louis Armstrong's reply to the woman who asked him to explain swing: 'Lady, if you have to ask you ain't got it'. In Australia there has been little question that the Big Three, Bart Cummings, Tommy Smith and Colin Hayes, have the touch of the caravan people, and would have been outstanding in any country.

Tommy Smith's record has been the most remarkable of all, and at the time of our visit this little man with the incorrigible grin and the riotously competitive approach had become the first ever trainer to land more than two million dollars in a single season (1979-80). Sadly, his luck

was out as far as we were concerned. He was still on crutches after a hip-breaking kick from a two-year-old; his latest super crack, Kingston Town, had broken down a few days before the Melbourne Cup, and an airline strike prevented our visiting Tulloch Lodge, the stables named after his first and greatest champion, the little 15-hand New Zealander he bought for just 750 guineas before decimal days, and trained to become the first Australian winner of over £100,000.

For all their success, Smith and Cummings still train on the race-track, American style. So, having failed to make the Tulloch Lodge rendezvous, getting to Colin Hayes's establishment in South Australia became crucial. Lindsay Park is not only unique in Australia as a top-class training operation miles from any race track, but unique to the world in having cradle-to-grave-supervision, the same set-up also containing an eight-stallion, 400-mare stud complex.

Allowances will have to be made for our rose-tinted spectacles, but after 10 days whirling through overnight flights, Honolulu stop-overs, Sydney heat and heavy doses of Melbourne Cup fever, to climb out of the six-seater Cessna and taste the sweet air of Angaston, 100 miles from, and 1,500 feet above, Adelaide, was like dropping

Hawkesbury is happily informal in many things (Top Right) and horses competing at the track have their racing plates put on in the stalls beforehand (Top Left) and taken off immediately afterwards. Nonetheless the practical controls spread to pre-race dope testing and the usual whistling for a urine sample afterwards (Bottom Left). But Hawkesbury has its holy of holies (Above) where president Bob Charley presents a prize to a winning jockey.

into paradise. Lindsay Park, which Colin Hayes started as a stud only in 1965, and as a training establishment in 1970, was the most stimulating place we visited in this whole whinnying trot around the globe, and so the perfect place to grapple with two of the great imponderables of Australian racing—how their training methods, and their horses, compare with the rest of the world.

The big thing about Australian racehorses is that they have to work for their corn. Take the Melbourne Cup winner, Beldale Ball. While he may be able to look back on his British record without shame—two victories in seven races over 12 months—he must also remember it as a holiday, since on Cup day he was running for the fifth time in five weeks and had been second in a highly competitive handicap only three days before becoming the toast of Australia. A British trainer might occasionally give such a programme to some little pot-boiler, but as a preparation for a big race would consider it unthinkable.

What's more, if a British horse did have such a programme you could bet on his having the gentlest of routines between races. Not so with Beldale Ball and his fellows. After running on the Saturday, he was led out on Sunday. On Monday morning he was out for nearly two hours, and did a mile-and-a-half spin. Monday afternoon he was walked down to the Marynigong River, and then swum behind a rowing boat for nearly two minutes. Before winning the Cup on Tuesday he had a long sharp trot, and then swam again on Wednesday afternoon. Some schedule by British standards, but almost mild by Australian. Some commentators wondered why Beldale Ball wasn't galloped on Tuesday before racing, or run again on Thursday like many of his rivals.

Beldale Ball's winning time, carrying 49.5 kilos (about 7st 8lbs) was 3min 19.8sec for the 3,200 metres, which would have set a record anywhere in Britain. That in itself is in no way conclusive, because British going, tracks and race tactics all tend to slow things down. But since Bob Charley, who runs Australia's version of Timeform, assessed Beldale Ball's improvement at a stone-and-a-half after arriving Down Under, it prompts the question whether British and European trainers are too soft on their horses.

Colin Hayes is far too wise a bird to be drawn into comparisons, saying: 'In different places, with different tracks, you develop different systems. I am just happy when we get things right. Mind

Tommy Smith, (Left) the most prolific trainer of recent times with over 50 successes in major classics and the producer of champion horses from Tulloch, in 1952 (the first horse to win £100,000 in Australia) to Kingston Town in 1980 (first to win one million Australian dollars); Bart Cummings (Right), 'the Cup King' and second only to Tommy Smith in the number of big races won. These two trainers, together with Colin Hayes, winner of the 1980 Melbourne Cup, over 200 races in the season and creator of the Lindsay Park Stud and training complex, make up Australia's big three.

you, not all horses adapt, and for a long time Beldale Ball couldn't run a leg down here'.

Interestingly enough, Hayes is a great admirer of Britain's top trainer, Dick Hern, whose methods (his 1979 Derby and record-stake winner, Troy, had only seven runs all season) would seem to be diametrically opposed to the Australian system. 'Dick has been to stay with us here and we visit him in England', says Colin. 'I have learnt a lot from some of the things he does. I like to think he has appreciated some of our ways, too'.

In many different aspects, those 'ways' echo Hayes's gentle but firmly-repeated assertion: 'Tradition is the enemy of progress'. In his own country's eyes, no off-track training centre has ever worked; the sharp undulations on all his gallops (up to 150 feet in three furlongs) seems pointlessly different from the flat tracks on which racing takes place. In 'traditional' British eyes, a basic riding time each morning of only 50 minutes would be held insufficient for top-class conditioning. The shortness of most work-outs (three to four furlongs) would seem suitable only for sprinters, the emphasis on daily swimming and 'technological' aids like weighing and timing are only just being appreciated, and the lack of concern at horses getting too close to each other either at exercise or in neighboring 'cage' boxes, would be thought dangerously casual.

But the motto beneath the Lindsay Park motif is: 'The future belongs to those who plan for it', and having spent 20-odd years as a supremely successful racecourse trainer down at Adelaide, Hayes didn't make this move without planning every tiniest detail. 'Down on the racecourse', he says, 'you are often in the hands of the Philistines.

Up here, we just have to be self-sufficient'. He can say that again. Lindsay Park not only grows almost all its own foodstuffs, but also has its own saddlers, butcher's shop, slaughterhouse and one of the most up-to-date laboratory units outside a university.

The Hayes answers to the doubters are precise. On hills: 'I like them, horses get through work without knowing it'. On short exercise and gallops: 'Long gallops tire horses'. On new aids: 'They are just aids, but all information is food for thought'. And on the lack of screened boxes (most of the colts are in 30ft adjoining sanded pens, with only one end covered, like giant retriever kennels): 'The horse is a herd animal; we try to make his imprisonment as bearable as possible'.

There is no need to justify with words. The winners do that. There were more than 200 of them, including the brilliant but ill-fated Dulcify, in the 1979-80 season. It is plain exciting to see and hear someone at the very top of his profession enthuse at the success of ideas. The swimming pool where up to five horses at a time do a couple of circuits to cool down after work-outs, the sandpit for them to roll in afterwards, the efficiency of change-arounds that saw 71 horses sent up the new grass gallop on the second morning we were there (the times automatically recorded over the last two furlongs), and the labour-saving feeding that can supply the 100-odd racehorses in 28 minutes.

On the stud side, the challenges to accepted wisdom are just as direct. The 120 miles of fencing are not traditional wooden post and rails, but wire with plastic topping. The mares and foals are driven along the network-between-fence pathway by outriders not on horses but on motorbikes:

When the horses hear the engine they know they are being gathered in'.

And who says you need trim green paddocks and a temperate climate to raise top-class horses? The fields have got long stalks of lucerne growing above the horses knees, and if they were still green in November, with part of the 28 inches of rain Lindsay Park gets annually, they will brown off in the summer. In any case, many of the yearlings are sent 50 miles north to the Murray River where, on an irrigated patch, they blossom in temperatures that this observer thought were normally conducive to the weak-necked animals you find in the tropics. 'People seem to forget the horse came from the desert. He loves the sun', says Hayes. 'It's what they eat that counts, and the lucerne is the best feed they can get. If anything, the problem up there is that they do too well'.

But if the balloon is about to go up on Australian bloodstock prices, they can take it from us that it won't be without some painful inflation problems. For the frequent, and in many ways justifiable, boast that Australian racing is the best in the world, is based on the system as at present. Horses run for good prize money, and as many of them are geldings, manoeuvering for a stud career is rarely applicable. If the value of Australian stallions suddenly takes off, all that will change.

Take the Kingston Town-Troy example. As a three-year-old gelding, Kingston Town in the 1979-80 season won 12 races (from 15 starts) and $A692,240, a rightly-acclaimed record for all concerned. In the 1980 European season, the three-year-old colt, Troy, won six out of seven races and a record £415,000 but, and here's the rub, he was then syndicated for £7.2 million and retired to stud. If there is that much money at the end of the classic rainbow, who's going to campaign on and risk all those juicy stallion fees?

The Australian system may be best for the race-goer who, in the end, just wants to watch the best horses race against each other. It may even be better for the horses. After all, Kingston Town and Dulcify were geldings, and Tommy Smith says that the Australian heat does not affect a gelding as much as an entire horse. But the British system offers more for the top horseman. Warwick Hobson's vivid statement – 'The British racing system has been going backwards for years – anything they do you are generally better doing

Lindsay Park, 100 miles north of Adelaide in South Australia, is one of the newest and certainly one of the most innovative training and breeding complexes in the world. One of Colin Hayes's sayings is 'tradition is the enemy of progress', and so horses are not hidden from each other in walled-in boxes but, like these colts, in adjoining sandy pens. 'The horse is a herd animal. We just try to make his imprisonment more bearable.' That's helped, too, by a swim in Lindsay Park's specially designed pool. Even away from home daily swimming is considered an important part of the training regimen; witness the horses taking an afternoon dip in the Marynigong River near Melbourne (Bottom Far Left).

in reverse'–will draw some support from those infuriated by European colts with bubble reputations who seem skilfully to avoid the cannon's mouth of confrontation. But what leading Australian horseman can put his hand on his heart, look at the Kingston Town-Troy comparison and not be tempted by how much more could be gained by doing less?

The Sangster syndicate has given Northern Hemisphere bloodstock its biggest single boost, but has also drawn the sharpest criticism for what, in sporting terms, is evasion but, in the business world, is sensible protection of assets. Now that Sangster is poised to send Australian prices soaring, how will the pricklier traditionalists react? Back here, in poor, beleaguered Blighty, we await events with interest.

The point was proved to me in much the same way as figures can be flipped out of the filing cabinet. This time I was whisked, by Comanche, over the gum trees and the scrub to see for myself, 100-odd head of horses, all in the baking heat, all looking tremendous. Through this, as through much of Australian life, one theme ran stronger than any other–they had achieved a lot, and they were going to get better.

Boom times have been with their racing for some time now–not just 400 racecourses (130 in Queensland) for only 14 million population, but a 40 per cent increase in foal production between 1975 and 1979, giving a final figure of 14,900. The track betting with its 6½ and 3½ per cent split between government and racing (Britain has approximately nine and one) has meant massive funds coming back into the business. Yet still Australia lacks the biggest jackpot that racing has to offer, the multi-million-pound syndication of a top stallion, like Troy, the 1979 Epsom Derby winner, or Spectacular Bid, his American contemporary, who went for $20 million in 1980. Just because of those prices, the richest stallion men in the world are looking for bargains, and with a record Australian syndication of SA2 million, why shouldn't they be in the land of opportunity?

At the same time, the old emphasis on stayers' races is being diluted in Australia with the six-furlong Golden Slipper at Rosehill, Sydney, only started in 1957 and now, at SA250,000 the richest two-year-old stakes in the world. The situation is not lost on the bright men, so it is no surprise to hear Sangster say that 'the Golden Slipper is the race to win in Australia', and to see him taking a substantial involvement in Lindsay Park.

At the moment, all eight stallions at the stud are imported, and while they are all beautifully bred (Brahms is by Round Table, the record-breaking Without Fear is by Round Table's son Baldric, and Bright Finish is by Nijinsky) none of them was a super champion. The question is, can their genes, combined with Australian environment and training methods, produce a star other countries would want? Colin Hayes allows the look of steel to shine through his spectacles as he says: 'I am damned sure they can'.

It's only 140 years since the Scottish Angas family, aided by a band of persecuted German Lutherans, trekked up from Adelaide. They planted their settlement at the top of the valley, where the grey-skinned gum trees seemed biggest. Today this Borassa Valley is strung across with some of the best vineyards in Australia. Angaston is an orderly, white-verandahed tribute to its founders, with a Lutheran bookshop still in the street, and the word Brathaus (hotel) still painted on the side of the village hostelry.

So it is fitting that in the house that Angas built should be a man who has done his own piece of creation. Up there, where only the parrots and cockatoos used to call, it is, like so much of Australia, a good place for believing.

Timeless beauty and modern-day methods, the classic ingredients for stud success. Horses at Lindsay Park graze beyond the gum trees in lucerne paddocks lined with the blue of 'Salvation Jane', the hardy weed which saved a starving sheep population in pre-irrigation days. Today, mares and foals are now driven between some of the 120 miles of fencing by grooms on motorbikes.

15
NEW ZEALAND

'In April, 1979 Alan Jones pulled off one of the most brilliant betting coups in history. He and Linda were making a much-publicised tour of Australia, taking with them a grey stayer called Northfleet: "The press gave us a VIP reception when we arrived, but none of them bothered to take any notice of the plain-looking pony tagging along at the back." Anyway, if they had, and if they had been told that he had been brought over to land a massive gamble and that his name was Shady Deal, no doubt they would have dismissed it all as a joke'.

CALL IT sentimental. More correctly, call it anthropomorphic, but let's admit to a bit of embarrassment when we went all the way to New Zealand to see an old equine friend and found him 'on the job'.

Of course, it's as much the fault of us racing writers as anyone, but the game ascribes so many human characteristics to its leading horses that sometimes you think that the nags need a psychiatrist more than a trainer. So while it's grand to talk of a horse as 'kind', 'courageous' and to be 'trusted with your grandmother,' it's as well to remember that he remains just a horse.

Never more so than when he progresses to be a stallion. In this instance it was Balmerino, hero of all Australasia in 1975, and all but hero of the whole world in 1977 when only a rapidly-shrinking length-and-a-half separated him from victory in the Prix de l'Arc de Triomphe. Now we all got very fond of him, and were often filing articles about 'the gallant Kiwi', 'seasoned traveller,' and even 'the fastidious old gentleman'.

Somehow, when you've penned those sort of lines, you rather expect Balmerino to come rushing up to greet you like a dog in quarantine kennels. Reality was a bit more earthy, for the Middle Park Stud manager, Norman Atkins, called out cheerily: 'He'll be covering a mare in a minute. Do you want to come and watch.'

Sentimentality apart, Balmerino's past and future exploits are central to New Zealand racing life. On the racecourse, his 23 victories in three different continents showed that a horse of apparently ordinary breeding could come from those rich Waikato grasslands 100 miles south of Auckland and take on the world. At stud, the question is going to be whether he at last can break through the bias caused by the fact no home-produced stallion has topped the New Zealand list since Stepniak in 1908.

Balmerino's story is already one of the most international and romantic of recent times. His owner, Ralph Stuart, originally spent just 60 guineas to buy Balmerino's grandam Caste who, despite being a venerable 19 years old, promptly bred to the ex-Italian and English sire, Duccio. Their produce, called Dulcie, was too crazy to race, but in 16 years at stud produced 15 foals, including Balmerino and the Adelaide Cup winner, Fulmen, among the colts; and Micheline, one of the fillies, produced Surround, the outstanding Australian champion of 1978.

Stuart's horses had to run with the sheep on his farm at Tangaroa, and is it simply coincidence that this is just 10 miles from the rather more imposing Trelawny Stud, where in 1946 the incredible Tulloch, the first New Zealand horse to win more than £100,000, was born? You don't have to look at the statistics to know that this is horse-rearing country. In fact it boasts such a growth of grass that it sustains eight-and-a-half million cattle and 78 million sheep—a higher animal-to-grass ratio than

anywhere in the world, including Ireland, and it is no surprise that the figures, 5,234 foals to three million people (1979 figures), show that New Zealand has the highest proportion of thoroughbred-to-human population. Britain's figures at the same time were 4,552 thoroughbred foals to 54 million population.

As Peter Willett has pointed out in his impeccably erudite survey: 'The thinking that has guided most New Zealand stallion-selection is that if you cannot afford to buy both pedigree and performance in a potential stallion, you should give priority to pedigree'. The idea being that if the right blood is there, New Zealand's perfect horse environment will do the rest.

The big horse farms, especially the Middle Park Stud, where Balmerino holds court in succession to his French-bred sire, Tric Trac, are clean, lush-grassed and efficient. But in complement to the figures quoted above, it's sheer number of horses around that impresses the first-time visitor, who also cannot help but notice the workaday New

Zealand attitude towards animals. The thoroughbred racehorse is accorded no big deal, and seems none the worse for it.

Leading trainer Dave O'Sullivan proves the point. In 1979 he was the first New Zealand trainer

(Preceding Spread) A land of space and the highest ratio of horses to humans in the world, New Zealand racing is determinedly independent. The 'do-it-yourself' spreads even to the racecourse paddock, where the jockeys have to vault on to their horse's back without the usual helping hand.

Journey's end for Balmerino (Bottom Left), the most internationally-successful New Zealand horse at the Middle Park Stud, near Cambridge in North Island. He is owned by Jack Atkins (Left). In his career Balmerino won 23 races in three different continents, was champion of Australasia in 1975, also won in America and was only narrowly beaten in the 1977 Arc de Triomphe. Now he is back within a few miles of where he was bred by sheep farmer Ralph Stuart, who now has a whole room full of trophies to remember him by, while the first visible product of Balmerino's new lifestyle was seen in one of the 1980 crop of foals (Far Left).

ever to top half-a-million dollars. His My Blue Denim's $NZ112,000 total was a best ever for a New Zealand-based horse, and yet the only prepossessing things about O'Sullivan's yard were the relaxed well-being of the horses, and the clear, competitive wisdom of their trainer. The O'Sullivan stable is about half a mile from Matamata racecourse, but light years away either from the on-track racing barn, or the original English 'crack regiment' stable discipline. More than anything else, it reminded me of successful family jumping yards back home, short on ceremony but long on stablecraft.

More than 300 horses are trained on the Matamata track, one of the leading country courses, and a million dollars go through the betting windows each meeting. But O'Sullivan only uses it twice a week, preferring to get his 55-odd horses out in groups of three and four to hack around the farm. Sitting in O'Sullivan's car while a couple of horses cantered around us, we seemed all of the 3,000 miles separating us from Melbourne, or the 12,000 from Newmarket. Yet there was regret as well as realism in the trainer's voice as, tweed hat tilted back, he said: 'It's the same as everything else, we have become a bit more factorified, I suppose. When I was apprenticed we used to have to walk for an hour before we worked, and then an hour afterwards, but sure, if you were going to do that today, you would just be going downhill. You couldn't do it. But then nobody can do it now, so it doesn't matter a damn'.

His horses go out for only 45 minutes, but they then go straight into one of the paddocks that stretch away to the back of his yard, and don't start to get brought in until 2.30: 'Of course, I can only compare it with Australia, but our horses are certainly a lot more settled than those trained on the tracks over there, stuck in the box for the rest of the day. If they do that, they often start to think a bit'.

The opportunity to turn horses out whenever they want a break during the day, or even a complete rest, a 'spell from training', is the one element Britain's trainers lack – because of weather in winter, and lack of opportunity in summer. One week after his Melbourne Cup triumph, Beldale Ball was turned out at Lindsay Park, and in an adjoining paddock was the Sangster classic hope Our Paddy Boy, who had just run third in the Victorian Derby.

In South Australia in November it was warm enough for the horses to need no protection, but the eye-catching thing about New Zealand horses is that although many people don't seem to bother with the more finicky point of presentation (some manes and tails wouldn't have won prizes), most racehorses out in the field seemed to be wearing rugs however balmy the weather. 'Oh yes', said Dave O'Sullivan, 'I have mine rugged twelve months of the year. The only time we take the rugs off them is when we bring them in at half-past two in the hot weather, but we would put them back on at seven o'clock for the night. If they go out with no rugs in the summer their coats get burnt, because the rays are very direct here. Up in Singapore you can sit out by a pool and get a great tan, but here you burn very quick'. As one who got painfully grilled in Singapore, and escaped unmarked from Matamata, I shall just have to take O'Sullivan's word for it.

Interestingly enough for those who remember the late great George Colling's remark: 'If I had a stable full of geldings I would have the bookies screaming for mercy,' O'Sullivan has only two colts

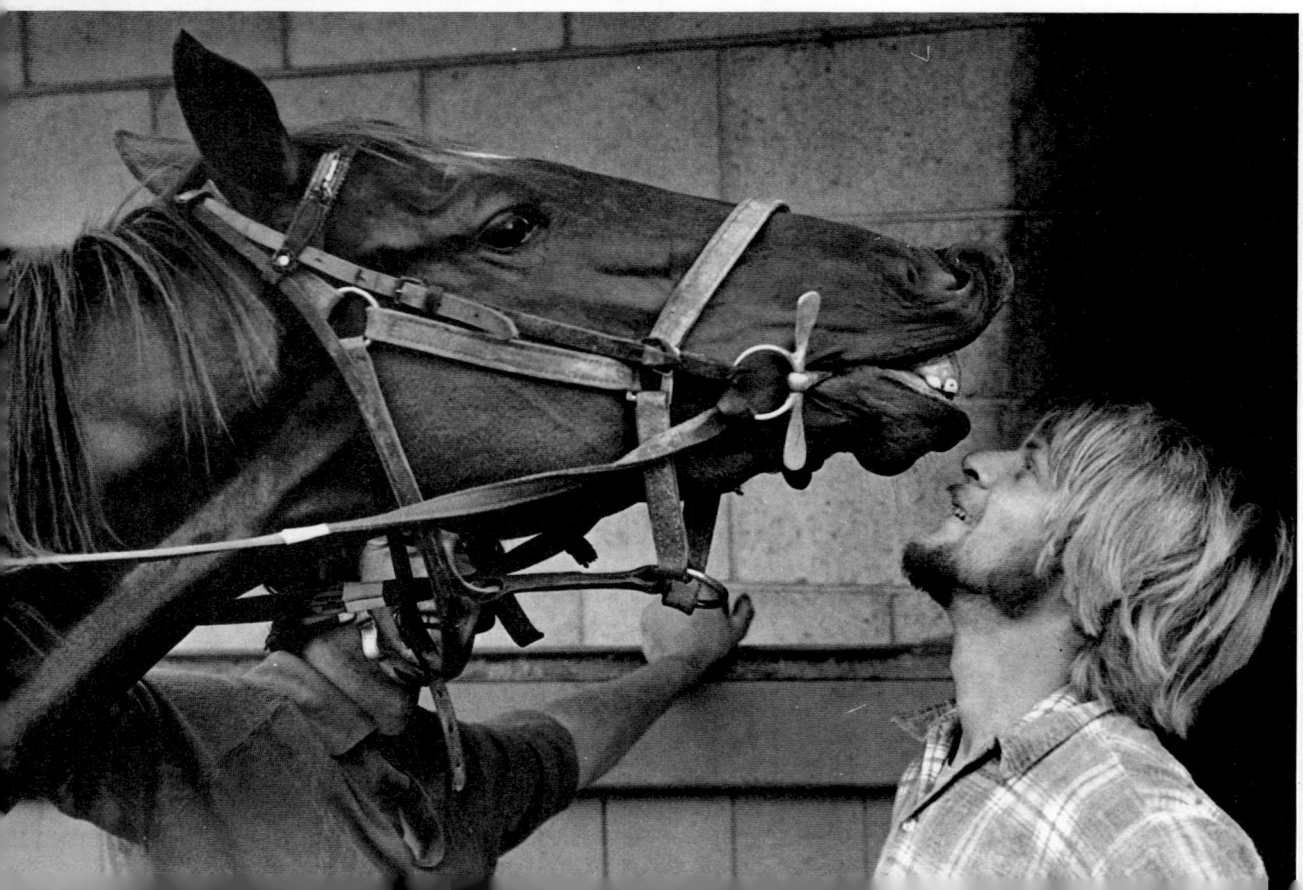

among his 55 horses: 'It makes this turning-out job much easier, and what's the point of keeping them 'bulls' as the Aussies say, when nobody wants a New Zealand pedigree, and all our stallions are imported?' Balmerino, now's your chance.

For O'Sullivan and other top men like Ray Verner, the training of horses is clearly no problem, even if labour can be. He and his staff start work at 4.45am, and the last of his feeds is at 7pm. There is also, with that extraordinary 5,000-a-year foal-rate, no shortage of horses. The problem is the lack of money in New Zealand racing. My Blue Denim set a record for a horse racing in New Zealand. Says O'Sullivan: 'She won 112,125 dollars, but 93,000 of that was for winning the Auckland Cup, which at 150,000 overall was the first race valued at more than 100,000 dollars ever run in New Zealand. But the previous record-holder was Uncle Remus, who won the Derbys, the bloody lot. He won just under 112,000. Yet you can take a horse over to Australia and win that in a month. Take that Golden Rhapsody of mine, he won a welter at Randwick and three at Brisbane, plus a second which was worth 112,000 Australian, which is about 120,000 in New Zealand money by the time you get it home'.

So the pattern is set. If you want money you have to get to Australia, and at present O'Sullivan has a happily successful system whereby his eldest son goes out with a select band of seasoned campaigners and he himself flies in just before a big race. And while O'Sullivan, Verner and company make their presence felt from Brisbane to Adelaide, even more so do the New Zealand-bred horses. Despite the dominance of Australian-born Kingston Town, who alone won almost $A700,000, the New Zealand animals collected

almost eight million dollars in stakes during the 1979-80 season, and their 13 Group One victories included Hyperno in the Melbourne Cup, Dulcify in the W. S. Cox Plate at Moonee Valley and Big Print in the Victoria Derby.

Most of these animals would have been bought on the market at places like the Trentham National Yearling Sales, where in January 1980 no fewer than 80 per cent of the 360 lots went for export, 62 per cent to Australia. The impression of boom-time ahead for Australasian bloodstock was certainly confirmed by those same Sales' overall figures, which showed the aggregate price of $A6,484,750 (up by 55 per cent and the average of $A18,013 (up by 51 per cent). But while all New Zealand rejoiced at an unprecedented five lots making six figures, that is still modest compared with European and North American sales, where bids of double that price are nothing unusual.

All that confirms Robert Sangster's contention that Australasian bloodstock prices are under-valued and ready for take-off, and it was no surprise to see the big Australian training guns at the centre of the action. Tommy Smith paid 120,000 guineas for a Zamazaan colt, and Colin Hayes topped the sales with 140,000 guineas for an In The Purple filly bought with Aucklander Don Dick, who is an executive in one of Australasia's largest transport firms, and a protagonist of the theory so coherently argued in Ross du Bourg's excellent work, 'The Australian and New Zealand Thoroughbred', that their horses can take on the world.

We broke some wine together on the night of the Melbourne Cup, and there is no doubt that Don Dick is not one of nature's born losers. Sadly, the first venture north, with a full brother to champion filly Surround bred to Northern Hemi-

sphere time (birthday January 1st), failed when the colt, called Le Monarc, had training problems. But Dick's Australian operation looks set fair. At Colin Hayes's Flemington stables, just up from the racetrack, Don showed us the freshly-landed New Zealand filly, Polar Air, and in the day we went racing at Te Rapa, Hamilton, on North Island, a week later, a cheer went up in the weighing room when the news came through that Polar Air had won the Sandown Guineas in New South Wales.

Yet it must be said that this emphasis on exports, and on bigger, richer events far away, also leaves a sense of wistfulness and depression that can be part of New Zealand life as a whole, and certainly affects its racing. An editorial in the October 1980 edition of The New Zealand Blood Horse, in detailing the lack of money in the industry and asking how long a major race club like Wellington can go on making losses of 140,000 dollars, says: 'The signs are already there that the system is breaking down–falling attendances, TAB holdings not keeping pace with inflation and race clubs as well as individuals in financial trouble. It is harder to get people to the track when the good horses are in Australia, and clubs can't keep improving facilities. It is harder to keep the horses here when the stakes are so much higher across the Tasman'.

Sad stuff if we weren't used to similar problems

For a leading trainer like Dave O'Sullivan (Left) winning in New Zealand is not enough. Each year a large part of his prize money (in 1979 he was the first NZ trainer to top half a million dollars) comes from raids on Australia and, the 112,000 New Zealand dollars collected by My Blue Denim was the highest-ever for a New Zealand-based horse. His base at Matamata (Below) lacks nothing in fun as well as expertise.

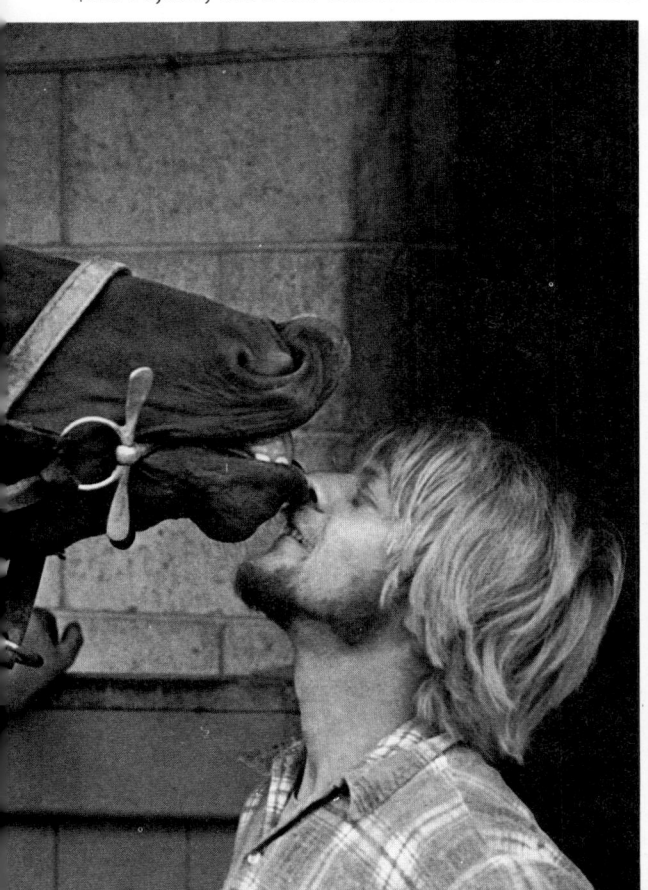

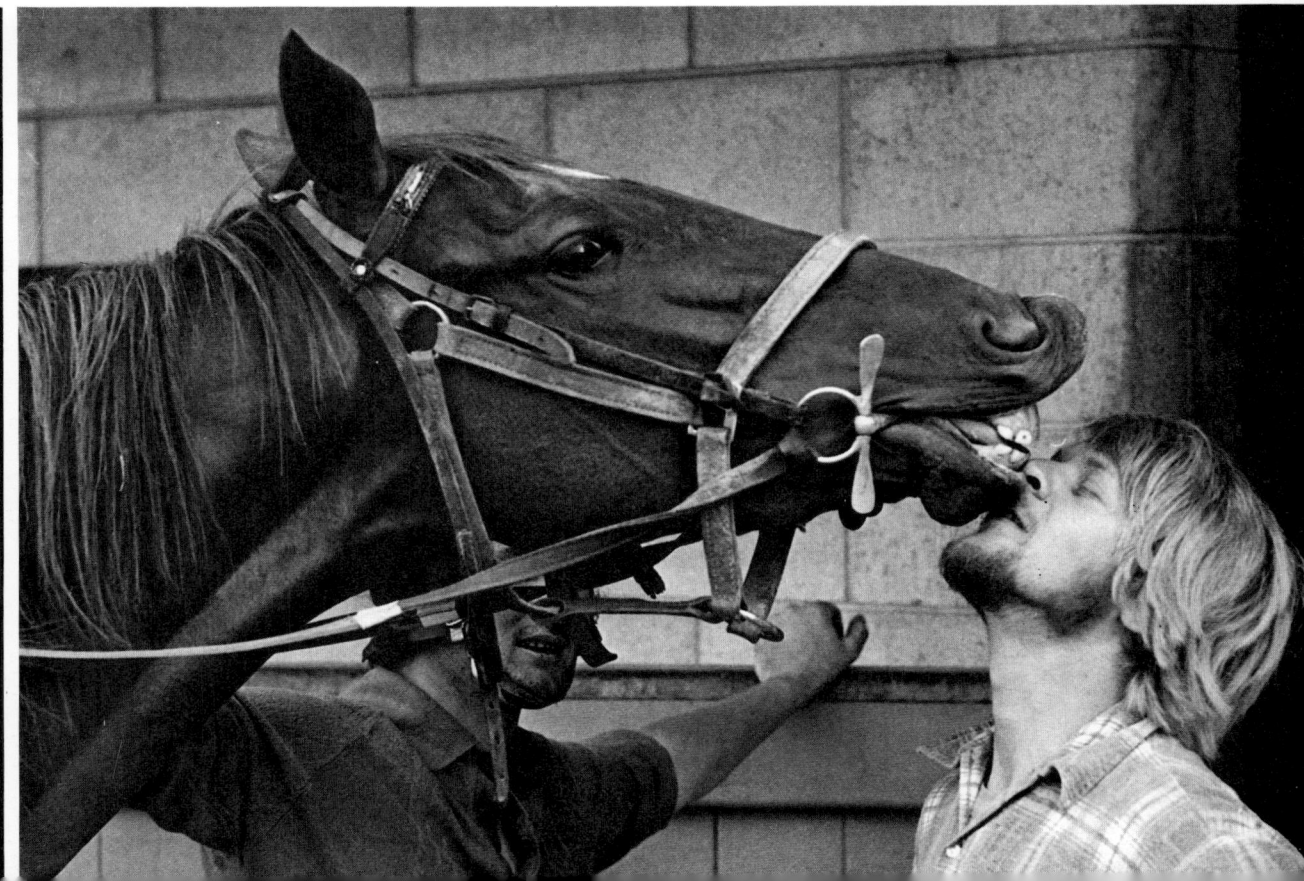

back home, and some of it was certainly borne out by our visit to Te Rapa for Waikato Cup day on November 15th 1980. Not that the course, with its newly-laid turf track, elegant tree-lined paddock and litterless stands, didn't look fit for the Queen, who in fact visited it three years before. Nor, with 10 races and 152 runners, could you say there was lack of sport. But the figures for attendance and betting were down, and with only three of the 29 Tote-only betting windows in the cheap ring taking as high as 10 dollars, it was a far cry from the feverish bookmakers' ring at Hawkesbury, and the prize-money didn't tell a much better story.

Admittedly, the Waikato Cup had 20,000 dollars in total prize-money and the Guineas 12,000, but some of the minor races were worth as little as 1,950 or 1,450 dollars to the winner. And, worse still, although there were three meetings and 39 races, including the 40,000-dollar New Zealand Cup at Riccarton that Saturday, the lack of opportunities can be such that trial races, without betting, are held to get a horse entered. In fact, a big, meaty chestnut called Dignify, carrying Ralph Stuart's green-and-crimson silks like his three-parts brother Balmerino, actually ran in the Waikato Guineas with only two such trial races as previous experience.

Lack of money, too, was the root cause of the amazingly cluttered jockeys' changing room. At only 25 dollars a ride, there is not enough cash to hire valets to clear up and quicken the changing process between races. So what would have been a handsomely-appointed locker room is jammed with suitcases in which each rider brings all his worldly goods, from saddle to sweat shirt.

This scrum was made infinitely worse by there being precious little restriction on entry. At practically every other racecourse in the world, only the riders are allowed in, but at Te Rapa all sorts of trainers, owners, lads, and even visiting hacks like me, were pushing around, asking questions, eating the sandwiches and generally hindering the jockeys. 'I know it's ridiculous', said Lionel Brown, an ex-jockey and now their racecourse representative. 'But I guess we have got used to it now.'

The sight of the Guineas favourite cantering to the start clearly sore on the very firm going was another minus, but there was also plenty to impress, nothing more so than the quiet civility of the racegoers. The grey suits and hats and flower-

The starting gates at Te Rapa, near Hamilton, North Island, are without the overhead struts normally used worldwide. Some visiting jockeys have thought them a trifle unstable but seeing is believing: with just three handlers this 13-strong field for a five-furlong two-year-old race loaded as quickly and calmly as anything around the globe. But it is the English heritage symbolised in the form of the pink-coated rider, that has meant that even if the horses sport few frills (note the lack of nosebands in the picture of the turn) there is plenty of action on the track as well as considerable public interest, including that of immigrant Polynesians.

Forgetting Cave's natural but biased enthusiasm for a minute, his patented Waikato Electric Starting Gates were mighty impressive in the field. Two-year-old races can be notoriously difficult to load, with some horses backing off and rearing up as if the stalls were cow-killing pens. There were 12 runners in the Ruakura Juvenile Handicap. All bar three walked straight in by themselves, and the others only needed a lead from one of Bob's sons. The race was over five furlongs, with a 180-degree bend after a furlong, and all jumped out for the fairest of breaks with little signs of the one criticism that Lester Piggott made, that the horses swerve away from the single-door opening at the front as they come out.

Quite apart from their efficiency and simplicity, these gates have an especial attraction for British tracks. First is the reduction in the eight-man team needed for what have admittedly become admirably well-drilled starting-stall assistants, and second the much easier transport. While the present British stalls are towed lugubriously from track to track like great beached whales, the Waikato gates can be stacked up and put on the back of an ordinary truck. It's no surprise to find that financially-pressed British racecourses are studying the Cave invention very closely.

Although in general the New Zealand jockeys looked like rather less polished versions of their better rewarded and more intensely pressured Australian counterparts, there were at least two superb pieces of race riding–Chris McNab coming from last to first to land top-weighted Drum a stylish winner of the Waikato Cup, and David Peake, long legs, spurs and all, almost stealing a race without ever going for the whip. And in at least three ways the jockeys also challenged what has become accepted wisdom in Britain. The first that they need a leg up in the paddock, the second that they cannot give a good account of themselves at disciplinary hearings and third that women jockeys have no place in racing.

In British terms, New Zealand jockeys don't mount in the paddock at all. The 'paddock' is a tree-shaded ring round the back of the stand where the horses do the preliminary parade, but a quarter of an hour before start time they are brought to the ring in front of the weighing room which in all Australasia is called 'The Birdcage'. To uninitiated eyes, what follows is a funny sight. For instead of gathering out in the centre of the ring for last-minute planning and giving the jockey a leg-up, the connections stay chatting by the weighing room until the mounting signal is given, and then the jockey marches across alone and vaults on board Cossack style. 'Oh yes', says trainer Dave O'Sullivan. 'If they can't jump up, I am damned if I am going to leg them up. It's the first thing kids get taught out here. We haven't many people around, and if they fall off they have got to know how to get back on again'. British pony clubs please note.

The disciplinary system is run on British lines.

patterned dresses in the stand reminded me of England 20 or 30 years ago, and the general politeness and ease were also of a bygone age. Even the more informal Polynesian element in the cheap ring were genial to the point of passivity compared with other disgruntled punters round the world.

You couldn't find anyone more solidly old-fashioned looking than 57-year-old engineer Bob Cave, with his collar and tie and short hair-cut above the white overalls, as if he was still in the

Royal Navy, with which, as a lad, he marched in King George V's Jubilee celebrations in London. Yet in the happy twist that keeps putting New Zealand back in the game, loyal, honest, provincial Bob has perfected what looks like a major advance to horse racing's largest single mechanical aid. In short Bob Cave has invented a new system of starting gates. Since starting stalls, rather than the old-fashioned barriers, became the accepted method of dispatch–and England's adoption of stalls in 1965 was about 20 years behind the United States and Australia–no one seems to have challenged their greatest drawback, the fact that horses don't like going in them. True, careful schooling from an early age, and the assistance of numerous hefty handlers, can usually get them loaded up without too much fuss, but racehorses are wary of walking into what looks, with its big overhead superstructure, all too like some sort of transit cage.

Cave's solution is simple. If the reason why the horses back away is the superstructure, do away with it. To those who say that the resulting smaller, lighter, detachable set of gates would not stand up to wear, he points out that he has been working on the system for some 20 years: 'Look at the gates we are using now. We have had them three years and three months, started 55,000 horses through them, and they are still in great shape. The proof of the pudding is in the eating'. He adds: 'I have seen gates the world over, and don't think any compare. Look at today. My three sons, all directors of this company, and I were the only men on the gates. Just four men, and we had 150 horses starting, and it was easy, just a skive'.

That is, the professional stipendiary stewards put their case against a jockey, and a panel of honorary stewards act like lay magistrates in giving judgment. I was most impressed by the Australian system where, in Melbourne at least, the team of six hawk-eyed stipendiaries put their charges, and the jockey makes his defence before the film is shown to see who is right, but the Te Rapa proceedings were conducted with elaborate correctness. So elaborate, in fact, that jockeys are clearly being equipped for second careers as barristers, there being little question of forelock-tugging dumbness when asked if they have anything to say. 'Yes sir,' answered the jockey, 'there are three points I would like to put to Mr. McNab...'.

Which leaves us with the ladies. For one stuck with the sporting stereotype of New Zealanders as either giant All Black rugby players or lean, leathery athletes, meeting their leading apprentice was a bit of a shock. She was green-eyed, red-haired, freckle-faced, and altogether the comeliest professional horseperson you have ever clapped eyes upon. And before anyone suspects another of those sniggering male-chauvinist 'Reincarnation-of-Lady Godiva' pieces, let me say that from all that could be gleaned 19-year-old Debbie Stockwell's 22-winner, table-topping success was well deserved. Lacking some punch perhaps, she looked to be outridden in the two-year-old race, but showed the style and confidence to make horses run that a young rider needs in any country.

It is particularly interesting that while in England no girl apprentice has cut any ice in the five years they have been eligible on the Flat, and in a good old men-only stand at Melbourne there wasn't a pigtail in sight, in New Zealand Debbie Stockwell was not only seventh in the overall jockeys' list, but was followed by at least half a dozen other successful girl apprentices.

Debbie has no heavy philosophy. 'I was working away in a yard like thousands of other girls, I suppose', she says. 'And when I realised we could get rides if we were apprentices, it seemed crazy not to try.' Maybe British girls are less adequate, the competition more intense, our trainers more prejudiced against the fair sex. But maybe not, for there must be something wrong when girls can make a definite impression in the more muscular sport of jump racing, and not get near that figure on the Flat.

You could almost say that out in New Zealand boys and girls are treated exactly the same, were it not for the memory that while all the men were heaving themselves unaided into the saddle, there was always a gallant hand waiting to grab Debbie's elegantly-turned ankle and leg her up. To find the real reason for this break-through, you have to leave Debbie and her girl-only dressing room (fastidious British commentator Robin Gray has never recovered from riding his first winner at about the 4,000th attempt in, of all places, Czechoslovakia, and being congratulated in the

unisex changing room with a kiss from a topless jockette) and travel to a little yard and ranch-house 20 miles the other side of Hamilton to meet Debbie's inspiration, the remarkable Linda Jones. With her striking blonde hair, pink jump-suit and gold ankle-chain above bare feet, 28-year-old Linda made Debbie look like the little sister who hasn't left school.

While in Britain the emancipation of lady jockeys was pushed through by a group of enthusiastic amateurs (if Ms Judy Goodhew will pardon the phrase), in New Zealand it was the single achievement of Linda Jones, a trainer's wife who wanted to earn a living in the saddle, and was not scared to take the fight to the highest courts in the land. Once licensed, she succeeded to the extent of winning a classic (the Wellington Derby on Holy Toledo), and was second on the list when a terrible fall sidelined her in the spring of '79.

What Linda had was a quality almost all women jockeys lack, the ability to galvanise a tired horse. Baby Clare was crashing around on the floor, and we were all goggling at a TV recording of Miss World, but shrewd-eyed Alan Jones looked admiringly across the room at his wife curled catlike in her chair, and murmured in affectionate reminiscence: 'Ah yes, Linda could hit them all right. She could really make them go'.

It might be added that Alan Jones is nobody's patsy, and in April, 1979 he pulled off one of the most brilliant betting coups in history. He and Linda were making a much-publicised tour of Australia, taking with them a grey stayer called Northfleet: 'The press gave us a VIP reception when we arrived, but none of them bothered to take any notice of the plain-looking pony tagging along at the back'. Anyway, if they had, and if they had been told that he had been brought over to land a massive gamble and that his name was Shady Deal, no doubt they would have dismissed it all as a joke.

However unlikely, the story is fact. Alan Jones had bought the little gelding by the imported stallion, Palm Beach (French-registered but bred by the Queen, being by her Two Thousand Guineas winner, Pall Mall, out of her Cheshire Oaks winner, Mulberry Harbour), and won several public trials with him. And despite this being the age of computers and horse-jets, the Australian rules blockheadedly allow an unraced horse such as Shady Deal to change its name on arrival. So when Shady Deal appeared on Seymour race-course, Victoria, for the first division of the maiden race, he had no form to his name, which now appeared as Torbek.

He also arrived under the care of small-time trainer Barry Fawdry, who operated at Bendigo 40 miles away from Seymour, and was hardly the man to land coups with unraced maidens. Torbek's price drifted out to 20-1, before the boys struck with such an avalanche of money that he was 5-2 favourite at the start. It was never a race, Torbek

coming home by three lengths with his head in his chest. No one tells exactly what the bookies paid but, in happy contrast to their panicky attitude over the fairly similar Gay Future coup in Britain, pay they did, well into six figures. And it was only after some super sleuthing by Melbourne Herald journalist David Jewell that everybody realised that although no rules had been broken, Alan Jones had been the man behind the coup, and it had been something of a 'Shady Deal'.

Torbek went on to become one of the top sprinters in Australia, and his string of successes was crowned by the Group One Marlborough Cup at Caulfield in April, 1980. As he thought back, Alan Jones had the slow smile of the man who has conjured racing's most coveted trick, and said gently: 'You see, there's no prize money here, so you've got to think of something. But you must find the right horse. It might take two or three years before you find him. When we do, we'll go to war again'. He was speaking 18 months after the Seymour coup. You have been warned.

Some people will tell you that New Zealand is small, empty and far away, and that its economy is in a mess because it lacks natural resources. But when you remember Alan Jones looking out to the future, and Ralph Stuart, now old and frail, guarding his glorious past in a special Balmerino trophy room, you know that quality horse flesh is one resource those two lovely islands need never be short of.

Jockeys with a difference. The modest expectations of New Zealand riders mean the most crowded dressing rooms in the world. With no valets to help them, jockeys block the gangways with their luggage. But the way is not blocked for women, and a girl like green-eyed Debbie Stockwell (Left) could head the apprentice list in 1980 following the trail blazed by Linda Jones. Linda (Below, with husband Alan and baby Clare) was the first woman to get a jockey's licence in Australia and she and Alan masterminded one of the most successful (and legal!) racing coups of the century.

A WORLD OF FIGURES

The statistics included here relate to the year 1981. They were compiled from research by French racing's Société d'Encouragement, are provided courtesy of its director-general Jean Romanet, and with the assistance of the International Racing Bureau in London. Where no information was available a dash has been inserted. When making comparisons within the statistics it is important to bear in mind that they cover not only racing on the flat but over jumps and also trotting. This is particularly important in relation to betting, where the figures clearly encompass all three disciplines and it is for this reason, plus their intrinsic interest, that the figures for each form of racing are given. The sterling sums are conversions from the original French franc figures and were calculated at a rate approximate to that at the end of 1981 (i.e. £1 = 10.92F).

Countries	Racecourses	Number of Races				Number of Horses			
		Flat	Jumping	Trotting	Total	Flat	Jumping	Trotting	Total
Argentina	40	8,520	–	1,271	9,791	11,356	–	1,456	12,812
Australia	606	23,674	246	15,049	38,969	32,464		15,280	47,744
Austria	1	216	8	–	224	265	29	–	294
Belgium	7	1,065	128	2,268	3,461	1,235	271	2,030	3,536
Brazil	23	10,148	–	915	11,063	13,289	–	100	13,389
Canada	117	8,206	–	35,781	43,987	10,800	–	22,900	33,700
Cyprus	1	213	–	–	213	228	–	–	228
Czechoslovakia	16	287	181	177	645	1,107		153	1,260
Denmark	10	431	–	4,540	4,971	731	–	3,212	3,943
France	273	4,174	2,050	8,044	14,268	8,127	4,777	10,778	21,452*
Great Britain	59	2,844	2,511	–	5,355	6,818	9,662	–	16,480
Greece	1	1,083	–	–	1,083	900	–	–	900
Holland	15	295	–	3,420	3,715	349	–	2,159	2,508
Hong Kong	2	446	–	–	446	735	–	–	735
Hungary	4	521	14	955	1,490	452	50	385	887
India	9	2,002	–	–	2,002	1,950	–	–	1,950
Ireland	28	722	1,022	–	1,744	4,505		–	4,505
Italy	33	3,705	388	9,629	13,722	2,866		4,918	7,784
Japan	10	2,779	187	–	2,966	4,789	374	–	5,163
Malaysia	4	843	–	–	843	1,266	–	–	1,266
Mexico	2	3,718	–	–	3,718	3,583	–	–	3,583
Morocco	3	327	18	36	381	375	20	36	431
New Zealand	73	3,275		1,940	5,215	6,324		–	6,324
Norway	1	250	60	–	310	260	40	–	300
Pakistan	3	891	–	–	891	656	–	–	656
Panama	1	1,714	–	–	1,714	955	–	–	955
Poland	3	714	42	–	756	722	78	–	800
South Africa	15	3,795	–	–	3,795	6,351	–	–	6,351
Spain	7	440	43	–	483	534	60	–	594
Sweden	32	549	25	8,614	9,188	791	75	8,801	9,677
Switzerland	10	84	40	172	296	289	122	269	680
Trinidad & Tobago	4	492	–	–	492	577	–	–	577
Tunisia	2	364	19	33	416	289	10	9	308
Turkey	4	477	–	–	477	343	–	–	343
USA	527	62,820	191	85,845	148,856	72,250	450	51,046	123,746
Venezuela	3	1,750	–	–	1,750	2,000	–	–	2,000
West Germany	48	2,008	282	8,453	10,743	2,682	344	6,161	9,187

*2,229 engaged in both Flat and Jumping

Number of Runners				Number of Stallions		Number of Mares		Number of Births 1981	
Flat	Jumping	Trotting	Total	Thoroughbred	Trotting	Thoroughbred	Trotting	Thoroughbred	Trotting
59,782	–	9,561	69,343	1,565	61	1,645	546	8,333	271
219,483	2,181	150,548	372,212	3,655	1,322	43,987	18,152	17,710	11,553
2,016	71	–	2,087	10	–	69	–	28	–
10,239	1,003	25,360	36,602	57	179	502	2,841	222	1,304
82,293	–	7,632	89,925	887	18	8,823	170	4,739	30
–	–	–	–	280	890	2,700	8,800	2,500	5,500
1,350	–	–	1,350	25	–	196	–	102	–
2,295	1,594	1,449	5,338	40	7	656	63	299	34
3,879	–	50,358	54,327	55	95	426	2,150	239	1,227
45,211	23,548	114,341	183,100	469	703	6,177	14,090	3,103	7,661
32,648	30,299	–	62,947	785	–	10,900	–	4,871	–
7,969	–	–	7,969	60	–	477	–	295	–
2,639	–	33,500	36,139	12	65	168	1,646	94	1,250
4,636	–	–	4,636	–	–	–	–	–	–
4,829	118	9,272	14,219	33	19	412	263	212	182
15,200	–	–	15,200	197	–	2,033	–	639	–
8,558	14,740	–	23,298	300	–	7,000	–	3,525	–
24,132	2,372	79,652	106,156	190	401	1,900	5,820	998	3,135
29,973	1,610	–	31,583	455	–	13,040	–	7,726	–
9,273	–	–	9,273	7	–	50	–	18	–
30,115	–	–	30,115	178	–	1,502	–	894	–
2,473	72	236	2,781	88	3	232	12	118	3
42,025		25,069	67,094	495	285	12,279	6,774	5,600	–
2,200	300	–	2,500	9	–	21	–	13	–
–	–	–	–	85	–	492	–	50	–
1,010	–	–	1,010	62	–	509	–	216	–
4,890	226	–	5,116	23	–	448	–	250	–
44,419	–	–	44,419	475	–	6,914	–	3,507	–
3,888	245	–	4,133	58	–	314	–	203	–
5,353	75	102,055	107,660	49	241	429	7,520	211	4,350
1,652	366	2,300	3,718	11	6	90	30	22	20
5,785	–	–	5,785	48	–	378	–	153	–
2,648	128	170	2,946	12	–	200	–	102	–
3,299	–	–	3,299	47	–	239	–	132	–
502,560	1,414	848,988	1,352,962	7,200	2,500	77,042	38,000	38,499	17,438
17,500	–	–	17,500	426	–	3,341	–	1,455	–
20,146	2,695	84,500	107,341	122	278	2,246	3,284	1,114	2,392

Countries	Prize Money (in £'s Sterling)				Average Prize Per Race (in £'s Sterling)			Average Prize Per Horse (in £'s Sterling)		
	Flat	Jumping	Trotting	Total	Flat	Jumping	Trotting	Flat	Jumping	Trotting
Argentina	11,698,705	–	387,099	12,085,804	1,234			943		
Australia	35,551,909	638,153	13,412,000	49,602,062	1,513		891	1,115		877
Austria	210,745	8,555	–	219,300	979		–	746		–
Belgium	2,609,604	362,138	2,852,404	5,824,146	1,683			1,647		
Brazil	5,947,813	–	25,901	5,973,714	540			446		
Canada	16,848,342	–	30,681,582	47,529,924	1,080			1,411		
Cyprus	448,098	–	–	448,098	2,103	–	–	1,965	–	–
Czechoslovakia	434,237	213,743	94,998	742,978	1,152			590		
Denmark	435,410	–	2,292,175	2,727,585	549			692		
France	28,325,628	11,746,806	26,609,253	66,681,687	6,786	5,730	3,308	3,485	2,459	2,469
Great Britain	13,292,422	5,785,320	–	19,077,742	3,563		–	1,158		–
Greece	4,089,811	–	–	4,089,811	3,776	–	–	4,544	–	–
Holland	382,326	–	2,815,268	3,197,594	860			1,275		
Hong Kong	4,111,543	–	–	4,111,543	9,221	–	–	5,594	–	–
Hungary	205,521	6,463	140,081	352,065	236			397		
India	3,081,885	–	–	3,081,885	1,539	–	–	1,580	–	–
Ireland	1,933,037	1,593,231	–	3,526,268	2,022		–	782		–
Italy	10,634,103	1,462,769	17,961,594	30,058,466	2,191			3,862		
Japan	73,204,614	7,676,214	–	80,880,828	27,269		–	15,665		–
Malaysia	1,206,885	–	–	1,206,885†	4,660†	–	–	2,404†	–	–
Mexico	7,663,758	–	–	7,663,758	2,061	–	–	2,139	–	–
Morocco	513,559	22,950	19,924	556,433	1,460			1,291		
New Zealand	5,243,857		2,919,029	8,162,886	1,565			–		
Norway	421,440	76,547	–	497,987	1,612		–	1,660		–
Pakistan	–	–	–	–	–	–	–	–	–	–
Panama	2,652,226	–	–	2,652,226	1,547	–	–	2,751	–	–
Poland	168,319	8,328	–	176,647	236	198	–	233	107	–
South Africa	9,718,155	–	–	9,718,155	2,561	–	–	1,530	–	–
Spain	839,927	61,525	–	901,452	1,866		–	1,518		–
Sweden	881,777	39,133	10,510,484	11,431,394	1,244			1,183		
Switzerland	142,788	90,260	230,048	463,096	1,564			681		
Trinidad & Tobago	1,643,827	–	–	1,643,827	3,341	–	–	2,849	–	–
Tunisia	444,819	14,726	12,695	472,240	1,135			1,533		
Turkey	527,949	–	–	527,949	1,107	–	–	1,539	–	–
USA	189,865,743	421,887	109,894,090	300,818,720	2,017			2,426		
Venezuela	26,363,095	–	–	26,363,095	15,065	–	–	13,182	–	–
West Germany	5,335,765	7,026,263	13,667,218	19,705,606	1,834			2,145		

†Singapore only

Tote Betting Turnover (in £'s Sterling)			Distribution of Tote Turnover: Amount of Deductions on Betting (in £'s Sterling)				
On-course	Off-course	Total	Returned to backers	Received by government	Retained for expenses	Returned to racing	Other deductions
122,904,374	378,299	123,282,673	66,465,285	12,024,987	44,792,401		–
234,966,667	1,188,541,667	1,423,508,334	1,209,982,083	113,880,667	49,822,792	49,822,792	–
–	–	–	–	–	–	–	–
8,274,784	74,809,973	83,084,757	59,821,025	4,584,114	8,458,976	10,220,641	–
72,642,916	–	72,642,916	49,506,147	3,155,024	19,981,745		–
751,648,414	–	751,648,414	–	60,518,352	–	–	–
2,819,250	2,523,635	5,342,885	3,501,346	23,019	909,865		–
304,314	48,633	352,947	242,856	–	110,091		–
24,817,097	2,158,008	26,975,105	18,882,574	1,888,257	–	6,204,274	–
290,395,807	1,822,543,667	2,112,939,474	1,531,919,877	382,535,450	100,364,625	98,119,521	–
24,900,000	–	24,900,000	19,401,800	966,000	3,391,500	1,110,700	–
62,372,056	13,013,472	75,385,528	60,344,910	5,722,228	4,951,280		4,412,898
25,031,486	3,808,563	28,840,049	21,630,037	721,001	2,451,404	4,037,607	–
337,833,333	619,330	957,163,507	791,003,338	78,267,816	87,892,353		–
6,646,930	821,524	7,468,454	5,203,604	146,593	649,084	1,469,172	–
21,901,833	–	21,901,833	13,672,341	3,475,624	–	4,753,865	–
12,711,289	–	12,711,289	10,798,324	–	1,243,331	669,634	–
60,548,662	22,135,966	86,284,628	57,383,132	4,134,231	21,167,265		–
1,137,490,663	2,205,498,854	3,342,989,517	2,483,478,577	409,506,357	308,861,501	141,143,082	–
38,485,234†	25,289,856†	63,775,090†	47,007,955	9,566,264	6,377,509	823,362	–
127,854,280	21,967,095	149,821,375	117,013,182	12,022,797	9,692,001	9,594,403	1,498,993
199,879	29,876,515	30,076,394	21,053,476	4,782,147	1,503,820	2,105,348	631,604
70,028,010	190,604,543	260,632,553	208,952,112	23,170,661	24,105,935	4,403,844	–
3,230,769	–	3,230,769	2,261,538	969,231			
–	–	–	–	–	–	–	–
8,323,500	11,755,758	20,079,258	14,155,877	592,338	–	5,331,043	–
–	–	–	–	–	–	–	–
88,100,799	151,240,421	239,341,220	189,476,293	25,742,436	24,428,949		–
6,309,940	759,154	7,069,094	4,948,363	706,907	353,451	1,060,374	–
133,226,777	92,783,852	226,010,629	162,727,653	22,601,063	18,080,850	18,080,850	4,520,213
914,704	1,586,538	2,501,242	1,465,292	37,731	767,532	218,393	18,294
16,466,058	–	16,466,058	9,870,001	1,608,072	–	4,987,984	–
710,897	6,601,190	7,312,088	5,306,342	898,777	142,179	964,789	–
–	–	–	–	–	–	–	–
5,171,567,527	869,924,119	6,041,491,646	5,083,517,617	234,856,710	–	362,489,496	360,627,822
49,047,619	220,714,286	269,761,905	161,857,143	26,976,190	44,142,857		36,785,714
133,688,407	6,855,606	140,544,013	117,120,006	936,960	6,746,117	15,740,929	–

Bookmakers

Of the 37 countries listed in the chart, only eight had legalised book-making in 1981 and only the following sums relating to such betting were available for publication.

On-course turnover

Australia	£961,333,333
Belgium	£25,272,594
Great Britain	£172,950,000
India	£58,235,480
Ireland	£44,367,417
Italy	£95,306,648
South Africa	£106,894,366
West Germany	£29,538,462

Off-course turnover

Great Britain	£2,360,198,000
Ireland	£85,000,000
Italy	£239,423,794
South Africa	£128,427,668

Received by government

Belgium	£1,263,630
Great Britain	£190,223,000
India	£954,956
Ireland	£17,665,299
Italy	£16,736,522
South Africa	£13,067,447

Returned to racing

Belgium	£2,742,076
Great Britain	£16,733,000
India	£2,157,128
South Africa	£5,210,404

In Great Britain, of the total book-making turnover of £2,533,148,000, a sum of £1,819,557,400 was returned to backers and in South Africa, of a total turnover of £235,322,034, a sum of £129,376,471 was returned. The remaining figures available were for sums retained for expenses and in Great Britain this amounted to £506,629,600, in Italy to £37,489,810, and in South Africa to £87,667,713.

INDEX

Note. Name entries in italics refer to names of horses. Bold page numbers indicate illustrations.

Front endpaper: They're off! A start at Newmarket, the course that is the ancestral home of modern flat racing.

Half-title: A waiting game. Lead horses held ready to take thoroughbred runners to the start at Aqueduct, New York State.

Title: Close enough to the action to be heart-stopping, this picture was shot at Happy Valley, Hong Kong.

Contents: Cool consideration. Trainer Ian Balding keeps a practised eye on a dawn patrol at Kingsclere in Hampshire.

Back endpaper: Returning home. A string wends its way to its Newmarket stables after exercise on the famous heathland.